The Elderly:
VICTIMS AND DEVIANTS

The Elderly

VICTIMS AND DEVIANTS

Edited by

Carl D. Chambers, Ph.D.
Professor, School of Health and Sport Sciences
College of Health and Human Services
Ohio University

John H. Lindquist, D. Soc. Sci.
Professor, Department of Sociology
Trinity University

O. Z. White, Ph.D.
Professor, Department of Sociology
Trinity University

Michael T. Harter, Ph.D.
Professor, School of Health and Sport Sciences
College of Health and Human Services
Ohio University

OHIO UNIVERSITY PRESS
Athens, Ohio
London

Library of Congress Cataloging-in-Publication Data

The elderly : victims and deviants.

Includes bibliographies.
1. Aged—United States.   2. Aged—United States—Abuse of.   3. Aged—United States—Crimes against.   4. Aged offenders—United States.   5. Aged—United States—Drug use.   I. Chambers, Carl D.   [DNLM: 1. Aged.   2. Social Environment—United States.   WT 30 E37]

HQ1064.U5E52   1987   305.2'6'0973   86-33269

ISBN 0-8214-0844-5
ISBN 0-8214-0845-3 (pbk.)

If we're not together,
We're too far apart.

Contributors

Tim Bien, R.Ph.
Adjunct Instructor of Clinical Pharmacy
College of Pharmacy
University of Cincinnati
Cincinnati, Ohio

Carl D. Chambers, Ph.D., L.N.H.A.
Professor and Coordinator
Health Services Administration Programs
School of Health and Sport Sciences
College of Health and Human Services
Ohio University
Athens, Ohio

Robert J. Cluxton, Pharm.D., R.Ph., M.B.A.
Associate Professor and Director
Clinical Pharmacy Programs
College of Pharmacy
University of Cincinnati
Cincinnati, Ohio

Michael T. Harter, Ph.D.
Professor
Health Services Administration Programs
and Dean
College of Health and Human Services
Ohio University
Athens, Ohio

Barbara Hurford, Pharm.D., R.Ph.
Clinical Pharmacy Programs
College of Pharmacy
University of Cincinnati
Cincinnati, Ohio

James A. Inciardi, Ph.D.
Professor and Director
Criminal Justice Division
Department of Sociology
University of Delaware
Newark, Delaware

John H. Lindquist, D. Soc. Sci.
Professor
Department of Sociology
Trinity University
San Antonio, Texas

David M. Petersen, Ph.D.
Professor
Department of Sociology
Georgia State University
Atlanta, Georgia

Kathryn S. Felton Pribble, M.HSA, R.T.R.
Health Services Administration Program
School of Health and Sport Sciences
College of Health and Human Services
Ohio University
Athens, Ohio

Harvey A. Siegal, Ph.D.
Professor and Director
Substance Abuse Intervention Services
School of Medicine
and
Professor
Department of Sociology and Anthropology
Wright State University
Dayton, Ohio

Suzanne K. Steinmetz, Ph.D.
Professor
Department of Individual and Family Studies
College of Human Resources
University of Delaware
Newark, Delaware

O. Z. White, Ph.D.
Professor
Department of Sociology
Trinity University
San Antonio, Texas

Contents

Preface

Our efforts at understanding the problems of an aging society have been hampered by a lack of behavioral, medical, and social data pertaining to our older citizens. In fact, one is hard pressed to find a consistent definition of what constitutes being old, being elderly, or being a senior citizen. In the past few years entire disciplines and subdisciplines in the academic training grounds have emerged as if we had suddenly discovered the "Aging of America" or that indeed there were older persons living among us. How many of you can count among your colleagues, friends, or acquaintances even one clinical gerontologist or geriatrician? Unfortunately, in our youth oriented culture, we almost reached the point of denying there were any old persons in our culture and certainly most of us were unwilling or unable to look ahead to the time *they might even outnumber us.*

The present volume is a step toward a more comprehensive understanding of our elderly. Criminologists have for some time been talking about the high rates of crime victimization among the elderly and health scientists have for some time been talking about the accumulation of chronic health problems among the elderly. They do so in the current volume as well. Additionally, however, an important advance in our knowledge of the elderly comes in discovering they are also deviants . . . . they are not only robbery victims, they rob people as well; they not only drink, they drink alcohol to excess and get arrested for DWI offenses just like the 18 year old; they not only take a great deal of medications, they also abuse these drugs for their euphoric effects. In all probability, the elderly have always been both victims and deviants. The distinct advantage to the present volume is that it presents the elderly as they really are: *a great deal like the rest of us only older.*

The contributors to the volume do not contend this single volume contains all the answers or even asks all the questions about how we are going to live with our elderly and how they may choose to live with us. What they do contend is that being old does cause some problems, exacerbates some problems, and may even prevent others from happening. What they argue for is inclusion rather than exclusion of the elderly in our assessments of diseases, crimes, alcoholism, drug abuse, domestic violence, suicide, and any other problems which create social casualties.

The reader should complete the volume believing that an attempt was made to compare and contrast exceptionally complex personal and social problems. While it is unlikely the reader will recognize his/her parent or grandparent described here, at least he/she will be exposed to someone else's parent or grandparent who just might be a drunk, a thief, or a victim. Everyone is getting older! No one is immune. Everyone is vulnerable.

Introduction

Imagine one of your aging parents being physically addicted to a life threatening "safe" drug prescribed to him or her over the years by a trusted family physician. *Imagine* your other aging parent being given a wide variety of both prescription and over-the-counter nonprescription drugs for several chronic health problems and that none of these medications had ever been tested clinically with an elderly population. *Imagine* how you would feel if you had "shopped" for the best nursing home in which to place an aging relative only to find out later that the relative had been unnecessarily heavily sedated so as to permit the "home" to function with fewer staff or had been underfed deliberately to increase profits. *Imagine* becoming so frustrated or angry with an elderly relative living in your home that you would become physically abusive with them. *Imagine* an elderly neighbor being beaten and even killed because of refusing to surrender a meager monthly social security check. If you can imagine these happenings, you are among the few who understand some of the realities of being that part of our population we call the elderly. Certainly, if you can imagine these realities, you can "see" some of the ways our elderly are *victimized*. But, let us extend our imaginations somewhat. *Imagine* an impoverished, homeless elderly person who perceives that all his options have vanished and that he must turn to theft to survive. *Imagine* an elderly man coping with the boredom and frustration of retirement by drinking too much too often and being arrested for DWI. *Imagine* his elderly wife trying to cope with him by staying "intoxicated" and therefore "insulated" with her prescription tranquilizers and sedatives. Obviously, the existence of elderly persons who abuse alcohol and other drugs and who commit crimes presents us with a view of the elderly as *deviants*.

It is difficult to conceive of a more controversial contrasting relationship than that which has been pursued in this volume. The volume, in fact, represents a reality which we as a society have been unable or unwilling to acknowledge, confront, and change. As a society, we have been ill prepared for the aging of our population. We were not prepared emotionally, intellectually, or socially for the aged population to increase both in numbers and as a proportion of the total population. We have yet to become prepared for the aged to live longer or for the death rate for the aged to continue to fall. Most of us do not even know that the fastest growing segment of our population is the population aged 85 and above, let alone the consequences of such a reality.

As the contributors began to discuss the potential content of the volume, it became obvious there was a need for a presentation which would describe some problems the elderly experience just because they have become old. It was equally obvious that there needed to be a "balance," a presentation which would describe problems the elderly bring upon themselves specifically as well as problems foisted on the elderly by their society. Finally, the contributors came together in a belief that describing the basic realities of an aging population would generate new personal and social roles for both the young and the old; new ethics would emerge surrounding distributive justice and the allocations of all types of resources; and, in all probability the system itself . . . society . . . would undergo some major revisions as economic and power bases shift to reflect the demographic shifts.

The professional literature does devote *some* space to the deteriorating health of our elderly, the burdensome cost of providing health care to our elderly who will never get well, the basic economic problems of our elderly in an inflationary society, and to the criminal victimization to which large numbers of our elderly are exposed. This literature does not, however, offer much for the student who is concerned with the problems the elderly might be bringing upon themselves or be forcing upon others. Both the contributors to this volume as well as the readers of it must now begin to view our elderly population from a more comprehensive perspective. Indeed, the elderly are both victims and deviants. Once this volume is in the literature, it should motivate others to research and to write on similar topics.

Carl D. Chambers, Ph.D., LNHA

Our Prejudices Against the Elderly

O. Z. WHITE, Ph.D.

Professor
Department of Sociology
Trinity University
San Antonio, Texas

I was introduced to the study of aging by a bright, open-faced young man who came to our campus as chair of the department of sociology. We were close friends, but we had little to do with each other professionally; I followed my interests and he followed his. I don't remember reading a paper of his or critiquing any of his research; I am sure he had little if any interest in my activities at that time.

David Oliver has been able to accomplish with boyish enthusiasm what most sociologists avoid like the plague. He is also a caring human being who has a passionate concern for his "variables." To him they are not only the objects of research but also friends, confidants, co-conspirators, partners in mischief, and playmates. I remember one of his annual Christmas parties. I doubt that there was a soul in the ball-room (other than Dave and his assistant) under 70 years old. Dave stood on the piano and lustily (and slightly off key, but who cared?) led the group in Christmas carols. Later, he made it a point to dance with every female in the room—all the while encouraging the other men present to do likewise.

To me, a product of the staid Parsonian tradition, it was an enlightening, if unnerving, experience. I shall always be grateful to David for teaching me something about the possibilities inherent in sociologist's relationship to their discipline, to other human beings, and to themselves. And more than that. For me he placed in perspective a basic attitude concerning older people: For the most part, they are like all of us—only older.

This is not to deny the very real problems that accompany the aging person. But, in the light of my friendship with David Oliver (now a nationally recognized gerontologist who holds a prestigious endowed chair in a respected institution) and what he taught me, I have been led to question whether "process" has not often been in actuality the self-fulfilling prophecy operating in the fertile ground of age-related stereotypes.

Erving Goffman (1963) wrote an extended essay on "spoiled identities," his term for those individuals who in some situations are disqualified from full social acceptance. Social disqualifications and the personal problems that result are related to mental and physical illnesses, racial minority, ethnic minority, disfigurements, alcoholism, drug addiction, homosexuality, prostitution, and more. Although Goffman did not mention aging per se, certainly many (but not all) the elderly suffer from spoiled identities. Brubaker and Powers (1976) pointed out that this negative connotation has been central to the study of aging since in the early 1950s. In early gerontological literature the term *stereotype* was used to convey attitudes (more often negative than positive) toward the status of the aged. Lippman (1922) defined stereotype as a rigid and factually incorrect perception produced by illogical reasoning. The concept has been softened somewhat in the past half century. Ian Robertson (1977), in his introductory textbook, introduces the term in the following manner: "Prejudiced thought always involves the use of a rigid mental image that summarizes whatever is believed to be typical about a group. This kind of image is called a *stereotype*."

Stereotypes are functional: they order expectations in such a way that behavior is constructed or anticipated in an orderly and predictable manner. An orderly society depends on the predictability of behavior. This, of course, is part of what socialization is all about. Most sociologists have heard countless dissertations on anomie—normlessness—and the dire consequences that occur when anomie is present and behavior is not predictable. Most of the time we are aware of societal expectations in relation to ourselves and others. And we know that most people behave as expected most of the time. Much of our behavior is based on anticipated actions of others, which in turn are based on internalized patterns. Our expectations focus on certain attributes (positive or negative) that we have attached to occupants of a particular status.

Thus, I know that an adolescent is likely to have certain attributes; when I deal with one I have not known before, I interact with him in the light of these behavioral expectations. The adolescent, for his part, knows that I have this image, and relates to it. In other words, stereotypes help us to cope with subjects with which we are not familiar. Except in the broadest sense, we are generalizing creatures, and stereotypes are a part of a greater learning process that social beings acquire for the sake of information management.

Often when we get to "know" the stereotyped individual, we find that he/she does not conform to our preconceptions. When that happens we often dismiss it—thinking "That's the exception that proves the rule"—and continue to act on the basis of earlier beliefs. More often than not, we tend to single out those actions that reinforce the stereotypes. For example: I once had a black graduate student (a Canadian) who had a passion for watermelon; I doubt I would have remembered that fact at all had he not been black.

The elderly have many attributes that make them prime candidates for stereotypical interpretation and reinforcement. First, they are easily identified by physical appearance. The hair tends to be gray and thin (or absent, in the case of males). Posture is slumped and shoulders become stooped. Speech tends to be slower and more deliberate, and some tonal range is lost. Given the speed, intensity, and pressure with which most of us live out our lives, who has not been irritated waiting behind an elderly person in a cafeteria line, where certain items are discounted for "senior citizens" but not all? Or tried to wait patiently while they boarded a bus or subway? Or, grumbling, followed their automobiles while they deliberately held to the speed limit during rush hours?

Second, they are an isolated group. Retired from the mainstreams of the marketplace and workplace, they have become more observers than participants. The detached observer role is in evidence on the park benches and around the mall fountains of the cities throughout the United States.

This isolation is more profound than most people realize, for many elderly Americans are either institutionalized or living in "retirement communities." Both groups are, for a number of very sound reasons, isolated from the larger population. They are like the invisible poor— there somewhere, but out of sight. When they live in a total community setting, they have limited interaction and thus are isolated from any meaningful relationship to the concerns of other groups. They often get only partial representations from the media, so that when they do attempt to participate, their conceptions seem naive, unsophisticated, and bland.

Third, the elderly are set apart by their problems with time. On one hand, they see about them family and peers who are dying off. Part of growing old is the realization of mortality, of time slipping away. Our socialization process is weakest at this point. We anticipate the other rite of passage well; death we avoid as long as we can. The life of the older person is lived under an ill-defined yet unavoidable shadow. And there is too little time.

On the other hand, there is a sense of too much time. Regular schedules, once centered around work and its satellite activities, no longer have any meaning. There are long, empty periods in what formerly had been busy and productive days. Few Americans have consuming leisure activites that easily carry over into retirement. There is thus created a gerontological time warp—on the one hand an anxiety related to time running out, and on the other hand an anxiety related to the long, dull, empty days that are left.

A fourth factor leading to stereotyping of the elderly is the general perception of their powerlessness. They are considered to be recipients rather than participants. The statuses they presently hold and the ill-defined roles they play are not significant to the production or decision-making process. They are consumer variables rather than production variables. In terms of the Protestant work ethic, they are the somewhat useless recipients of the somewhat optimistically planned largesse of the day. It is therefore not surprising that Social Security and Medicare were among the first targets for budget cuts. Of all political categories, the elderly were considered less capable of a powerful response to these propositions. Happily, the general population did not support the leadership in this direction.

The elderly are in many ways a minority, subjected to the same negative stereotypical behavior as racial and ethnic minorities. Gerontologists have used the term *ageism* as a counterpart to the more familiar *racism* and *sexism*. Ageism first appeared in the literature when Robert N. Butler, then director of the National Institute on Aging, specified it as "a process of systematic stereotyping of and discrimination against people because they are old" (1975). There is ample evidence that ageism exists—avoidance of elderly people on an individual level, discrimination, derision through hostile humor, complaints that they "don't do their part" or "take more than they deserve," and the assertion that they are a danger to society as a whole. And all this in spite of the fact that most of the more than 23 million people over 65, are functioning well on their own and getting along on their available financial resources.

A major difference between ageism and the other "isms" is that ageism is relatively new in our culture. The literature on aging that has a historical perspective often points out that in history the older person has often been the object of respect. Being elderly in contemporary society has often been seen as a regrettable trait, characteristic of contemporary urban industrialized populations. There is some evidence, however, that this earlier "respect" for the elders was motivated in part at least by economic considerations: the patriarchal nature of traditional social systems led to inheritance-related decisions, and property ownership rested with the individual until the end of his days. Even so, there is evidence that the veneration of elderly wisdom sometimes met with serious objections, even in the patriarchies of the ancient Hebrews. "You are old," the leaders of Israel told Samuel, "and your sons do not walk in your ways" (1 Sam. 8:4–5).

The elderly elite in contemporary society do not share the same problems as other categories of older citizens. For the particularly talented, retirement is not mandatory. Many individuals simply ignore the 65-year cutoff point; and, since they have obvious power, others ignore it as well. The late W. W. McAllister, a highly respected multi-term mayor of San Antonio, did not enter politics until he was in his early 70s—after a successful career as chief executive of a savings and loan association. Rather than retiring, high-level corporate and financial executives are often "kicked upstairs" to positions that require less energy, but they still retain power and prestige.

In the absence of educational enlightenment or personal experience, most people will get their information concerning aging and the process of aging from the mass media. The television set of the average American family is on an average of six hours a day. Gerontologists have ascertained that the media have, more often than not, reinforced negative physical and behavioral stereotypes of the elderly (Allen, 1981). This is supported by general findings across the various disciplines of behavioral science that media humor can generally be seen as an indicator of societal attitudes. Johnny Carson's Aunt Blabby is a stubborn, narrow-minded, vitriolic old woman. Tim Conway and

Carol Burnett, in their regular comedy routine, used an old couple with vacant faces who had problems (both physical and mental) dealing with routines of everyday life. To capture and maintain interest, television uses the stereotype in order to collapse time. The very process requires simplification and thereby leads to inaccuracies.

Palmore (1971) sought to study attitudes toward the aging by an analysis of 264 jokes collected from ten popular joke books. He found that over half the jokes reflected negative views, dealing with such things as physical ability or appearance, age concealment, sex, and mental abilities. Those dealing with men were more positive. More recent studies have indicated that not only is the male role more positive but males appear much more often than women. Smith (1979) found negative attitudes toward elderly persons in his study of cartoons in eight magazines. Joke humor was found to have more negative presentations than cartoon humor, and negative cartoons involved sexual impotence, being social reactionaries, mental incompetence, and physical infirmity. Positive presentations were often departures from the negative stereotypes.

Pamela Patten-Goldner (1984) had reported that negative stereotypes have become "ingrained in the belief systems of all age groups, including the elderly themselves" (see also Bengston, 1971; Bennett, 1976; Harris, 1975; Hickey and Kalish, 1968; Peters, 1971). Although there is some contradiction, there is evidence that children generally have clear views on aging as early as six (Marks and Newman, 1978; Seifeldt et al., 1981)—and many of these views are negative. Adolescents, themselves the recipients of stereotypical images, internalize these negatives when they are young, and continue to hold on to them. We need to provide children in their early years with information about the aging process, from childhood throughout life. This would be realistic and meaningful preparation for their own life experiences, if, indeed, the educational experience will dismantle the negative stereotypes.

We have implied but not yet articulated the profound and pervasive nature of the self-fulfilling prophecy: People are likely to become what others say they are, if the message is delivered in a consistent and structured way. And one way to keep minorities "in their place" is to infantilize them—label them "children" and then tell them over and over again that is how they act and that is who they are. People soon learn that it is best to behave as expected, that it will lead to the avoidance of pain (the most likely scenario) or the gaining of pleasure.

Why keep minorities "in their place"? There are positive reasons (cheap labor) and negative ones (social cost, economic pressures, or fear). When I was in South Carolina in the 1950s an elderly black friend once said to me, "Please don't call me 'mister.' I've been a boy all my life. It's too late for me to be anything else now." "Second childhood" is an all-too-familiar term in our culture. We allow outrageous behavior by elderly individuals that we would never anticipate from so-called mature adults. Birthday parties in most nursing homes will quickly prove my point. The inevitability of it all seems to prompt most of the clientele to relax and enjoy it as much as they can.

Why segregate the elderly? Because our society seems to work better that way. We have major space problems—social space, economic space, and (perhaps most importantly) emotional space. And we also have major time problems: time is crashing down on us, smothering us, and we see in the elderly a condition in which we will soon participate. We are, in the words of the old proverb, "too soon old and too late smart." This is frightening to us: gerontophobia, the fear of aging, is a common neurosis in our day. One way to deal with the fear is to make the feared object harmless and then keep it out of sight.

The human life cycle is therefore as much a social as a biological process. Life expectancies within a given society are related to a number of social and demographic factors such as health care and health-related influences, activities that either prevent or contribute to accidents, and violence and attitudes toward conflict. While a person born in the United States at the turn of the century could reasonably expect to live 47 years, average life expectancy today is 74 years.

The content of the life cycle is affected by other social factors as well. Relatively new social inventions, such as compulsory schooling and the relatively new life-cycle position called "adolescence," have kept large numbers out of the work force; and another social invention, compulsory retirement, has served the same purpose. However, youth are propelled by strong dynamics of deferred gratification—looking forward to a bright, rosy, satisfying future—while retirees are faced with empty, nonproductive roles—scarcely comforted by the platitudes describing the "golden years" and threatened by myths, which they themselves often believe.

Why have these myths arisen? One answer may lie in the research process. In actuality, only 6 percent of those 65 and over reside in long-term care institutions. But because they are a readily available captive audience, this group has been the target of much of the early, and some of the later, research concerning older Americans. So what are the *facts* about elderly people? Atchley (1980, p. 225) has listed 23 *accurate* beliefs. According to him, older people:

1. Are able to learn new things;
2. Have poor coordination;
3. Walk slowly;
4. Need glasses to read;
5. Are *not* unproductive;
6. Are useful to themselves and others;
7. Do *not* become less intelligent;
8. Are able to concentrate;
9. Are set in their ways;
10. Do not die soon after retirement;
11. Are not bedridden much of the time;
12. Worry about their health;
13. Are not helpless;
14. Are not in their second childhood;
15. Have to be careful about their diets;
16. Are more interested in religion;
17. Are more likely to have friends;
18. Can manage their own affairs;
19. Get love and affection from their children;
20. Do *not* feel neglected by their children;
21. Are interested in the opposite sex;
22. Are not a nuisance;
23. Worry about finances.

How to combat negative stereotyping—that's the challenge. Certainly most would agree that the arbitrary nature of the American social system forces older Americans into molds that might well be undeserved. Life, liberty, and the pursuit of happiness are not rights that should be subject to forfeiture because a person belongs to a specific age category. Social change that involves deep-seated values and is not perceived as urgent is always slow and deliberate; the old ways are comfortable—why bother to change? So far, the elderly have not been able to generate much of a sense of urgency.

There is some evidence, however, that our *political structures* are reacting to the presence of a growing population of elderly Americans. For the most part, there have been reactions to the increasing numbers drawing Social Security benefits. Mandatory retirement has been raised to 70 for many occupations, and the minimum age for receiving full Social Security benefits will soon be 67. It is to be hoped that these changes will soon be so widespread that 65 will no longer be the magic age for retirement. As those in the retirement categories increase and thus become more significant as special-interest voters, we can expect an increase in gerontopolitical activity.

In the early 1960s I participated in a study at a sizable elderly housing project—a study that reveals some interesting attitudes toward religion. When questioned about their religious preferences, many of the elderly expressed ambivalence about religion in general and churches in particular. Now they were "recipients" rather than "cheerful givers." Now they were passive listeners rather than active worshippers. Indeed, even in worship they had become dependent. Families or well-meaning strangers came to the complex to pick them up and deliver them to churches, where they felt like strangers, even in the old and familiar surroundings in which they had earlier felt proprietary pride.

The church and its various activities have often been colored by ageism. Youthful pastors are in demand, while church programs are geared toward youth and their activities. Older church members need far more than bland condescension—they need vigorous programming directed toward their needs. They should be integrated into the congregation, so that they can share in the enterprises, cope with the problems, and reap the rewards of discipleship. Little in the life of congregations is age specific. A conscious effort by congregations to break down age barriers could lead to new levels of mutual understanding and respect. Negative stereotyping could hardly survive in such an environment.

Education is another natural context for fighting ageism. This implies education in its deepest, most meaningful sense: a blending of experience, insight, and decision making. It implies morals and values. The advantages of enlisting older people into the various educational enterprises of communities has ample documentation. In the mid

1960s, the late Vera Burke, a social worker far ahead of her time, founded a "foster grandparents" program in San Antonio, which continues to operate successfully today. In such programs, young children are in touch with their own histories in a vibrant and meaningful way as they learn crafts and hear stories from people who actually participated in "historical" activities and events. In the process, children learn that the people involved are not just "old folks" whose skins no longer fit, but real people who have led exciting lives, know important things, and are real and important links with the past. Those older Americans who participate in the education of the nation's young thus become role models—not objects of ridicule and scorn. As different individuals teach different skills and tell different stories, children also learn that no two people are really all that much alike, even if they are old.

A new area of intergenerational activities involves older people and college students. At Trinity University, for example we have an APO social club that is dedicated to social service. One of its most successful efforts over the past few years has been a telephone reassurance program, which provides daily contact for elderly persons who live alone. To set up the program, members located isolated older people through churches and various social agencies and secured basic information about them in an initial interview. This information included nearest living relative or friend, physician's name and telephone number, medications, and the time they would prefer being called. The depth and meaningfulness of some of the relationships that developed were surprising. And often the young people found that they benefited as much from the relationships as did the elderly.

The advantages of these activities are several. Young people have great mobility and are thus able to participate in a broad range of activities. Young college students themselves have histories and are able to share meaningful experiences with older friends. Exciting relationships develop as a response to the needs of both generations. With the college group, the goal is mutual respect and mutual support arising from a relationship that had, as its original purpose, help and concern for the elderly.

Building on the success of telephone reassurance we are now attempting to move into the area of housing. The elderly often have critical problems with housing. Those who live alone are still largely self-sufficient and have no desire to live in an institution. However, loneliness, fear of crime, and fear of a sudden debilitating illness are three of the concerns that they often express. One answer to the problem is shared housing, a solution that has met with some success. A few colleges are beginning to experiment with intergenerational dormitories. Their initial reports have been enthusiastic. One drawback to intergenerational dormitories, however, is that two separate cultures tend to develop side by side and daily interaction does not take place.

In San Antonio, however, we are beginning another type of program, which would place college students in homes of the elderly. Each arrangement is made after careful screening, and each has its own contract. Some older people are motivated to participate in the program simply because they live in a big house and are lonely. Some express the need for only minimal help, such as grocery shopping, and lawn mowing. This is noted in the contract, and rent is adjusted accordingly. We stressed that we are not interested in providing general domestic or health-related services.

Students are motivated to participate in the program for a number of reasons. Some are faced with financial problems. Some face a shortage of space in the most desirable dorms at their institutions. Some need a quieter environment in which to study. Some are interested in gerontology as a profession.

All our students will be required to do some reading in preparation for their new experience, to keep a journal during the first year, and to meet with an assigned advisor regularly. The advisor is usually a professor, but is sometimes a social worker or an administrator. At the end of the year, students meet with their advisors, submit brief critiques, and are assigned grades. Three semester hours credit are earned, in addition to the other rewards gained from the experience. Anyone planning a program such as this should be prepared for some dismal failures. No matter how careful the screening process, some mistakes will be made. The rewards, however, make it all worthwhile.

Please remember that while we know something about the stereotypes, we know little about the majority of the aged who are "really out there." Gerontologists have generally had as the subjects for their studies those older people who are either isolated or in some form of captivity. Little is known about the 85 percent who are relatively healthy and mobile, and we have little information about the 75 percent who are not poor or the 70 percent who are not living alone.

REFERENCES

Allen, B. J. "Knowledge of Aging: A Cross-Sectional Study of Three Different Age Groups." *Educational Gerontology* 1981: 49–59.

Atchley, Robert C. *The Social Forces in Later Life.* Belmont, Calif.: Wadsworth, 1980.

Bengston, V. L. "Interage Perception and the Generation Gap." *Gerontologist* 11 (1971): 85–89.

Bennett, R. "Attitudes of the Young Toward the Old: A Review of Research." *Personnel and Guidance Journal* 55 1976: 136–39.

Brubaker, T., and Powers, E. "The Stereotype of "Old": A Review and Alternative Approach." *Journal of Gerontology* (1954) 9:243–46.

Butler, Robert N. *Why Survive? Being Old in America.* New York: Harper & Row, 1975.

Goffman, E. *Stigma: Notes on the Management of Spoiled Identity.* Englewood Cliffs, N.J.: Prentice Hall, 1963.

Harris, L. *The Myth and Reality of Aging in America.* Washington: National Council on the Aging, 1975.

Hickey, T., and Kalish, R. "Young People's Perceptions of Adults." *Journal of Gerontology* 23 (1968): 215–20.

Lippman, W. *Public Opinion.* New York: Harcourt Brace, 1922.

Marks, R., and Newman, S. *Children's Views on Aging.* Document Resume (1978) Ed 190 850, CE 026 377, pp. 1–20.

Palmore, E. "Facts on Aging: A Short Quiz." *Gerontologist* (1977): 17 315–20.

Patten-Goldner, P. "Literature Review on Children's Attitudes Toward the Elderly." Unpublished paper, Trinity University, 1984.

Peters, C. "Self Conceptions of the Aged, Age Identification and Aging." *Gerontologist* 11 (1971): 69–73.

Richman, J. "The Foolishness and Wisdom of Age: Attitudes Toward the Elderly as Reflected in Jokes." *Gerontologist* 17 (1977): 210–19.

Robertson, I. *Sociology* New York: Worth, 1977.

Selfeldt, C.; Jantz, R.; Galper, A.; and Serock, K. "Children's Attitudes Toward the Elderly and Aging." *Educational Gerontology* 7 (1981): 43–47.

Smith, M. D. "The Portrayal of Elders in Magazines' Cartoons." *Gerontologist* 19 (1979): 408–12.

Health Status of the Elderly: Infinite Need and Finite Resources

CARL D. CHAMBERS, Ph.D.

Professor
Health Services Administration
School of Health and Sport Sciences
Ohio University

KATHRYN S. FELTON PRIBBLE, M.HSA

Health Services Administration Program
School of Health and Sport Sciences
Ohio University

THE SETTING

> Whatever one feels is right—or wrong—about American society today can be illustrated by health care (Levine, 1979).

Anytime we talk about health care in general or specifically for the economically dependent, such as the elderly and the poor, we inevitably reveal our basic emotional, intellectual, social, and ethical assumptions about the proper relationship of government to its citizens, citizens to government, and citizens to citizens. As our country grew and matured, most people came to assume that everyone had a "right" to treatment when ill or injured. In quite recent times, people also came to believe this right has expanded to include mental as well as physical health. Thus, we believe that all our citizens have a right to the resources that will permit them to be as healthy and happy as possible—including quality primary, secondary, and tertiary preventions and interventions. Most important, we came to believe that if one could not secure this care through personal effort in the competitive marketplace, it was the responsibility of the government either to provide the services directly or to "pay" for them through appropriate providers.

13

Both the providers and consumers began to think of health care as an unlimited resource to which everyone had unlimited access.

While this may be philosophically commendable, it is and always was an economic fantasy. Most analysts have come to accept several restrictions on this belief:

- "Deserving" is a philosophical concept, but "providing" and "consuming" are economic realities.
- Economic reality means limited availability, which ultimately means limited accessibility.
- Those consuming "most" of a limited resource are providing the "least" to that resource pool.
- At a minumum, elderly consumers of available health care resources will probably never be in the position to "pay back" the resource pool.

The reality of the situation is that *the elderly are the primary consumers of our limited health care resources.* At a time when they are only some 12 percent of the total population, they account for close to one-third of our health care expenditures (Waldo and Lozenby, 1984; Surgeon General, 1979). This is understandable given the physical and mental health status of the elderly, the result has produced a society that has become bankrupt due to these expenditures. From all indications, we can expect the disparity between the size of the elderly population and their disproportionate consumption of health care resources to increase, and at an accelerated pace. Without forceful intervention, what is now a current overburden will become a system-destroying economic disaster. In all probability, intervention will mean fewer resources for the elderly. "Health care cost containment" will become the bureaucratic euphemism for restricting health-care services to the elderly.

There is absolutely no question that the current size of the older population has placed an unprecedented burden on our available health care resources. As the aged population increases in numbers—and it most assuredly will—the composition will change also, to include more of the "old-old." These unprecedented stresses will necessitate unprecedented solutions. Providing for the medical needs of our older citizens already is producing a major social and ethical dilemma for most of us. Unfortunately, it is a dilemma the system cannot tolerate. Resolution is vital. The elderly are probably destined to become *victims* in any resolutions. We have no solutions to this pending victimization. We see no scenario where the elderly will not lose. We present the case of the elderly—infinite needs and finite resources—in the hopes of reducing their losses, not preventing them.

HEALTH STATUS OF THE ELDERLY: INFINITE NEED

To make rational decisions about health care resource allocation, the prudent analyst will first make some determination of need. For example, if it is true that the elderly consume a disproportionate share of the available resources, are their "needs" also disproportionate? Are the elderly somehow inappropriate overconsumers who could be "cut back" without being placed in any significant jeopardy? Are they consuming resources at a rate commensurate with their actual need? Or are they indeed underconsumers who are already being victimized?

"The elderly have more health problems than their juniors, and tend to have more complicated and severe disease that require longer periods of hospitalization and more extensive utilization of home health care and extended care facilities" (*Statistical Bulletin*, 1984).

For the young, being ill is a transitory problem. For the old, being well is generally just as transitory. For most people, being old *means* having health problems that don't go away; health problems are chronic and progressively debilitating, necessitating constant and ever-increasing health care.

We can assume this situation will only get worse—the number of people who survive to become elderly is increasing and the pool of the very old is increasing even more rapidly. *We are becoming older but not healthier.*

Between 1982 and 2000 the population of persons aged 65 and over will increase by 30 percent and may even increase by 150 percent by the year 2050. By comparison, demographers project a 110 percent increase in the population of persons aged 85 and over by the year 2000 and an increase of 557 percent by the year 2050 (*Statistical Bulletin*, 1984). By the year 2020 the elderly population will constitute 20 percent of the total population (Pegels, 1980).

"Future growth in the numbers of elderly is in part a reflection of the Post-World War II 'baby boom' bulge. However it is also spurred by the marked reductions in death rates of the elderly in the past 15 years. Heart and cerebrovascular death rates have witnessed particularly steep declines for the elderly in recent years" (Davis, 1984).

It is rather ironic that our successes in delivering quality health care have created such expectations and demands on the delivery system that we now must contemplate restricting access to this care. Progress toward containing one set of problems may be creating even larger ones.

The elderly currently consume 30 percent of the available health care resources. Do they actually "need" all these resources? Just how sick are they?

Studies have shown that the majority of our population aged 65 and above is *not* in good health, that an individual's health worsens with age, and that the elderly poor have the worst health of all (Tissue, 1972; Derraro, 1980; Chambers, 1982; Chambers et al., 1984; Waldo and Lozenby, 1984). More specifically these studies suggest that:

- Some 30 percent of all our elderly perceive themselves to be in only fair health.
- Among the rural elderly, 30 percent feel they are in good health, 25 percent feel they are in marginal health, and 45 percent feel they are in poor health.
- Among the urban elderly, 44 percent feel they are in good health while 56 percent feel they are in poor health.
- Among the elderly poor, 40 percent feel they are in good to excellent health, and 60 percent feel they are in only fair to poor health.
- Among persons under age 70, some two-thirds perceive themselves to be in good health but this drops to 45 percent after age 70.

The 1981 assessments distributed by the Health Care Financing Administration (Waldo and Lozenby, 1984) seem to indicate that these resources are being consumed legitimately. Consider these data on the noninstitutionalized elderly:

- 30 percent are in no better than fair health.
- 22 percent are experiencing limitations in their major daily living activities because of their health.
- 18 percent are unable to carry out their major daily living activities unassisted because of their health.

- Each elderly person averages 42 activity-restricted days a year because of poor health.
- Each elderly person averages 13 bed-disability days a year because of poor health.
- On any given day, the "average" elderly person will report 1.1 acute health problems and 3.3 chronic ones.

We assume it is the chronic health problems that result in the disproportionate consumption of the available health care resources. Because they are chronic, they don't "go away." Resources may not always be available, but the need will always be there. To a very large degree, these chronic debilitating conditions are part of the aging process itself. Status management and symptom relief are the best we can hope for. "Cures," which would reduce care needs, are not possible. This inability to significantly reduce the demand for resources is clearly shown in the data below, which illustrate both the extent and the nature of chronic health problems in the elderly.

Health Problem of
Persons Aged 65 and Above
1981 Rate per 1,000 Persons

Arthritis	464.7
Hypertension	378.6
Hearing impairments	283.8
Heart conditions	277.0
Chronic sinusitis	183.6
Visual impairments	136.6
Deformities or orthopedic impairments	128.2
Diabetes	83.4
Varicose veins	83.3
Hemorrhoids	65.9
Diseases of the urinary system	56.1
Hay fever without asthma	51.9
Chronic bronchitis	46.1
Eczema, dermatitis, uritcaria	30.9
Asthma	28.6

Obviously our elderly, as a group, do present a great "need" for our available health care resources.

Are the elderly overconsumers, in the sense of consuming health care resources needlessly or inappropriately? Although the elderly do consume a disproportionately large amount of the available health care resources, our research indicates that, based on actual need, they are *under*consumers.

Consider: during a 1979 nationwide survey assessing the health status of the general population, 90 percent of those aged 65 and above reported they had some existing problem with their health (Chambers, 1980). Of these, 90 percent reported multiple problems; the average was 4.1 per person. Virtually everyone who had a "current" or existing problem also reported at least one significant "chronic" problem. But the elderly in this study were not overconsuming health care resources; only 30 percent of the health complaints were even presented to a primary-care provider. They were self-treating 40 percent of their health complaints and ignoring the remaining 30 percent. Other surveys conducted on a more restricted basis have confirmed the multiplicity of the physical and mental health problems among our elderly (Chambers, 1982).

Lest we misunderstand the "seriousness" of these many untreated health problems, consider the conditions reported by the elderly during the nationwide study and a regional survey in southeast Ohio (Chambers, 1980 and 1982).

In both surveys, elderly respondents considered heart disease, high blood pressure, diabetes, or some combination their principal health problem. Of the elderly reporting these as current conditions, less than one-half had seen a physician about these problems within the past six months (48 percent in the national survey and 41 percent in the regional survey).

Such data have led us to contend that the elderly actually *under*consume health care resources.

THE ABILITY OF THE SYSTEM TO PROVIDE COMPREHENSIVE HEALTH CARE FOR THE ELDERLY

In 1977, average per capita health care spending for persons 65 years of age or over was 3.5 times that for the total population (Fisher, 1980). That ratio is even higher today and is expected to continue to rise in spite of the cost-containment activities currently in place. Per

Health Problems of
Persons Aged 65 and Above

Problem Condition	Nationwide	S.E. Ohio
Heart problem	58%	41%
Respiratory problem	49	48
Circulatory problem	31	50
Gastrointestinal		
Problem	35	34
Hypertension	49	59
Diabetes	16	11
Arthritis	64	73
Major hearing loss	21	25
Major vision loss	22	32
Mental distress	31	27
None	6	2
Total problems		
Range	0–10	0–8
Mean	4.1	4.0

capita health care expenditures have been increasing at a rate considerably in excess of overall inflation. For example, the increase between 1977 and 1978 was 13 percent (Waldo and Lozenby, 1984). Total health care expenditures for the aged are expected to rise from about $50 billion in 1978 to almost $200 billion in 2000, in constant 1980 dollars (Davis, 1984).

Health care costs for the aged are underwritten as shown in the following proportional distribution (Waldo and Lozenby, 1984):

Sponsors of Health Care Costs

Medicare	50%
Medicaid	13
Other government programs	5
Private industries	7
Elderly "out-of-pocket"	25

Thus, more than two-thirds of the current health care expenditures on the elderly are being borne through government programs, with the federally financed Medicare program bearing the lion's share. Current and projected deficits in this program keep its soundness and actual survival in constant jeopardy. In 1984 the Health Care Financing Administration projected that the Medicare trust fund could be exhausted as early as 1989 if the current laws, reimbursement practices, and coverage are not modified (Waldo and Lozenby, 1984).

In recent years, we have seen more and more costs being shifted to the elderly consumer through higher premiums, deductibles, and co-payments. As the "public" monies become more threatened, this shift will undoubtedly accelerate.

LIMITED ABILITY OF THE ELDERLY TO PAY FOR CARE: FINITE RESOURCES

There are an estimated 27 million elderly people in this country; of those at least one-fourth exist either below or slightly above the poverty level. At the very time when health problems demand an ever-increasing share of the individual's available income, this income is decreasing. Most people can now anticipate spending some 15 years, or 20 percent of their lives, on retirement. Unfortunately, income during these retirement years is normally less than half the amount of pre-retirement income (Jones, 1977). It is not hard to imagine what occurs when health worsens, health care costs increase, and income becomes fixed.

We must not lose sight of the fact that the elderly directly purchase 25 percent of all the health care services and goods they consume with "out-of-pocket" monies. In 1984, the aged consumed $4,202 of health care per capita. Of this amount, $1,059 was in the form of direct patient payments. The elderly are already spending a greater proportion of their available dollars for health care services and goods than the non-elderly and the trend is for the system to shift an even greater share of these costs to them. At what point does this become an impossible burden which the elderly cannot bear? For the elderly generally and the economically dependent elderly specifically, this "point" has probably already been reached. Additional health care costs must be met through sacrifices in other basic living areas, such as housing and food.

COMMENT

Spending for health care has understandably become a source of major concern for increasing numbers of Americans. Among our elderly citizens, this is almost universally the case. Surveys among the elderly have always identified health and health care as primary concerns. As one gets older, concerns for physical and mental health and the ability to secure care if needed are the principal causes of stress, anxiety, and depression. Such concerns are both real and justified.

From 1977 through 1982, annual personal health care expenditures for all Americans rose at an annual rate of 14 percent, or 1.5 times the rate of growth of the gross national product. Over the same period, the health care expenditure portion of the gross national product rose 8.8 percent to 10.5 percent. It is expected to rise to 15.0 percent by the year 2000, in spite of all our attempts to prevent it from doing so.

Health care is expensive—too expensive. The elderly consume a disproportionate amount of this expensive care, and they are unable to share in its cost. Since it seems economically disastrous for this situation to continue, we are faced with two options. First, we could simply restrict the elderly's access to comprehensive health care by making these services available on the basis of ability to pay. Second, we could aggressively pursue innovative and creative ways to finance and deliver economical health care services.

While we agree that the elderly are disproportionate consumers of the available health care resources in this country, we do not necessarily agree they are overconsumers. If need is the criterion for allocation, they are not overconsumers of these limited resources. On the contrary, they are underutilizers now and could never hope for parity in the distribution or redistribution of limited resources. Any reallocation of resources that is restricted solely to health care resources will mean that the elderly will lose.

We believe that health care availability and access must be determined within the context of total available resources. Typically however, those who cannot afford to pay do not get to make decisions about what should be provided, to whom, and how. Being economically dependent makes one dependent in most other things as well. To a very large extent, the elderly have been, and will continue to be, *social casualties* in their competition for available health care resources.

Have the elderly been "victimized" by all this? Certainly. Is this "victimization" likely to continue? Probably. Is this "victimization" necessary? No.

It seems to us that a realistic retrenching strategy could be found in a model in which society is committed to providing a specific level of health services as a *right*. In order for there to be a movement toward such a model, there must be some definition of an acceptable minimum standard in personal medical services. We believe such a minimum "right" might be guaranteed access to both primary outpatient and inpatient care, while restricting access to the more limited-benefit, low-return services such as coronary bypass operations and the high-technology services such as organ transplants. Specific inclusions and exclusions should be a matter of preadoption negotiation among consumers, providers, and financers. Such a strategy should help to reduce the "losses" we see accruing to the elderly and, simultaneously, buy society the time needed to create innovative models for both financing and delivering care to everyone, including the elderly.

REFERENCES

Chambers, C. 1980. *A report of the physical and mental health status and therapy index for the general population*. Geneva, Fla.: Personal Development Institute.

Chambers, C. 1982. *A report of the physical and mental health status for the residents in southeast Ohio*. Athens: Ohio University College of Health and Human Services.

Chambers, C., O. White, J. Lindquist, and M. Harter. 1984. "Patterns and correlates of minor tranquilizers use within a tri-ethnic population of the noninstitutionalized elderly." Speech presented at the Southwestern Sociological Association Annual Meeting in Fort Worth, Texas.

Davis, K. 1984. The medical care challenge of an aging population. *Statistical Bulletin*. April–June, p. 13.

Derraro, K. F. 1980. Self-ratings of health among the old and the old-old. *J. Health and Soc. Behavior* 21 (December): 377–83.

Fisher, C. 1980. Differences by age groups in health care spending. *Health Care Financing Review*. HCFA Pub. No. 03045. Health Care Financing Administration. Washington: Washington; U. S. Government Printing Office.

Jones, R. 1977. *The other generation*. Englewood Cliffs, N.J.: Prentice Hall.

LeVine, C. 1979. Ethics and health cost containment. *Hasting Center Report* 9(1) (February): 10–13.

1980 United States DHHS Publication No. (PHS) 81–1232, Hyattsville, Md.: National Center for Health Statistics.

Pegels, C. 1980. *Health care and the elderly*. Rockville, Md.: Aspen.

1984. Projections of population growth at the older ages. *Statistical Bulletin*. Metropolitan Life Insurance Company, April–June.

Surgeon General. Healthy older adults. *Healthy People*. Washington: General Printing Office, pp. 71–76.

Tissue, T. 1972. The survey of the low-income aged and disabled: An introduction. *Social Security Bulletin* 40: 3–11.

U.S. Department of Commerce, Bureau of Census. 1985. *Statistical abstracts of the United States 1985.* Table 183.

Waldo, D. and H. Lozenby. 1984. Demographic characteristics and health care use and expenditures by the aged in the United States: 1977–1984. *Health Care Financing* 6(1) (Fall): 1–29.

Drug Use and Misuse In Old Age

DAVID M. PETERSEN, Ph.D.

Professor
Department of Sociology
Georgia State University
Atlanta, Georgia

Researchers have long focused their attention upon the use (and misuse) of drugs among populations of adolescents and young adults. This exclusive concentration on youthful drug use, with a corresponding lack of emphasis on other age groups, has provided an empirically inaccurate picture of the nature and extent of drug use in American society. While it is certainly true that the young represent a sizeable proportion of drug users, it is important to keep in mind that the young are not the only individuals who use and misuse drugs. The elderly have a greater number of chronic illnesses than do younger people, and, as a result, they receive disproportionately more medications than any other age group. While those over 65 years of age make up only about eleven percent of the population, they receive approximately twenty-five percent of all prescriptions written. Moreover, a significant share of all prescriptions received by the elderly is accounted for by psychoactive drugs, with four of the ten most frequently prescribed drugs for those 65 and over being psychotropics (Task Force on Prescription Drugs, 1968).

In contrast to the large amount of information available on drug use and misuse among the young, there is a lack of data on drug use patterns among adult and elderly populations. Although there is an increasing awareness of the problem of drug use among the elderly (including a flurry of research activity within recent years), there is much less information regarding drug use patterns among this population than for any other stage of the developmental life cycle. It is the purpose of this paper to draw together the available information on drug use and misuse among the elderly in order to provide some conclusions regarding our state of knowledge in this area. Because legal drug use represents the primary problem among the elderly, illicit drug use will not be reviewed here. Our discussion will center, then, on the use and misuse of legally prescribed drugs and legally purchased over-the-counter drugs. Where data permit we will concentrate our attention on psychotropic or psychoactive (mood altering) drugs.

At the outset, it must be noted that there are problems in doing a review of the literature in this area. In the first place, studies that have attempted to describe the nature and extent of drug patterns among the elderly lack a standard definition for drug use and misuse. For some, *use* implies "proper utilization" of drugs intended for therapeutic purposes, resulting in minimal or no adverse medical or social consequences (Atkinson and Kofoed, 1984). Our intent here, however, will be simply to examine studies that provide basic knowledge about the extent to which elderly persons *take* particular drugs. Moreover, we will be concerned with the various contexts in which drug use occurs and the purposes for such use. Inappropriate drug use will also be of concern. For our purposes, *misuse* will refer to the inappropriate use of prescription psychoactive (and other) drugs resulting from physicians' inappropriate prescribing practices and patients' failure to comply with instructions for taking medications.

In addition to problems with terminology, the literature offers considerable variation in classification of psychoactive drugs. In one study, for example, sedatives are combined with minor tranquilizers, while in another they are combined with hypnotics or grouped separately. Thus, direct comparisons between these studies are extremely difficult. Differences also exist with regard to *age* definitions. Many researchers have included all persons over middle age (often 45 to 50) as "elderly." Comparisons of findings from such studies with other investigations of persons over 60 or 65 present a problem.

We have made no attempt to reconcile these differences here; we merely note that it is difficult, if not impossible, to make direct comparisons between investigations. Given the diverse nature and variation among existing studies, we will review individual studies separately and provide linking commentary when appropriate.

PATTERNS OF PRESCRIPTION DRUG USE

For convenience, the studies to be discussed here can be grouped under four general categories. The first concerns drug use among representative samples of persons at *all* ages, from which we may extract data on the elderly. The second focuses on drug use in the *general elderly* population. (Although no national studies have explored the extent to which older people use psychoactive drugs, selected regional investigations have been directed at the elderly.) The third category examines drug-use patterns for elderly persons residing in *institutional* settings (nursing homes and hospitals treating psychiatric patients). The final category contains studies that have attempted to contribute to our understanding of the influences that lead the elderly to drug use. In examining the fourth category, we will consider the contextual, attitudinal, and personal correlates related to drug use in the aged.

Epidemiology of Drug Use

Patterns of psychotherapeutic drug use during the year preceding the interview were obtained by Mellinger and his associates (1971) from a probability sample of 1,104 adults aged 18 and over in San Francisco, California. Seven major therapeutic classes of drugs were included: major tranquilizers, minor tranquilizers, antidepressants, stimulants, sedatives, hypnotics, and antispasmodic–gastrointestinal drugs. The results reveal that both individual drug use and type of drug used are highly correlated with age. The highest proportion of nonusers of any psychotherapeutic drug were persons 60 and over: 65 percent of the females and 75 percent of the males reported no use within the year preceding the survey. Nonetheless, elderly men (60 and over) were somewhat more likely to be using a psychotherapeutic drug than were young persons aged 18 to 29 (17 percent versus 12 percent), while elderly females and their younger counterparts were equally likely to use these prescription drugs (27 percent versus 28 percent). In addition, persons 60 and over were more likely to use prescription hypnotics than were those aged 18 to 29. The younger group was more likely to use minor tranquilizers, sedatives, and stimulants.

Chambers (1971) investigated drug use in the general population of New York state during 1970, examining the use patterns for 17 categories of drugs (including some illicit drugs). He found age to be a significant factor in the regular use (at least six times per month) of selected drugs. Persons aged 50 and over were more likely than any other age category to be regular users of barbituate sedative-hypnotics (58 percent); nonbarbituate sedative-hypnotics (58 percent); major tranquilizers (48 percent); and minor tranquilizers (42 percent). For the 50 and over and the 18- to 24-year-old groups, a bimodal age relationship was found for regular users of amphetamines and noncontrolled narcotics/prescription nonnarcotic analgesics. Regular use of the remaining 11 substances (e.g., antidepressants and diet pills) was fairly evenly distributed by age group. The data reveal, then, that the use of general depressants is more prevalent for the middle-aged and elderly than for any other group.

In another examination of psychoactive drug use patterns, Parry and his associates (Parry et al., 1973; Mellinger et al., 1974) interviewed a national household sample of 2,552 persons aged 18 to 74. The study concentrated on drug use during a one-year period preceding the interview and, with the exception of antispasmodics, used the same therapeutic drug classification as Mellinger and his colleagues (1971). While most respondents reported that they had not used a psychoactive drug during the last year, both elderly men and women were more likely than any other age cohort to have used a prescription psychotherapeutic drug. Almost one-fifth (21 percent) of the older men and one-third (32 percent) of the older women had used at least one prescription psychotherapeutic drug during the last year. As to specific drugs used, the minor tranquilizers/sedatives and the hypnotics were the drugs most frequently reported by both elderly men and women. Moreover, for both men and women, the use of these drugs was more prevalent among the elderly than among members of any other age group.

In addition to determining prevalence rates, Parry and his colleagues attempted to determine levels of use—how often psychoactive drugs were taken and in what pattern. A duration-frequency index was constructed based on usage of one or more drugs in any category, and respondents were classified according to "high" and "low" patterns of drug usage. An examination of high-level use among those who took all prescription psychoactive drugs within the last year revealed that roughly one-third (32 percent) of those aged 60 to 74 fell in that category. When compared to the two middle-aged groups (39 percent for ages 30 to 44, and 42 percent for ages 45 to 59), the level of psychoactive drug use for the elderly was somewhat lower. Thus, while the elderly appear to use more drugs than any other age category, they are some-what less likely to report a high level of use than are middle-aged persons.

Warheit and his colleagues (1976) investigated patterns of drug use among 1,633 noninstitutionalized adults in Alachua County, Florida. They found a significant positive relationship between age and drug use, with the greatest percentage of overall drug use occurring among those persons aged 60 and over. The proportion of individuals who were using some type of drug (prescription or over-the-counter) at the time of the interview ranged from a low of 45.3 percent in the age group 18 to 29 to 75.6 percent in the 60 and over group. Persons 60 and over were most likely to be taking prescription drugs for somatic conditions (for example, high blood pressure, diabetes, heart disease) and to report undifferentiated drug use (no positive identification of drug being taken). The elderly were also more likely than younger persons to be using prescription psychotropic drugs (sedatives, tranquilizers, and stimulants): 17.5 percent of those 60 and over, compared to 4.8 percent of those between 18 and 29.

The study findings also point to age differences among users of the three classes of psychotropic drugs. Sedatives were used most frequently by those persons 60 and over, with roughly one-third (34 percent) reporting use of these drugs. In contrast, sedative use was lowest for the 18 to 29 age category, with 20.8 percent reporting that they took these drugs. While use of tranquilizers was greatest for the 30 to 59 group, more than one-third (35.3 percent) of those 60 and over had used these drugs. Stimulant use was most common among persons under 20 (22.6 percent) and was negatively related to age, with only 3.5 percent of those 60 and over reporting use. Further, frequent use (every day, all the time, or often) of both sedatives and tranquilizers also generally varied by age. Persons 45 and older were found to be the most frequent users of these drugs. Frequent use of the sedatives ranged from a low of 7.5 percent among the 18 to 29 group to 20.0 percent among those 60 and over. For tranquilizers the range was from a low of 55.2 percent for those under 30 to a high of 86.4 percent among those aged 45 to 59, although nearly as many persons over 60 reported the frequent use of these medications (83.1 percent). In sum, the elderly were more likely than younger persons to be using sedatives and tranquilizers and to be using them frequently.

Approaching psychoactive drug-use patterns from another direction, Zawadski and his colleagues (1978) compared utilization rates of both the aged (60 and over) and the general Medicaid populations in California during the fiscal year 1975–76. Specifically, they examined drug expenditures and drug profiles among several groups and subgroups, including the general Medicaid population of 2 million eligible state residents—the Medicaid elderly, composed of 361,000 eligible persons; the approximately 60,000 institutionalized elderly in long-term care facilities; and some 300,000 noninstitutionalized elderly. The study reveals that prescription drug expenditures were more than twice as high for the *aged* Medicaid population as for the general Medicaid population. The aged, who comprise about one-sixth (16 percent) of the Medicaid population, accounted for 35 percent of all paid prescription dollars. Among the elderly, more than twice as much was spent on those institutionalized in residential nursing facilities as on the noninstitutionalized or community elderly. Analysis of expenditures for psychotropic drugs (antidepressants, major and minor tranquilizers, stimulants, sedatives, and hypnotics), as opposed to nonpsychotropic drugs, revealed that the major difference in use among the elderly was a much higher level of psychotropic drug use among those who were institutionalized. (They spent 17 times more on psychotropic drugs than did the community elderly.) Between the noninstitutionalized elderly and the general population, there was little difference in the level of psychotropic drug use. In sum, psychotropic drug use was found to be more related to institutional residence than to age.

The Task Force on Prescription Drugs noted in the *The Drug Users* (1968) that the elderly in the United States received 262 million prescriptions from all sources, for which they paid over $1 billion. A comparison of an average person over 65 with one under 65 revealed that the amount of money the former spent on prescribed drugs was three times the amount spent by the latter. It has also been reported by the National Council on the Aging (1970) that 20 percent of the elderly's out-of-pocket expenditures are for medications.

The data reveal in the main that the elderly are more likely than the young to be using drugs, including psychoactive drugs. Persons over 60 are likely to be taking prescription drugs for somatic conditions, but they also receive a disproportionately high number of psychotropic medications. Approximately one-fifth of older men and one-third of older women reported the use of a psychoactive drug. The highest prevalence of use occurs for sedatives, minor tranquilizers, and the hypnotics. Much lower rates of consumption are reported for stimulants, antidepressants, and other drugs. Moreover, the elderly are more likely to be using sedatives, minor tranquilizers, and hypnotics than any other age group. Among the aged who use prescription psychotropic drugs, at least one-third report that their drug use is at a "high" level. In addition, the elderly are more likely than younger persons to be frequent users of sedatives and tranquilizers. Prescription drug expenditures have also been found to be higher for the aged than for the general population.

Studies of Drug Use by the Elderly

In recent years the extent and patterns of drug use by the elderly have concerned a number of researchers. A study that Vener and his colleagues (1979) conducted on drug use and health characteristics of 55 community-dwelling, retired elderly persons residing in Michigan revealed that 37, or two-thirds (67 percent), of the respondents reported that they had taken a prescription drug in the week preceding the interview. For those who reported using any drugs (prescription, over-the-counter or social) the average number taken was 5.6, while the overall number of prescription drugs was two per person. The average number of drugs taken was higher for men than for women (7.5 and 4.7, respectively).

Hale and his colleagues (1979) examined drug-use patterns in a geriatric hypertension-screening program for persons 65 and over in Dunedin, Florida. The study included 1,711 patients who had visited the clinic during the three years that preceded the study. The findings reveal that 76.6 percent of these patients were regularly using drugs, with a higher proportion of women users (79.4 percent to 72.0 percent). There was a consistent increase by age category (from "under 70" to "over 84") in the percentage of patients who used at least one drug. By age 85, more than three-fourths (85 percent) of these patients reported using at least one drug on a regular basis. In addition, there was a consistent increase in the average number of drug classes used by age category. The typical patient was using 1.9 drug classes, ranging from 1.6 in the under–70 group to 2.6 in the over–84 group. Men used an average of 1.7 drug classes, compared to 2.0 for women. The most common drug categories used by these elderly patients were antihypertensive agents (30.7 percent), vitamins (26.7 percent), analgesics (24.0

percent), cardiac drugs (15.3 percent), cardiovascular dilators (12.7 percent), diuretics (9.4 percent), laxatives (9.1 percent), and tranquilizers (8.7 percent).

During 1977 and 1978 a special Citizen's Task Force on Seniors and Substance Abuse in Michigan conducted a study on the nature and scope of drug-abuse problems among persons 60 years old and older (Michigan Offices of Services to the Aging and Substance Abuse, 1979). Interviews were conducted with 371 elderly persons, and the results indicate that the majority (71 percent) were currently using prescription medications. The most commonly reported were cardiovascular drugs (69 percent), diuretics (50 percent), psychotropics (16 percent), and vitamins/nutritional supplements (10 percent). The data reveal that these elderly persons took an average of 2.9 different drugs and that they had been using their prescriptions for an average of 31 months. The rate of psychotropic drug use for these elderly respondents (16.0 percent) was more than twice the rate among the general population (7.3 percent).

An exploratory study by Chien and his colleagues (1978) was undertaken to determine the dimensions of drug use among 242 noninstitutionalized persons aged 60 and over living in the capital district of New York state. Subjects for this study were contacted through 23 volunteer agencies in the community, including senior centers, a geriatric day care center, and so on. The data indicate that these community-dwelling elderly were using a total of 301 different types of prescription and over-the-counter drugs, which the researchers grouped into 32 different categories. Exactly three-fifths, or 60 percent, of all drugs used were prescription medications. The average number of drugs taken per respondent was 3.8, with a range from 0 to 15 drugs. Eight of 10 respondents (83 percent) reported they were currently taking two or more drugs, with 14 percent taking between 7 and 15 drugs. Only 8 percent reported no drug use. The drug categories most frequently used were (in order of frequency): analgesics (66.6 percent), cardiovascular drugs (33.5 percent), laxatives (30.6 percent), vitamins (29.3 percent), antacids (26.4 percent), antianxiety agents (22.3 percent), and diuretics (16.5 percent). In addition, one-third (33.1 percent) reported taking medications that they could not identify by name.

A second exploratory investigation into drug use among a sample of persons 60 and over was conducted in the Washington, D.C. metropolitan area by Guttmann (1978). Almost two-thirds (62 percent) of the

447 noninstitutionalized elderly persons surveyed reported using prescription medications, with females reporting much more frequent use than males (72.2 percent to 27.2 percent). The three drug classes most frequently reported as being used—cardiovascular drugs (39.3 percent), sedatives/tranquilizers (13.6 percent), and anti-arthritic drugs (9.4 percent)—made up more than one-half of all prescriptions taken in the 24 hours prior to the interview. More than one-third reported using between 2 and 4 prescription drugs, while roughly 5 percent reported using as many as 5 to 9 drugs.

Three investigations into the correlates of elderly drug use, which will be discussed at greater length in another section, provide additional information of the drug-use patterns of the aged. Back and Sullivan (1978) inquired into the drug-use patterns of 502 members (aged 45 to 70) of a health insurance plan in Durham, North Carolina. At the time of the interview, drugs most frequently being used to deal with specific ailments included high blood pressure medicine (10.2 percent), pills to make one lose water or salt (6.6 percent), and nitroglycerin tablets for chest pain (4.0 percent). The three most frequently reported medicinal drugs used for nonspecific complaints included vitamin or iron pills (17.5 percent), tranquilizers (15.7 percent), and painkillers (11.2 percent). Eve and Friedsam (1981) reported on the use of two psychoactive drugs—tranquilizers and sleeping pills—among a sample of 8,061 persons 60 and over surveyed in Texas during 1974. Their results indicate that 22 percent had taken tranquilizers in the past month and 12 percent had used sleeping pills. Whittington and his colleagues (1981) conducted a survey of 199 older residents of a suburban county near Atlanta. They found that three-fourths (77 percent) of their respondents reported taking at least one prescription drug during the year preceding the interview. Almost two-thirds (62 percent) reported using 1 to 4 drugs, and 15 percent reported using five or more drugs. Almost one-half (42 percent) of these elderly reported the use of a prescription psychotropic during the last year, including sedatives (13 percent), tranquilizers (17 percent), and narcotics (17 percent).

Studies of elderly populations reveal that approximately two-thirds are using prescriptions on a regular basis. Typically, an elderly person uses an average of two prescription drugs. Although there is some variance between investigations, the highest prevalence of use is evident for cardiovascular drugs, analgesics, and psychotropic medications. Psychotropic use among the elderly ranges from a low of one-fourth of all respondents to more than two-fifths and includes primarily sedative and minor tranquilizer use.

The Institutionalized Elderly

The studies we have reviewed up to now have reflected only prescription drug-use patterns in the noninstitutionalized elderly population. However, to provide a more comprehensive profile of drug patterns among the elderly, it is desirable to examine their drug use in other contexts as well. Here we will examine two settings for the institutionalized elderly in which data appear to be reasonably useful: hospitals and nursing homes.

Hospital Inpatients

In a study of drug administration practices at 12 Veterans Administration hospitals, Prien and his colleagues, in their 1975 and 1976 studies, reported on the use of psychoactive drugs for 2,682 patients aged 60 and over. Of the total sample, 1,276, or 48 percent, had a primary diagnosis of mental disorder; 197, or 7 percent, had an associated diagnosis of mental disorder; and 1,209, or 45 percent, had no diagnosis of mental disorder. Drug-use data were obtained from the patients' medication records and included only those drugs in use on the day of the survey.

More than one-third (37 percent) of all 2,682 patients received at least one major tranquilizer, minor tranquilizer, or antidepressant. The five most frequently prescribed drugs—thioridazine (Mellaril), chlorpromazine (Thorazine), diazepam (Valium), chlordiazepoxide (Librium), and amitriptyline (Elavil)—accounted for 63 percent of all psychoactive drug orders. Psychiatric patients were more likely to receive at least one drug than were nonpsychiatric patients (56 percent as compared to 16 percent). In addition, patterns of use differed in the two groups. For the psychiatric patients, major tranquilizers were the most frequently prescribed psychoactive drug category (69 percent), followed by antidepressants (17 percent) and minor tranquilizers (14 percent). Among the nonpsychiatric patients, minor tranquilizers accounted for 52 percent of all psychoactive prescriptions, with major tranquilizers accounting for 33 percent and antidepressants 15 percent.

Examining psychoactive drug use only for the 1,276 psychiatric patients with a primary diagnosis of mental disorder, we find that the majority (61 percent) received some psychoactive drug. The most frequently prescribed drug categories included antipsychotic drugs (44 percent), antidepressants (11 percent), and antianxiety drugs (10 percent). The most frequently prescribed drugs were thioridazine and chlorpromazine, which accounted for well over one-half (61 percent) of the antipsychotic drug orders for these patients. Further analysis reveals that for major tranquilizers, minor tranquilizers, and antidepressants, the percentage of psychiatric patients receiving a psychoactive drug, as well as the average daily dosage, declined as age category increased. This finding was contrary to the finding for the general population. In addition, about one-sixth (16 percent) of the patients received a combination of two or more psychoactive drugs. The proportion of patients receiving two or more drugs also decreased with age. Data on prevalence of psychoactive drug use by diagnostic category reveal that more than two-thirds (70 percent) of the patients classified as schizophrenic received prescriptions, followed by 66 percent of those with other mental disorders and 55 percent of those with organic brain syndrome. The authors conclude that drugs prescribed to, and prescription practices observed with, these elderly patients were generally appropriate.

Data regarding the elderly patient can be extracted from the 1973 investigation that Laska and his colleagues conducted into psychoactive drug use at all ages among 587 schizophrenic patients in a state hospital. Drug-use information collected from the hospital's Drug Monitoring System produced results that generally echo the findings of Prien and his associates (1975). For patients 65 and over, 70.5 percent were using major tranquilizers, 13.8 percent antidepressants, and 8.2 percent minor tranquilizers. The percentage of women using all three drug types was substantially higher than that for men. About one-half (57.5 percent) of the men received a major tranquilizer, compared to slightly more than three-fourths (78.0 percent) of the women. Older female patients received antidepressant drugs more than four times as frequently as did the men (19.3 percent to 4.2 percent). In addition, minor tranquilizer use among females was essentially double that of males—9.9 percent compared to 5.1 percent. Among patients 20 and older, Laska and his colleagues found a general decline in the percentage of psychiatric inpatients receiving a drug and in the average daily dose of the drug as age category increased. This was true for all three drug categories examined.

Among elderly psychiatric patients, then, it appears that major tranquilizers, minor tranquilizers, and antidepressants were the most frequently prescribed drugs. Major tranquilizers seem to be used in psychiatric inpatient settings much more frequently than any other class of drug. In one study, more than two-thirds of all psychoactive drugs used by patients were the major tranquilizers, with about one-sixth of patients receiving two or more psychoactive drugs. Although this study was based on a cross-sectional design and cannot be taken to reflect an aging effect, the data do reveal that the use of prescription psychoactive drugs among psychiatric inpatients tends to be less at higher ages. This pattern was evident for the percentage of persons using one drug, for those using two or more drugs, and for the average daily dosage of drug administered.

Nursing Home Residents

In 1975 Beardsley and his colleagues conducted an investigation into drug use among 270 residents in five nursing homes in the Minneapolis–St. Paul metropolitan area. Drug-use data obtained from patient charts and medication records included only drugs prescribed by a physician within the month prior to the study. The results reveal 1,109 incidents of drug use for an average of 4.1 per resident (with a range from 0 to 15 per patient). Psychoactive drugs accounted for one-fifth (20.1 percent) of all cases. The psychoactive drugs prescribed included hypnotics (9.1 percent), major tranquilizers (5.4 percent), minor tranquilizers (3.6 percent), and antidepressants (2.0 percent). The investigation contains information regarding the individual psychoactive drugs most frequently prescribed. Where hypnotics are concerned, the most frequently prescribed was chloral hydrate, which was administered to 12.2 percent of the residents. The most frequently prescribed major tranquilizer was Mellaril, with 11.1 percent of the patients receiving it. Valium was the most frequently prescribed minor tranquilizer (9.3 percent) and Tofranil was the most frequently used antidepressant (2.2 percent).

A second investigation into drug use in nursing homes was conducted by Ingman and his colleagues (1975), who studied 131 residents of a Connecticut institution. The study focused on psychoactive drug prescriptions following a change in the institution's drug policy. The new policy required physicians to rewrite drug orders every month rather than renew previous orders. Drug prescribing was examined for one day before and one day after this policy change, and a followup survey was conducted 10 months later. The average number of drugs prescribed for these residents was 2.1, but this was found to differ from the average administered (1.3), due to a substantial number of discretionary (p.r.n., or according to need) prescriptions. Over one-third (34.4 percent) of the residents received prescriptions for major tranquilizers, one-quarter (25.2 percent) for hypnotics, one-fifth (19.9 percent) for minor tranquilizers, and one-tenth (10.7 percent) for antidepressants. Moreover, the data reveal that 4.6 percent were simultaneously receiving more than one major tranquilizer, 2.3 percent were receiving more than one hypnotic, but less than one percent (0.8 percent) were receiving more than one minor tranquilizer or antidepressant.

In sum, available data show that major tranquilizers and hypnotics are the classes of drugs most frequently prescribed in nursing homes. The average number prescribed is between two and four. More than one-fourth of these elderly received hypnotic drugs, one-third a major tranquilizer. Moreover, in one study almost 5 percent of the residents were simultaneously receiving more than one major tranquilizer, and over 2 percent were receiving more than one hypnotic.

Correlates of Elderly Drug Use

Investigations that attempt to examine the factors or forces resulting in drug use among the elderly are exceedingly scarce. Here, we will examine some of the known regularities.

When it has been appropriate in the preceding sections of this review, we have indicated sex differences in drug-use patterns for the aged. With one exception (Vener et al., 1979), the data have shown that elderly females take more drugs than males. Indeed, one investigator (Guttmann, 1978) reported female prescription drug use at a level two and one-half times that of the males (72.2 percent vs. 27.2 percent). Whittington and his colleagues, in the 1981 investigation discussed earlier, focused on this issue of sex differences. Their concern was whether females, who are reported to take more drugs at all ages than men, continue this pattern into old age. Their findings indicate that the average number of prescription drugs taken by females during the year preceding the survey was significantly higher than the number taken by males (2.97 compared to 2.17). This pattern was the same for the average number of psychotropic drugs (0.73 compared to 0.47). However, psychotropic drug-use levels ("high" versus "low" use) for sedatives, tranquilizers, and narcotics were not significantly different. Nonetheless, the findings do not suggest that there is a shift toward "equality" of overall drug use in old age, as some researchers have suggested might be the case (Nathanson, 1977). The most likely explanation for differential drug use, the authors suggest, is not related to individual male-female differences, but to the different ways in which other status definers (such as physicians) treat older women and men.

For their sample, Chien and his colleagues (1978) attempted to determine if elderly drug-use patterns were related to medical illness. To make this determination, they related total drug usage to symptomatic and asymptomatic groups for each of 13 body systems (for example, skeletomuscular and cardiovascular systems). In general, they found that more drugs were used by the symptomatic than by the asymptomatic group. Statistically significant results were found from these comparisons for 8 out of the 13 systems studied. Physician-prescribed medications were found significantly more frequently in the group with psychiatric symptoms than in the nonsymptomatic group. Guttmann (1978) also provides data regarding medical reasons and drug use. His respondents cited poor health (by 21.1 percent) as the leading reason for drug use during the year preceding the survey. This finding was consistent with the fact that more than one-fourth (26.6 percent) reported that they could not perform normal daily activities without their drugs. Not surprisingly, the use of prescription drugs was negatively correlated with health: persons who used more prescription drugs tended to be less healthy. There was also a positive relationship between physical disability and prescription drug use, with disabled persons tending toward greater use.

Back and Sullivan (1978) examined the notion that views of drugs and the behavior associated with their use may be related to variation in drug-use patterns among the elderly. To relate personality traits and drug use, Back and Sullivan conducted a factor analysis of 35 statements related to sickness and drug use and isolated five factors: (1)

insecurity, (2) tendency to adopt the sick role, (3) fear of medicine or drugs, (4) fear of the loss of personal control, and (5) curiosity about mind-changing drugs. For women, the use of medicine for specific ailments was significantly related to three factors—insecurity, sick role, and fear of medicine. For men, none of these factors was significant. For both males and females insecurity was found to be strongly correlated with the use of drugs for nonspecific complaints. These data suggest that to some extent, drug use by the elderly may be related to their attitudes and personality traits.

In their investigation of sedative and tranquilizer use among the aged, Eve and Friedsam (1981) attempted to identify potential predictor variables related to the use of these psychotropic substances. Two theoretical frameworks—a model for use of health care services and the social epidemiological framework of the etiology of mental disorders—guided their investigation. The results indicated that while both models were useful in predicting elderly drug use, the variables in the social epidemiological framework proved to be more predictive. In the health care use model, "need" variables (such as assessment of general health and appetite) were the best predictors of tranquilizer and sleeping pill use. Among the predictor variables in the social epidemiological model, health variables (assessment of general health, assessment of appetite, and physician visits within the past year) were the most predictive of the use of both drugs. However, the variables related to income, housing, and transportation also had an effect. In the main, the findings reveal that subjective assessments are more predictive of tranquilizer-sedative use than objective assessments.

For drug use among the elderly, in contrast to drug use by the young, there are not at present any established statistical regularities (generalizations). Nonetheless, the few existing studies of the influences on elderly drug use suggest some possible conclusions. Patterns of sex differences appear to substantiate that females continue taking more drugs than males into old age. Several studies of the elderly have highlighted the important connection between drug use and health status. Poor health, physical ability, and perceptions of general health have all been found to be related to overall, as well as psychoactive, drug use. One study found that certain attitudes and personality traits are related to drug use among the elderly. This suggests that some elderly are predisposed to drug use and that these predispositions may influence the extent of use.

PATTERNS OF OVER-THE-COUNTER DRUG USE

Even less is known about elderly people's use of over-the-counter (OTC) drugs than about their use of prescription drugs. Still, we do have some limited data regarding what representative samples of individuals do in this regard. From these data we can extract data on elderly cohorts. In addition, a few studies concerned with prescription drug use by the elderly have also gathered information on OTC drug use.

In their investigation of patterns of use in San Francisco, Mellinger and his associates (1971) found that the elderly were less likely than any other age category to have used a psychoactive OTC drug during the year preceding the survey. The 18 to 29 group was four times as likely as the 60 and over group to have used OTC psychotherapeutic drugs: 27 percent of the younger males and 23 percent of the younger females had used these drugs, compared with 6 percent of the older men and women. The elderly user, according to these researchers, depends more on conventional medical sources in obtaining drugs than does the younger one (under 30), who typically bypasses the medical system and hence has a greater consumption of OTC drugs.

Additional data on elderly OTC use is contained in the national psychoactive drug use survey by Parry and his associates (1973) and Mellinger and his colleagues (1974). In the 60 to 74 category, only 9 percent of men and 7 percent of women reported using any OTC psychotherapeutic drugs within the last year. Both males and females aged 18 to 29 were about three times more likely to report that they used a stimulant, sleeping pill, or tranquilizer than were those 60 to 74. Over-the-counter sleeping pills were the most frequently used drug for both men and women, but the percentages are not very high (7 percent and 5 percent, respectively). In contrast to the pattern for prescription psychoactive drugs, the young tend to use more nonprescription psychoactive drugs than the elderly.

In their regional survey of a southern county, Warheit and his associates (1976) also addressed the issue of OTC drug consumption, in which 26.6 percent of the sample were found to be using *any* type (e.g., laxatives, hormones) of nonprescription drug at the time of interview. Although smaller age differences were reported for the use of OTC drugs when compared to prescription medications, those persons 60 and over had the highest percentage of OTC drug use. The proportion of OTC use ranged from a low of 24.5 percent among those aged 18 to 29 to a high of 33.3 percent among those 60 and over.

The survey of 371 community-dwelling elderly, conducted in Michigan by the Citizen's Task Force on Seniors and Substance Abuse (1979), revealed that 60 percent of the elderly were currently using any OTC medications (compared to 71 percent using prescriptions). Chien and his colleagues (1978) reported that of the known medications used by their elderly sample in New York state, 40 percent were OTC preparations. Guttmann (1978) reported that 69 percent of his community sample in metropolitan Washington, D.C. used a type of OTC drug. More than one-half (55.4 percent) of OTC drugs used were internal analgesics. Eight percent of this sample reported that they were unable to perform their normal daily functions without using their OTC preparations. One-sixth of these elderly consulted their physicians about the use of an OTC drug, while two-thirds relied on their own decisions. In sum, studies directed at the community-dwelling elderly reveal fairly high levels of consumption of all types of OTC preparations, in contrast to the national epidemiological investigations, which concentrated on psychoactive preparations.

Thus, use of any type of OTC drug by the elderly ranges from about one-third to over three-fifths in the populations surveyed. For the one study that provides comparative age data, persons 60 and over had the highest percentage of OTC drug use (although the age differences were small). Use of psychoactive OTC preparations by the elderly, however, is apparently not disproportionately high. Only 9 percent of elderly men and 7 percent of elderly women report any use of OTC sleeping pills, tranquilizers, or stimulant drugs, while young adults aged 18 to 29 are three times as likely to take these drugs. The highest prevalence of use for the elderly occurs with sleeping pills, but this is not very high (7 percent) for females and 5 percent for males).

PATTERNS OF DRUG MISUSE

In the main, the misuse of prescription drugs can take four forms—over-use, under-use, erratic use, or contraindicated use (Petersen et al., 1979). The individual who over uses drugs either takes more types of drugs than necessary, takes more than the prescribed amount, or takes a p.r.n. (according to need) prescription when it is not called for. Under-use refers to the patient's failure to acquire and take appropriate medications and the failure to take as much of the drug as the prescription calls for. Erratic use, on the other hand, occurs when the patient fails to follow instructions or makes a mistake and misses doses, takes double doses, or takes doses at the wrong time in the wrong way. Contraindicated drug use occurs when a patient is prescribed the incorrect drug by his physician, one that is either ineffective, produces an unwanted or deleterious side effect, or interacts harmfully with other medications already being taken. An older patient can experience any or all of these misuses. Although the actual extent of drug misuse among the elderly is difficult to determine, it is important to examine existing data on patterns of misuse. Here, we shall examine data on patient noncompliance, improper prescribing patterns, and drug-related adverse reactions.

Patient Noncompliance

The patient who administers his own medicine may undermine the physician's best efforts by failing to comply with his or her instructions for use. Hussar (1975), in a review of noncompliance studies, indicates that there is considerable variation between studies—with a range of noncompliance from roughly one-third to one-half of all patients surveyed. Most investigators of noncompliance have concerned themselves with compliance rates alone, and efforts to correlate demographic variables with noncompliance have often failed to produce any significant relationships (Davis, 1968; Boyd et al., 1974). However, Hussar (1975) hypothesized that the elderly are quite likely to be noncompliant, since noncompliance is known to be correlated with several traits more common to the elderly than to other age groups (for instance, chronic illness and living alone.).

Indeed, a few studies have apparently found that age is related to noncompliance. Latiolais and Berry (1969) examined 180 indigent outpatients at a university hospital and found that elderly patients were significantly more likely to fail to comply with drug orders than younger persons. Latiolais and Berry found 77 patients who were noncompliant with their medication order; of this number 59.8 percent were over 50 years of age and 28.6 percent were over 60. Looking at the data from the angle of correct and proper use of medications, they found that among 103 patients who did comply with instructions, only 34.9 percent were over 50 and 15.5 percent were over 60. Brand and his colleagues (1977), in their study of 225 discharged hospital patients, found that persons in their 70s were almost twice as likely not to comply with a physician's prescription directives as were those persons in their 40s (46 percent compared to 26 percent). For patients 80 and over, the rate reached a high of 62 percent.

Schwartz and her colleagues (1962) studied 178 elderly, chronically ill patients in a clinic and found that more than one-half (57 percent) of those aged 60 to 74 made medication errors. In addition, more than two-thirds (68 percent) of those over 75 made these same errors. However, further analysis using finer age breakdowns revealed that the relationship between age and noncompliance was less than consistent. Further, Clinite and Kabat (1969), in their study of 30 men released from hospital care at a Veterans Administration hospital, also found contradictory evidence regarding age and compliance. The highest rate of medication error was reported for those persons aged 81 to 90 (42.9 percent), but the lowest rate of any age group was reported for patients 71 to 80 (9.6 percent). That no clear pattern was evident for age is apparent from an examination of the other age categories used. Persons 41 to 50 and 51 to 60 had higher error rates than patients 61 to 70 (42.5 percent, 36.5 percent, and 27.6 percent, respectively).

Data regarding types of noncompliance are not clearly documented, but under-use of medications appears to be the most common form of medication error. Schwartz and her colleagues (1962) found that 47 percent of the medication errors committed by older persons in their sample were the result of a failure to take the medication as often as prescribed. The Michigan Offices of Services to the Aging and Substance Abuse (1979) found that 30 percent of the elderly in their study stopped taking a drug sooner than directed by their physicians. In their study of 67 prescription drug users in Fayette County, Kentucky, Raffoul and his associates (1981) reported an overall misuse rate of 43 percent among prescription drug users, and said that under-use of some type accounted for almost three-fourths (72 percent) of the instances of misuse that they recorded. Stephens and his colleagues (1981) surveyed 1,101 noninstitutionalized residents of Houston, Texas, aged 55 and over, in regard to their use of prescribed psychoactive drugs. Approximately 7 percent (6.9 percent) of the total were classified as "inappropriate users" of prescription psychotropics. This represented more than one-third (40.2 percent) of all instances of use of psychoactive drugs in the sample. The researchers also reported under-use as the most common form of noncompliance for their sample, with 87 percent taking less medication than they were directed to take.

Information on other forms of noncompliance is limited. Schwartz and her colleagues reported that after under-use, the next most frequent type of medication error was "inaccurate information" about their drugs, which accounted for 20 percent of the errors in the sample. Incorrect dosage accounted for an additional 10 percent of the errors and incorrect timing of the dose accounted for 4 percent.

On the basis of their study, Schwartz and her colleagues (1962) have suggested three possible reasons for noncompliance: (1) there were communication problems between physician and patient, (2) the patient was not competent to administer his or her drugs, and (3) there was inadequate supervision of the patient's drug-taking behavior by a professional or a family member. Brand and his co-workers (1977), on the other hand, found that the most frequent reason for noncompliance was economic. More than one-third (34 percent) reported that they could not afford to purchase the prescribed medication or that they could not take the drug as directed by the physician because of the excessive costs involved. Related data are provided by the Michigan Offices of Services to the Aging and Substance Abuse Services (1979). Asked why they had stopped taking a drug or varied its dosage, almost one-half (43 percent) of their subjects said that they "felt better" when they did. An additional 18 percent responded that they stopped because of unpleasant side effects from drug therapy, while 10 percent reported that they had simply forgotten. Doyle and Hamm (1976), in a study of 405 elderly persons residing in three Florida counties, indicate that older people do make decisions for themselves about the duration of prescription use or the discontinuation of medications. About 40 percent of the respondents reported that they do not continue to take medications that they do not like, whereas less than one-half (43.3 percent) reported taking their medication until receiving instructions from their physician to stop. The respondents in the study by Stephens and his colleagues (1981) were also straightforward as to their reasons for noncompliance: almost one-half (48.6 percent) reported that they "did not like" either the prescription or the dosage. Other reasons cited included taking the drug only when it was needed (23.0 percent), economic reasons (9.4 percent), getting better results with their own method of taking the drug (6.8 percent), bad side effects (4.1 percent), and forgetting or being too busy to take the drug (2.7 percent).

Data regarding noncompliance and age are mixed. Some investigations reveal that elderly patients are significantly more likely to fail to comply with drug prescription orders than are young persons and that the error rate is higher for the older-old than for the younger-old. Other studies show that the relationship is consistent when fine age breakdowns are used. Indeed, Prentice (1979) argues that existing findings are too inconsistent to allow any conclusive statements regarding the relationship between age and noncompliance. Nonetheless, underuse of medications clearly seems to be the most common type of noncompliance error among elderly persons, although data regarding other forms of noncompliance are limited. Reasons for noncompliance have been found to be quite varied, with economic considerations important to at least one elderly sample. Additional data suggest that the elderly often make decisions to discontinue or modify their drug regimen when they find that they "do not like" either the prescription or the dosage.

Improper Prescribing Patterns

In this section we shall describe the various types of misuse that can be traced directly to physicians and other health care personnel. We will be concerned here with contraindicated use and the mechanisms of physician-initiated misuse, including technical errors in the selection or prescription of drugs and behavioral errors in the process of prescribing and communicating appropriate instructions to the patient (Whittington, 1983). According to Whittington, technical errors in prescribing for the elderly patient include: (1) selecting an inappropriate medication, (2) prescribing too high or too low a dose, (3) prescribing too many different drugs at one time, and (4) failing to determine a drug's interactive, or side-effect, potential for causing an adverse reaction. Behavioral errors that might arise during the prescription process include: (1) failing to check the patient's drug history, current drug regimen, and drug-taking habits; (2) prescribing over the telephone without actually examining the patient; (3) failing to provide adequate instructions for how and when the prescription is to be taken; and (4) allowing automatic or telephone renewals of prescriptions without examining the patient.

Although it can be readily acknowledged that many of these errors happen with young patients as well as older persons, geriatric patients face special drug problems that make them more vulnerable to such mistakes. Drug interactions are a particular problem for elderly patients, who often suffer from several chronic conditions and—as a result—simultaneously receive a number of medications (Cadwallader, 1979). The elderly are also more sensitive to the effects of most psychoactive drugs than are younger adults (Ziance, 1979). Because the elderly have a slower rate of drug absorption, distribution, metabolism, and excretion, drugs taken concurrently have an increased chance of producing drug intoxification (Lamy and Vestal, 1976; Ziance, 1979). In addition, the risk of physical and emotional side effects is always present among the elderly (Lamy and Kitler, 1971; Ziance, 1979).

While many physicians are now paying attention to the special problems of drug selection and monitoring among the elderly (see, for example, Melmon, 1971; Learoyd, 1972; Triggs and Nation, 1975; Lamy, 1978, 1979), it is safe to say that the typical physician is inadequately trained in both geriatrics and pharmacology (Learoyd, 1972; Pfeiffer, 1973; Maddox, 1979). Much of the responsibility for physician-initiated drug misuse in elderly patients must be placed on the physicians themselves. Nonetheless, the extent of physician-related misuse is difficult to determine. No investigations provide us any direct data concerning the actual encounter between physician and elderly patient. And, unfortunately, only a few studies cast any light on those physician errors that result in the prescription of the wrong drug or the wrong dose. Those few studies that have addressed this issue have done so within an institutional setting (primarily with psychiatric inpatients and nursing-home residents).

In an early study of 27 patients in a geriatric hospital in Massachusetts, Kastenbaum and his co-workers (1964) reported no cognitive improvement among their patients through the administration of either a stimulant (Dexedrine) or a major tranquilizer (Mellaril). A few years later Barton and Hurst (1966) found that Thorazine, a major tranquilizer, brought little or no symptomatic relief to their sample of 53 hospitalized female geriatric patients. They concluded that 80 percent of geriatric mental patients may be receiving such tranquilizers unnecessarily.

Although Daniel (1970) disputes these findings, there is additional evidence that the elderly in institutional settings may receive medication when no therapeutic function is evident. The data suggest that elderly persons in nursing homes often receive too many prescribed drugs, including psychoactive medications. Testimony regarding the over-use of such drugs was presented in hearings before the Subcommittee on Long-Term Care of the U. S. Senate Special Committee on Aging (U.S. Senate, 1975). The report addresses evidence of errors in medication, the high incidence of adverse drug reactions, drug addiction in nursing home residents, and the consequences of the over-use of psychoactive drugs in these settings. The report of the subcommittee cites a 1971 study, conducted by the Department of Health, Education and Welfare into 75 nursing homes, that provides some information on these settings. The results reveal that most of the patients reviewed were taking one to four different drugs, almost half (40 percent) had not been seen by a physician for over three months, only 18 percent had had their prescription orders revised within the last 30 days, and more than one-third of those receiving cardiovascular drugs (37 percent) and tranquilizers (35 percent) had not had a blood pressure test within the last year.

At the time of the 1971 study, other reports began to appear in the professional literature documenting patterns of overprescription and over-use. Ingman and his colleagues (1975) reported that almost one-fourth (23 percent) of their sample of 131 patients in a nursing home had been prescribed at least one drug that the authors determined was not recommended. Statistically significant findings also revealed that patients with normal physical and mental abilities actually received more psychoactive drugs than did patients with diminished capacities.

Another investigation conducted by Beardsley and his co-workers (1975) examined whether p.r.n. (according to need) medications were justified among residents in five nursing homes. From an examination of patients' charts, they determined the appropriateness of prescribed drugs to the recorded patient symptoms. They found more than one-third of both tranquilizers (37 percent) and hypnotic prescription orders (35 percent) were not justified by patient charts.

While the data do not allow one to draw any conclusions as to the magnitude or intent of improper prescribing patterns in institutional facilities, they do call attention to the potential use of such drugs as "control" medications when no therapeutic function is being served. Townsend (1971), Learoyd (1972), and Moss and Halamandaris (1977) have all described the tendency of some nursing homes (and other geriatric residential facilities) to minimize the ongoing management and control of "difficult" patients through the use of such drugs. This practice, appropriately termed "chemical straitjacket" (U.S. Senate, 1975), calls to our attention the possibility of drug misuse in this setting other than that which we may attribute to physician mistake.

An additional problem of some note in long-term care facilities is the poor control measures in the drug distribution system that, in many cases, result in widespread medication errors (Kayne and Cheung, 1973; Thomas, 1979). Estimates of these types of errors range from 22 to 50 percent of all doses of medications administered in long-term care facilities (Crawley et al., 1971; Kayne and Cheung, 1973). These errors have variously been attributed to poor medication control procedures, heavy workloads, and lack of staff training (Stannard, 1973; Moss and Halamandaris, 1977; Thomas, 1979).

Although one can identify many technical and behavioral errors related to physician-initiated misuse, data regarding improper prescribing patterns are limited. There are no investigations in the nature of behavioral errors that might arise during the prescription process when patient meets physician. Those studies that do exist have addressed technical errors by physicians in nursing-home and psychiatric hospital settings. These data indicate that about one-fourth of nursing-home patients receive prescriptions that are not justified by diagnosis of their ailments. While one can question unnecessary prescribing of psychoactive drugs in these settings, these studies do not provide any information on motivations for such prescription patterns. Some authors have suggested, however, that existing prescription practices in nursing homes are intended to facilitate the management of difficult elderly patients and to minimize management problems.

Drug-Related Adverse Reactions

Many have assumed that the disproportionately high level of drug consumption by elderly persons is likely to lead to misuse, including drug-related problems such as acute drug reactions (Brady, 1973; Pascarelli and Fischer, 1974; Heller and Wynne, 1975; Petersen and Thomas,

1975). However, there is very little evidence to support this assumption.

Heller and Wynne examined data compiled from medical sources, including hospitals and emergency rooms, across the United States through the Drug Abuse Warning Network (DAWN). They found that for the first six months of 1973, persons over 50 constituted only 6 percent of the total cases of drug incidents involving barbituate sedatives, tranquilizers, and alcohol-drug interactions. Moreover, according to the DAWN data for 1974–75, people 50 and over, who make up 26 percent of the total population, accounted for only 5 percent of all drug incidents (including drug-related illness and death). That was the lowest proportion for all age groups and included drug incidents recorded at emergency rooms, crisis centers, inpatient units, and medical examiners' offices. The data reveal that the frequency of contact with the DAWN network for persons over 50 resulting from prescription psychoactive drugs, as well as all drugs, is comparatively low.

The 1975 study by Petersen and Thomas substantiates these findings. They gathered data from the patient records of 1,128 persons treated for acute drug reactions at a hospital emergency room in Miami, and found that only 5 percent of their total sample (N=60) were 50 or older, which compared to this age group's representation in the hospital catchment area of 39 percent. These elderly persons sought emergency-room treatment only because of adverse reactions to legal drugs, and 80 percent of these involved psychoactive drugs (primarily sedatives and minor tranquilizers). Inciardi and his colleagues (1978), in a followup study of the same research setting for a four-and-a-half-year period, found essentially the same pattern. Persons aged 60 and over comprised only 2.6 percent of the total sample of 9,975 persons. Although Inciardi and his co-workers conclude that acute drug reactions may not be a problem for the aged, Petersen and Thomas speculate that these data may well underrepresent the total number of elderly who experience these problems, because the elderly are disinclined or unable to seek help in this type of setting.

The data on drug-related adverse reactions among the elderly indicate that these people are less likely than those of other ages to be admitted to hospital emergency rooms and other such settings for drug problems. No data suggest that the disproportionate consumption of drugs by the elderly results in high levels of drug-related problems, at least not in incidents that are reported in institutional settings. At this time we simply do not know if the elderly are responsible drug users or if they prefer not to seek professional help for their problems in the settings that have been investigated.

DISCUSSION

Research on drug use and misuse in age cohorts other than young adults is comparatively sparse. We have attempted to summarize the existing work on drug patterns among the elderly. In so doing, however, we have done little more than provide an overview of the research in this area. In this final section our goal will be to identify basic issues that need to be confronted in further research.

The community-dwelling elderly have been found to have high rates of use for prescription and OTC drugs, as well as higher usage rates than any other age categories for several classes of prescription psychoactive drugs, including minor tranquilizers, sedatives, and hypnotics. The data on prescription psychotropic drug use in institutional settings (nursing homes and hospitals) reveal much the same patterns. Among the studies reported, major tranquilizers and hypnotics were the classes of psychoactive drugs most frequently prescribed. The limited nature of most of the available data, however, makes it impossible to say much more than this.

A great deal more information is needed on the nature and extent of drug use by the elderly. Extensive epidemiological studies of drug-use patterns among the general population of community elderly are needed. Past studies have tended to concentrate on small populations that have often been biased or highly selective. At the same time, however, studies of special populations of elderly that are usually underrepresented in current surveys are needed—studies of women, low-income, institutionalized, minority, and rural aged. The research design employed to date has been either cross-sectional or retrospective. Studies are needed that would examine drug-use patterns over time to assess duration and change.

Information is needed on the social and psychological factors that might predict and explain elderly drug use. In what key ways do drug users differ from nonusers? (Studies to date have also lacked control groups.) A wide range of factors needs to be examined in relation to drug use. Virtually nothing is currently known about structural variables and elderly drug use. What are the race, sex, social class, residence, and other demographic characteristics of aged drug users? Attitudinal variables that assess views about drugs and drug use have only recently been addressed by researchers. These findings are only suggestive, leaving much more to be done. Are some elderly persons more predisposed to take and depend heavily on drugs, while others seek to avoid their use?

Whereas previous investigations have often concentrated only on psychotropic drugs, greater knowledge is needed about the use patterns for all types of prescription drugs. Moreover, past research efforts have often employed broad categories of drugs and have often combined categories such as sedatives and tranquilizers. Future studies would do well to concentrate on specific drugs and drug classes. Finally, studies are needed to rigorously test the various explanatory models that have been advanced to account for elderly drug use and misuse (Glantz, 1981; Hochhauser, 1981; Mandolini, 1981). Explanatory models linking elderly stress to drug use as a coping mechanism or as an outcome of "learned helplessness," for example, have not yet been tested.

More information is also needed about the magnitude of, and the reasons for, the misuse of drugs by the elderly. In our review we have found that some researchers have looked for misuse in the health care system, while others have sought an answer in the elderly patient. As Maddox (1979) has correctly noted, however, the phenomenon includes misuse both *by* and *of* the elderly. Although both system and patient appear to be implicated, there is very little published research that documents the extent of misuse in the older population.

The studies regarding compliance, for example, are not comprehensive enough to allow firm conclusions to be drawn regarding the extent of, or reason for medication errors. Some studies conclude that the elderly are less likely than younger persons to comply with medication orders, while in other investigations compliance is greater for the aged. More research is called for to determine if advancing age leads to medication errors for prescription drugs in general and psychoactive drugs in particular. Some research suggests that the failure to take as many drugs as often as prescribed may be deliberate on the part of the elderly. Others have argued that medication errors are unintentional and the result of a variety of problems. More information is needed, both for different types of drugs and for different segments of the elderly population, to clarify the reasons for noncompliance.

As was noted earlier, there are no systematic studies of the interactive process between the elderly patient and physician. Such research is needed if we are to understand physician-initiated errors that occur in drug therapy with this population. What do physicians tell their elderly patients about the use of prescription medications? Is more time spent providing instructions for some drugs than others? Studies of the physician-patient relationship might perhaps also shed light on the problem of compliance rates. As to the technical errors that often occur in drug prescription, it has been suggested that in nursing homes, drugs are often prescribed and administered for purposes other than those suggested by the drug regimen. Despite increased concern, however, little is known about why the institutionalized elderly receive so many drugs. More study is needed to determine who initiates psychoactive drug orders in these settings and for what reasons. Finally, the appropriateness of prescribing practices needs to be examined in greater depth.

The data on adverse reactions among the elderly reveal that this population is less likely than other adults to be admitted to hospital emergency rooms and other settings for the treatment of drug-related problems. Are the elderly more responsible in their use of drugs than other age groups? Or can one conclude that many acute drug reactions among this population are less likely to come to public attention? The limited published studies shed no light on this issue.

In sum, although available data indicate that the elderly receive large numbers of drugs and are apparently at higher risk for potential drug misuse, we lack extensive data to document correspondingly high patterns of misuse either *by* or *of* the elderly.

REFERENCES

Atkinson, R. M., and L. L. Kofoed. 1984. Alcohol and drug abuse in old age. In C. Cassel and J. R. Walsh (eds.), *Geriatric Medicine*, vol. 2 of *Fundamentals of Geriatric Care*. New York: Springer-Verlag.

Back, K. W., and D. A. Sullivan. 1978. Self-image, medicine, and drug use. *Addictive Diseases* 3:373–82.

Barton, R., and L. Hurst. 1966. Unnecessary use of tranquilizers in elderly patients. *British Journal of Psychiatry* 112:989–90.

Beardsley, R., A. Heaton, H. Kabat, and J. Martilla. 1975. *Patterns of drug use in nursing home patients*. Minneapolis, Minn.: University of Minnesota.

Boyd, J. R., T. R. Covington, W. F. Stanaszek, and T. R. Coussons. 1974. Drug defaulting: Part II, analysis of noncompliance patterns. *American Journal of Hospital Pharmacy* 31:485–91.

Brady, E. S. 1973. Drugs and the elderly. In R. H. Davis and W. K. Smith (eds.), *Drugs and the elderly*. Los Angeles: Ethel Percy Andrus Gerontology Center, University of Southern California.

Brand, F. N., R. T. Smith, and P. A. Brand. 1977. Effect of economic barriers to medical care on patients' noncompliance. *Public Health Reports* 92:72–78.

Cadwallader, D. E. 1979. Drug interactions in the elderly. In D. M. Petersen, F. J. Whittington, and B. P. Payne (eds.), *Drugs and the elderly: Social and pharmacological issues*. Springfield, Ill.: Charles C. Thomas.

Chambers, C. D. 1971. *An assessment of drug use in the general population*. New York: State Narcotic Addiction Control Commission.

Chien, C., E. J. Townsend and A. R. Townsend, "Substance use and abuse among the community elderly: the medical aspect." Addictive Diseases 3:357–72.

Clinite, J. C., and H. F. Kabat. 1969. Errors during self-administration. *Journal of the American Pharmacological Association* NS9: 450–52.

Crawley, H. K., F. M. Eckel, and D. C. McLeod. 1971. A comparison of a traditional and unit dose drug distribution system in a nursing home. *Drug Intelligence and Clinical Pharmacy* 5:166–71.

Daniel, R. 1970. Psychiatric drug use and abuse in the aged. *Geriatrics* 25:144–58.

Davis, M. S. 1968. Physiologic, psychological and demographic factors in patient compliance with doctors' orders. *Medical Care* 6:115–22.

Doyle, J. P., and B. M. Hamm. 1976. *Medication use and misuse study among older persons*. Jacksonville, Fla.: the Cathedral Foundation.

Drug Abuse Warning Network. 1974–75. *Project DAWN III*. Rockville, Md.: National Institute on Drug Abuse.

Eve, S. B., and H. J. Friedsam. 1981. Use of tranquilizers and sleeping pills among older Texans. *Journal of Psychoactive Drugs* 13:165–73.

Glantz, M. 1981. Predictions of elderly drug abuse. *Journal of Psychoactive Drugs* 13:117–26.

Guttman, D. 1978. Patterns of legal drug use by older Americans. *Addictive Diseases* 3:337–56.

Hale, W. E., R. G. Marks, and R. B. Stewart. 1979. Drug use in a geriatric population." *Journal of the American Geriatrics Society* 27:374–77.

Heller, F. J., and R. Wynne. 1975. Drug misuse by the elderly: Indications and treatment suggestions. In E. Senay, V. Shorty, and H. Alksne (eds.), *Developments in the Field of Drug Abuse*. Cambridge, Mass.: Schenkman.

Hochhauser, M. 1981. Learned helplessness and substance in the elderly. *Journal of Psychoactive Drugs* 13:127–33.

Hussar, D. A. 1975. Patient noncompliance. *Journal of the American Pharmacological Association* NS15:183–90.

Inciardi, J. A., D. McBridge, B. R. Russe, and K. S. Wells. 1978. Acute drug reactions among the aged: A research note. *Addictive Diseases* 3:383–88.

Ingman, S. R., I. R. Lawson, P. G. Pierpaoli, and P. Blake. 1975. A survey of the prescribing and administration of drugs in a long-term care institution for the elderly. *Journal of the American Geriatrics Society* 23:309–16.

Kastenbaum, R., P. E. Slater, and R. Aisenberg. 1964. Toward a conceptual model of geriatric psychopharmacology: An experiment with thioridazine and dextroamphetamine. *The Gerontologist* 4:68–71.

Kayne, R. C., and A. Cheung. 1973. An application of clinical pharmacy in extended care facilities. In R. H. Davis and W. K. Smith (eds.), *Drugs and the elderly*. Los Angeles: Ethel Percy Andrus Gerontology Center, University of Southern California.

Lamy, P. P. 1978. Therapeutics and the elderly. *Addictive Diseases* 3:311–35.

———. 1979. Considerations in drug therapy of the elderly. *Journal of Drug Issues* 9:27–45.

——— and M. E. Kitler. 1971. Drugs and the geriatric patient. *Journal of the American Geriatrics Society* 19:23–33.

——— and R. E. Vestal. 1976. Drug prescribing for the elderly. *Hospital Practice* 11:111–18.

Laska, E., E. Varga, J. Wanderling, G. Simpson, G. W. Logeman, and B. K. Shah. 1973. Patterns of psychotropic drug use for schizophrenia. *Diseases of the Nervous System* 34:294–305.

Latiolais, C. J., and C. C. Berry. 1969. Misuse of prescription medication by outpatients. *Drug Intelligence and Clinical Pharmacology* 3:270–77.

Learoyd, B. M. 1972. Psychotropic drugs and the elderly patient. *Medical Journal of Australia* 1:1131–33.

Maddox, G. L. 1979. Drugs, physicians, and patients. In D. M. Petersen, F. J. Whittington, and B. P. Payne (eds.), *Drugs and the elderly: Social and pharmacological issues*. Springfield, Ill.: Charles C. Thomas.

Mandolini, A. 1981. The social contexts of aging and drug use: Theoretical and methodological insights. *Journal of Psychoactive Drugs* 13:135–42.

Mellinger, G. D., M. B. Balter, and D. I. Manheimer. 1971. Patterns of psychotherapeutic drug use among adults in San Francisco. *Archives of General Psychiatry* 25:385–94.

Mellinger, G. D., M. B. Balter, H. J. Parry, D. I. Manheimer, and I. H. Cisin. 1974. An overview of psychotherapeutic drug use in the United States. In E. Josephson and E. E. Carroll (eds.), *Drug use: Epidemiological and sociological approaches*. Washington, D.C.: Hemisphere.

Melmon, K. L. 1971. Preventable drug reactions—causes and cures. *New England Journal of Medicine* 284:1361–68.

Michigan Offices of Services to the Aging and Substance Abuse. 1979. *Substance abuse among Michigan's senior citizens: Patterns of use and provider perspectives*. Lansing, Mich.

Moss, F., and V. J. Halamandaris. 1977. Nursing home drugs: Pharmaceutical Russian roulette. In F. Moss and V. J. Halamandaris (eds.), *Too old, too sick, too bad*. Rockville, Md.: Aspen.

Nathanson, C. A. 1977. Sex, illness, and medical care: A review of data, theory, and method. *Social Science and Medicine* 11:13–25.

National Council on the Aging. 1970. *The golden years: A tarnished myth.* Washington, D.C.

Parry, H. J., M. B. Balter, G. D. Mellinger, I. H. Cisin, and D. I. Manheimer. 1973. National patterns of psychotherapeutic drug use. *Archives of General Psychiatry* 28:769–83.

Pascarelli, E. F., and W. Fischer. 1974. Drug dependence in the elderly. *International Journal of Aging and Human Development* 5:347–56.

Pfeiffer, E. 1973. Use of drugs which influence behavior in the elderly: Promises, pitfalls and perspectives. In R. H. Davis and W. K. Smith (eds.), *Drugs and the elderly.* Los Angeles: Ethel Percy Andrus Gerontology Center, University of Southern California.

Petersen, D. M., and C. W. Thomas. 1975. Acute drug reactions among the elderly. *Journal of Gerontology* 30:552–56.

Petersen, D. M., F. J. Whittington, and E. T. Beer. 1979. Drug use and misuse among the elderly. *Journal of Drug Issues* 9:5–26.

Prentice, R. 1979. Patterns of psychoactive drug use among the elderly. In *The Aging process and psychoactive drug use.* Rockville, Md.: National Institute on Drug Abuse.

Prien, R. F., P. A. Haber, and E. M. Caffey. 1975. The use of psychoactive drugs in elderly patients with psychiatric disorders: Survey conducted in 12 Veterans Administration hospitals. *Journal of the American Geriatrics Society* 23:104–12.

Prien, R. F., C. J. Klett, and E. M. Caffey. 1976. Polypharmacy in the psychiatric treatment of elderly hospitalized patients: A survey of 12 Veterans Administration hospitals. *Diseases of the Nervous System* 37:333–36.

Raffoul, P. R., J. K. Cooper, and D. W. Love. 1981. Drug misuse in older people. *The Gerontologist* 21:146–51.

Schwartz, D., M. Wang, L. Zeitz, and M. E. W. Goss. 1962. Medication errors made by elderly chronically ill patients. *American Journal of Public Health* 52:2018–29.

Stannard, C. 1973. Old folks and dirty work: The social conditions for patient abuse in a nursing home. *Social Problems* 20:329–42.

Stephens, R. C., C. A. Haney, and S. Underwood. 1981. Psychoactive drug use and potential misuse among persons aged 55 years and older. *Journal of Psychoactive Drugs* 13:185–93.

Task Force on Prescription Drugs. 1968. *The drug users.* Washington, D.C.: U.S. Government Printing Office.

Thomas, D. L. 1979. Clinical and administrative aspects of drug misuse in nursing homes. In D. M. Petersen, F. J. Whittington, and B. P. Payne (eds.), *Drugs and the elderly: Social and pharmacological issues.* Springfield, Ill.: Charles C. Thomas.

Townsend, C. 1971. *Old age: The last segregation.* New York: Grossman.

Triggs, E. J., and R. L. Nation. 1975. Pharmacokinetics in the aged: A review. *Journal of Pharmacokinetics and Biopharmaceutics* 3:387–418.

U.S. Senate Special Committee on Aging, Subcommittee on Long-Term Care. 1975. *Nursing home care in the United States: Failure in public policy. Supporting paper no. 2: Drugs in nursing homes: Misuse, high costs and kickbacks.* Washington, D.C.: U.S. Government Printing Office.

Vener, A. M., L. R. Krupka, and J. J. Climo. 1979. Drug usage and health characteristics in non-institutionalized retired persons. *Journal of the American Geriatrics Society* 27:83–90.

Warheit, G. J., S. A. Arey, and E. Swanson. 1976. Patterns of drug use: An epidemiologic overview. *Journal of Drug Issues* 6:223–37.

Whittington, F. J. 1983. Misuse of legal drugs and compliance with prescription directions. In M. Glantz, D. M. Petersen, and F. J. Whittington (eds.), *Drugs and the elderly adult*. Rockville, Md.: National Institute on Drug Abuse.

Whittington, F. J., D. M. Petersen, B. Dale, and P. L. Dressel. 1981. Sex differences in prescription drug use of older adults. *Journal of Psychoactive Drugs* 13:175–84.

Zawadski, R. T., G. B. Glaser, and E. Lurie. 1978. Psychotropic drug use among institutionalized and noninstitutionalized Medicaid aged in California. *Journal of Gerontology* 33:825–34.

Ziance, R. J. 1979. Side effects of drugs in the elderly. In D. M. Petersen, F. J. Whittington, and B. P. Payne (eds.), *Drugs and the elderly: Social and pharmacological issues*. Springfield, Ill.: Charles C. Thomas.

Medical Mood Alteration Among the Elderly: Victimization or Deviancy?

CARL D. CHAMBERS, Ph.D.

Professor
School of Health and Sport Sciences
College of Health and Human Services
Ohio University
Athens, Ohio

O. Z. WHITE, Ph.D.

Professor
Department of Sociology
Trinity University
San Antonio, Texas

JOHN H. LINDQUIST, D. Soc. Sci.

Professor
Department of Sociology
Trinity University
San Antonio, Texas

MICHAEL T. HARTER, Ph.D.

Professor
School of Health and Sport Sciences
College of Health and Human Services
Ohio University
Athens, Ohio

INTRODUCTION

In 1982, demographers estimated that there were 11 million noninstitutionalized men and 16 million noninstitutionalized women 65 and over in the United States (*Statistical Bulletin*, 1984). It was anticipated that these men would make 40 million visits to physicians' offices during the year, for a per-person average of 3.7 visits. It was anticipated the women would accumulate slightly over 60 million visits to their physicians, for an average of 3.9 visits per person. Of these more than 100 million office visits, more than 6 million would end in either a new or refill prescription for a minor tranquilizer or other antianxiety medication, some 3 million would end with a prescription for an antidepressant, and more than 1 million would end with a prescription for a major tranquilizer or other antipsychotic medication (Koch, June 1983).

Researchers have suggested that between 6 and 10 percent of all elderly persons' visits to physicians result in either the direct dispensing of, or a prescription for, a mood-altering drug (Koch, April 1983). At least half will be for benzodiazepine—a minor tranquilizer such as Valium (diazepam), Librium (chlordiazepoxide), Tranzene (clorazepate), and Dalmane (flurazepam). Although other benzodiazepines are beginning to erode its market share, Valium continues to be the most widely prescribed mood-altering drug and one of the most widely prescribed of all prescription drugs.

Physicians are much more likely to end an office visit for an elderly woman, than for an elderly man, by writing a prescription for one or more mood-altering drugs. A recent (1981–1982) two-year assessment compiled by the National Center for Health Statistics reveals that this sex difference persists even when controlling for the specific type of mood-altering drug. Elderly women more frequently receive prescriptions for minor tranquilizers and other antianxiety sedating medications, for antidepressants, and for major tranquilizers and other antipsychotic medications (see Table 1).

It is also interesting to note in Table 1 that, regardless of sex and probably age, about twice as many physician visits terminate with a prescription for an antidepressant as for an antipsychotic medication; moreover, twice as many visits produce a prescription for an antianxiety medication as for an antidepressant.

PREVALENCE OF USE: ANTIANXIETY MEDICATIONS

The minor tranquilizers are a group of anxiolytic sedatives that were introduced into medical practice during the 1950s with Miltown (meprobamate). They were designated as "minor tranquilizers," effective in

TABLE 1
**Sex Differences in the Rate at Which Mood Altering Drugs
are Prescribed for Elderly Patients by Office-based Physicians**

1980–1981 Rate Medications Provided per 1000 visits

		AntiAnxiety Medications	AntiDepressant Medications	AntiPsychotic Medications
Females	Ages 45–64 (157 million visits)	71	35	16
	Ages 65 and above (126 million visits)	69	30	13
Males	Ages 45–64 (109 million visits)	55	23	12
	Ages 65 and above (82 million visits)	49	13	8
Total	Ages 45–64 (266 million visits)	65	30	14
	Ages 65 and above (208 million visits)	61	23	11

Source: National Center for Health Statistics, H. Koch, "Utilization of Psychotropic Drugs in Office-Based Ambulatory Care, National Ambulatory Medical Care Survey, 1980 and 1981." *Advance Data from Vital and Health Statistics*, No. 90. DHHS Pub. No. (PHS) 83–1250. Hyattsville, Md.: Public Health Service, June 1983.

the reduction of anxiety and tension, as opposed to the "major tranquilizers," which are used in the treatment of severe mental disorders.

Ample data support the conclusion that the elderly are overrepresented among therapeutic users of the minor tranquilizers and other medications prescribed for the relief of anxiety symptoms (Chambers et al., 1975 and 1983).

In 1978 and 1979 Chambers and his associates conducted a statewide general population survey of medicine use and abuse in a major Midwestern state. In this state, where both rural and urban residents were surveyed, the total lifetime prevalence of minor tranquilizer use among those aged 60 and above was almost 40 percent. Not unexpectedly, the elderly women were more likely than the men to have used these drugs: "Recent and current use of the minor tranquilizers also was found to be prevalent . . . these data suggest that one out of every four seniors not institutionalized will have taken one or more of the minor tranquilizers within the last six months and one in the last five will have done so within the last month." These utilization prevalence data are presented in Table 2.

TABLE 2
Minor Tranquilizer Use Among the Elderly
(Midwestern State, Rural and Urban)

	% Males	% Females	% Total
Any lifetime use	35.5	44.0	37.8
Use during last six months	22.8	26.9	23.6
Use during last month	19.6	20.8	20.1
Has used daily for at least one week	27.4	30.4	28.8

While the consumption of these anxiety-reducing medications seems high, other data indicate that this level of use is understandable. During this same period (1979), the researchers were provided with a set of data obtained from a nationwide random sample of adults responding to questions concerning their mental and physical health. Some of the data reveal why the high tranquilizer use is understandable.

In a randomly selected population of 2,060 adults, 16 percent reported current emotional difficulties or other mental health problems—nervousness, restlessness, tension/stress reaction, depression, anxiety, and general unhappiness. When one controlled for age above 60, this incidence rate went up to 67 percent. Among the elderly who reported such emotional distress, half said their conditions were chronic and half reported multiple problems. It is noteworthy that only 15 percent were being treated professionally for these specific conditions or for distress.

Based on these two sets of data, we began to explore the correlations between perceived health status and tranquilizing medication. By 1983 we had selected San Antonio, Texas, as the site for assessing the basic epidemiology of minor tranquilizer use among the noninstitutionalized elderly. The study site was chosen to provide a tri-ethnic population for assessment. Senior citizen centers catering primarily to whites, blacks, or Mexican-Americans were selected as independent study sites, and a quota of 100 randomly selected interviews was assigned to each site. The interviews were conducted by graduate students trained and supervised by the senior researchers. The 305 valid interviews obtained provided considerable "new" information about the elderly and their use of minor tranquilizers.

The study population reported the following reasons for using anti-anxiety medications:

Have trouble sleeping	Often	14%
	Sometimes	41%
	Hardly ever	44%
Have felt very nervous	Often	11%
	Sometimes	36%
	Hardly ever	42%
Have felt on the verge	Often	4%
of a nervous breakdown	Sometimes	17%
	Hardly ever	79%

In this total study population, *44 percent were currently taking one or more of the minor tranquilizers.* Of these, 34 percent were taking them daily and 59 percent at least twice a week. Fully one-fourth had specifically requested them from the physician. Over half were taking Valium (diazepam). The vast majority (86 percent) believed the drugs were helpful to them, and only 7 percent reported any negative side effect.

When we studied prescribing practices in an earlier survey in Texas, we found a significant number of primary-care physicians (35 percent) reluctant to deny a patient's request for a minor tranquilizer. The current study of consumers reaffirms this.

- Among all current users of minor tranquilizers, at least 1 in 4 has requested the medication, as opposed to waiting for their physician to recommend it.
- Whites (38 percent) and blacks (34 percent) much more frequently ask for these minor tranquilizers than do Mexican-Americans (13 percent).
- Males (31 percent) more frequently ask for these minor tranquilizers than do females (24 percent).
- Persons who are enjoying good health (35 percent) more frequently ask for these minor tranquilizers than those who take them and are in poor health.

Ethnicity and Minor Tranquilizer Use

The white cohort is described in Figure 1, the blacks in Figure 2, and the Mexican-Americans in Figure 3. As the reader will note, the whites are noticeably older than either the blacks or Mexican-Americans.

Figure 1. 100 Elderly Whites

83% Women
73% Age 69 or older
61% Widowed
46% Good physical health

Have had trouble sleeping		*Have felt very nervous*	
Often	21%	Often	20%
Sometimes	41%	Sometimes	31%
Hardly ever	38%	Hardly ever	49%

		Have felt on verge	
Have awakened tired		*of nervous breakdown*	
Often	24%	Often	5%
Sometimes	32%	Sometimes	21%
Hardly ever	44%	Hardly ever	74%

Currently taking a minor tranquilizer	(42)	42%		
Daily			(11)	26%
Twice a week			(10)	24%
Once a week			(7)	17%
Less than once a week			(14)	33%
Believe the drugs help			(41)	98%

Possibly as a consequence, whites report a higher rate of symptomatology associated with active anxiety or depression and general poor
health. Additionally:

- 42 percent of these elderly whites were taking minor tranquilizers
  and 1 in 4 had requested them specifically from their physicians.
- 26 percent of all these tranquilizer users were taking this medication
  daily *and* fully 1 in 2 were taking it at least twice a week.
- Virtually every white user reported that the drugs were effective and
  helpful in relieving their symptoms.

The *black cohort* (Figure 2) was found to be much younger than the
other cohorts and almost equally distributed by sex. The inclusion of
younger males had an obvious effect on the data. For example, there
were significantly lower rates of self-reported poor health generally,
and symptomatology, specifically, associated with active anxiety/de-
pression. However, in spite of this "better" health status, the use of
minor tranquilizers was as high as among the much older, more ill
whites. The consumption rate was even higher. Forty-two percent of

Figure 2. 105 Elderly Blacks

52% Women
22% Age 69 or older
11% Widowed
76% Good physical health

Have had trouble sleeping		*Have felt very nervous*	
Often	7%	Often	5%
Sometimes	48%	Sometimes	39%
Hardly ever	45%	Hardly ever	56%

Have awakened tired		*Have felt on verge of nervous breakdown*	
Often	10%	Often	6%
Sometimes	50%	Sometimes	17%
Hardly ever	40%	Hardly ever	77%

Currently taking a minor tranquilizer	(44)	42%	
Daily		(18)	41%
Twice a week		(15)	34%
Once a week		(3)	7%
Less than once a week		(8)	18%
Believed the drugs help		(39)	87%

these elderly blacks were taking one or more of the minor tranquilizers, and 1 in 3 had asked their physicians for them. Forty-one percent of these medicators use the tranquilizers daily and fully 75 percent of all users do so at least twice weekly. Eighty-seven percent believed these medications to be helpful.

Generally speaking, the *Mexican-American cohort* (Figure 3) was found to be between the whites and blacks. The Mexican-American health status and active symptomatology were more evenly distributed, as were their basic demographic attributes. Interestingly, their use of minor tranquilizers was consistent with the prevalence noted for both whites and blacks.

• While 40 percent of these elderly Mexican-Americans were taking one or more of the minor tranquilizers, which is comparable to the other cohorts, the overwhelming majority (87 percent) were taking them at the suggestion of the physician, rather than at their own request.

Figure 3. 100 Elderly Mexican-Americans

57% Women
57% Age 69 or older
55% Widowed
59% Good physical health

Have had trouble sleeping		*Have felt very nervous*	
Often	16%	Often	9%
Sometimes	35%	Sometimes	37%
Hardly ever	49%	Hardly ever	54%

		Have felt on verge	
Have awakened tired		*of nervous breakdown*	
Often	16%	Often	0%
Sometimes	42%	Sometimes	14%
Hardly ever	42%	Hardly ever	86%

Currently taking a minor tranquilizer	(40)	40%	
Daily		(17)	43%
Twice a week		(9)	23%
Once a week		(2)	5%
Less than once a week		(12)	29%
Believe the drugs help		(36)	86%

- 43 percent of these users were taking tranquilizers daily and two-thirds were taking them at least twice a week.
- 86 percent believed the medicine to be helpful.

Sex and Minor Tranquilizer Use

The study groups contained about twice as many women as men. Given the fact that about half were at least 70, the sex distribution was anticipated. However, as noted earlier, this distribution was *not* consistent across ethnicity groups, with black males overrepresented and white males underrepresented.

- The males were found to be enjoying better general health, which one can attribute generally to their younger ages.
- 48 percent of the women and 33 percent of the men were reporting current use of one or more of the minor tranquilizers, and the overwhelming majority felt that the medications were helping.

- If one were using such a medication, the frequency of consumption was high, regardless of sex. For example, 72 percent of males and 57 percent of females were using tranquilizers at least twice a week.
- Virtually all users believed that the drugs were helping them "cope" with symptoms.

In this study group of the noninstitutionalized tri-ethnic elderly, 13 percent of the men and 16 percent of the women were daily users of minor tranquilizers.

TABLE 3
Levels of Current Minor Tranquilizer Use

	Elderly Men (N=97)	Elderly Women (N=208)
Currently take a minor tranquilizer	33%	48%
Use daily	13%	16%
Use twice a week	11%	11%
Use once a week	2%	5%
Use less than once a week	7%	16%
Among users: believe the drugs help relieve symptoms	100%	84%

Age and Minor Tranquilizer Use

The total study population was almost equally distributed between those under and above 70. Not unexpectedly, significant differences surrounding health and medication use emerge when the younger cohort is compared with the older one.

- The younger respondents were more likely to be healthy generally and to present fewer symptoms of an active anxiety/depression: 66 percent of the younger group, but only 44 percent of the older, reported good physical health.
- In spite of better health generally and fewer anxiety/depression symptoms specifically, the younger persons in this elderly population were consuming as many minor tranquilizers just as frequently as were their older counterparts.
- Sex does not seem to play any part in the faith a user has in the efficacy of these drugs.

TABLE 4
Levels of Current Minor Tranquilizer Use

	Persons Age 69 or Less (N=151)	Persons Age 70 and Over (N=154)
Currently take a minor tranquilizer	42%	46%
Use daily	13%	17%
Use twice a week	13%	13%
Use once a week	1%	6%
Use less than once a week	15%	13%
Among users: believe the drugs help relieve symptoms	84%	87%

Health Status and Minor Tranquilizer Use

Some 55 percent of these elderly respondents reported that they were in good physical health. Of these, 32 percent were found to use minor tranquilizers and fully 21 percent were using them at least twice a week. By way of contrast, 51 percent of those who saw themselves in poor physical health were using minor tranquilizers and fully one-third used the drugs at least twice a week. Obviously, poor health increases use and frequency of use of the minor tranquilizers.

In summary, when one discusses the use of minor tranquilizers by the elderly, our studies suggest that:

- 42 percent of the whites, 42 percent of the blacks, and 40 percent of the Mexican-Americans currently use them.
- 33 percent of the elderly men and 48 percent of the elderly women currently use them.
- 42 percent of persons ages 60 to 69 and 46 percent of those age 70 or above currently use them.
- 32 percent of the "well elderly," but 51 percent of those in poor health, currently use them.

Thus, altering one's mood, or chemically coping by using a minor tranquilizer, is quite prevalent among the elderly of all ethnic groups, regardless of health or age. However, there appear to be more use of these psychoactive medications in a major metropolitan area such as San Antonio than in a rural or smaller urban center such as one examined in the Midwest.

PREVALENCE OF USE:
ANTIDEPRESSANT MEDICATIONS

The introduction of antidepressants some 25 years ago and their increasing popularity among practitioners have greatly facilitated the management of a wide variety of depressive states. Generally referred to as "mood elevators," these drugs have chemical structures quite different from the amphetamines and other stimulants, which they have largely replaced in the treatment of depression.

With these drugs, the onset of therapeutic effect is quite delayed. Almost maintenance use is required for the medication to take effect. In clinical practice, the antidepressants are normally continued for three to six months after optimal improvement in the patient's condition.

Until the last 10 years or so, antidepressants were the least prevalent of all prescribed psychoactive medications. For example, in 1975 we were projecting only about 1 million persons as being current users of these medications (Chambers, et al., 1975). However, as these drugs gained in popularity, certain patterns became obvious: The elderly were significantly overrepresented in the use of these medications, and older women were more likely than older men to be using them.

Within the past 10 years, however, the total prevalence of *therapeutic* use of these substances has more than tripled. From all indications, the use of antidepressant medications now surpasses the use of the minor tranquilizers during the ambulatory management of emotional crisis. At least among the elderly, we expect the prescribing of antidepressants such as Elavil (amitriplytine), Tofranil (imipramine), and Siniquan (doxepin) will become even more common. As life expectancy increases, one accumulates more "chronic" depressions directly attributable to deteriorating lifestyle and health condition. In recent surveys of prescribing practices, primary-care physicians mentioned prescribing more than 30 *different* antidepressant medications for their patients. Antidepressants currently account for almost 30 percent of all mood-altering prescriptions (Koch, June 1983).

Compared with what we know about the epidemiology of minor tranquilizer use, we have significantly fewer data about the use of the antidepressant medications. Available national data suggests there are some 10 million new or refill prescriptions every year for these specific mood "elevators." Some 3 million of these represent consumption by the elderly (Koch, June 1983). The elderly are obviously overrepresented in their use of the antidepressants (Chambers, 1975).

Survey data on utilization in a major Midwestern state during 1979 revealed the following for persons 60 and older:

- 7 percent of the elderly men and 10 percent of the elderly women had at sometime used a prescription mood elevator (antidepressant). Because these drugs must be consumed over an extended period to be effective, some level of extended use was virtually universal.
- 4 percent of the elderly men and 5 percent of the elderly women were *current regular* users of these drugs.

PREVALENCE OF USE: ANTIPSYCHOTIC MEDICATIONS

The major tranquilizers are chemically classified in the phenothiazine group of drugs and have been available for therapeutic use since about 1880. However, the full appreciation of their efficacy in both acute and chronic psychotic symptoms did not occur until the early 1960s. The more common of these antipsychotic medications—Thorazine (chlorpromazine), Compazine (prochlorperazine), Mellaril (thioridazine) and Stelazine (trifluoperazine)—have almost become household words. "Major tranquilizers account for almost 15 percent of all the new prescriptions and refill prescriptions for tranquilizing, sedating and antidepressant medications" (Koch, June 1983).

Survey data on use of these medications in noninstitutionalized populations are limited. In the early surveys (1970–1975) we found that women generally were overrepresented in the use of these drugs but that the elderly as a combined group were not. Later surveys (1979) suggested that the following was probably typical of the current situation:

- 4 percent of the men age 60 and above had at some time been prescribed a major tranquilizer and 3 out of 4 had used them daily for a period of time. About one-half of these elderly men with histories of using these phenothiazine medications are expected to be *current regular* users (2 percent of all men age 60 and above).
- 6 percent of the women ages 60 and above had also been users of

these medications and about one-half of everyone with a use history were believed to be *current regular* users (3 percent of older women). As with the men, most of the women had been "maintenance" users for a period of time.

INDICES OF MISUSE AND ABUSE

Most epidemiologists who focus on the use, misuse, and abuse of psychoactive substances would agree that *misuse* relates to using the drug in some manner other than as prescribed—for example, by increasing the amount or extending the period of use—while *abuse* means using the drug nonmedically to produce a euphoric or intoxicating effect. In both cases, the behavior must be *deliberate* if it is to be considered a deviancy.

- Deliberate noncompliance or misuse of the antianxiety, antidepressant, and antipsychotic medication by the elderly is limited.
- Deliberate nonmedical use or abuse of the antianxiety, antidepressant, and antipsychotic medication by the elderly is limited.
- When deliberate misuse and abuse of these mood-altering drugs by the elderly does occur, it more often involves the antianxiety medications than the antidepressants or antipsychotic medication.

Table 5 reflects the levels of misuse and abuse among the elderly who are *current* users of these antidepressant medications:

TABLE 5
Current Users of Antidepressants
(Age 60 and above)*

Has Respondent ever	Minor Tranquilizers	Anti Depressants	Major Tranquilizers
Increased dose frequency	16%	11%	5%
Increased dose amount	25%	11%	7%
Extended period of use	10%	11%	7%
Used non-medically	5%	4%	2%

* 1979 survey data from a major Midwestern state.

While some levels of deviancy are apparent from these data, the standard for determining the presence or absence of deviancy is quite stringent (e.g., "Have you *ever*. . . ?"). Future surveys must focus more on the context of the deviancy, as well as on any consequences of it.

At present, there are precious few indications that the elderly pay much of a price for their noncompliance or abuse of psychoactive medications. They report few side effects or other negative reactions to the drugs. Stated somewhat differently, the limited deviancy among the elderly associated with these drugs seems far overshadowed by the therapeutic relief they believe the drugs bring them. Their perceived "distress" is extensive and their reliance on these medications for both short- and long-term relief seems to them quite appropriate.

INDICES OF VICTIMIZATION

The sheer prevalence with which mood-altering medications are prescribed raises the potential for victimization. As long-term observers of the increasing use of these drugs to cope with normal life situations, we are prepared to note a variety of concerns about possible victimization.

Our major concern is that *none of these drugs has been rigidly tested for use with the elderly*. Virtually all clinical trials have been completed with young adults, and neither providers nor elderly consumers appreciate how little we know about the absorption, excretion, and metabolism of these drugs in the aging and elderly body. We do a *major* disservice to the elderly, our principal consumer of some of these medications, by not insisting on good clinical trials specifically for the elderly. In the meantime we should be monitoring the use of the drugs better than we have in the past.

A second concern must be the increasing patterns of long-term use and even the lifetime maintenance use of some of these drugs. Many people in their 60s have had a minor tranquilizer prescription for 20 years or more. Nor is it uncommon to encounter an elderly person who has been a daily user of a minor tranquilizer for years. This situation occurs in spite of the fact that at least the minor tranquilizers have been approved for only short-term relief of symptoms. They are not indicated for maintenance management of, or for coping with, the stress of everyday life. We are not prepared to say that long-term use of these medications has or does not have any significant debilitating effects. What does concern us is that *we do not know the emotional or physiological consequences for even low-dose, long-term use*. And if we do not know it, obviously the elderly consumer does not.

Our third concern involves the widespread acceptance of the safety of these medications by their providers and consumers. This acceptance has lulled us into a false sense of security with them. The most widely used of these medications, the antianxiety drugs, are the very ones most likely to produce an acute overdose and death and both psychological dependence and physical addiction. Once addicted, a patient finds withdrawal from the medication to be life-threatening. We do a *major* disservice to the elderly by not making them appreciate the fact that these drugs are dangerous when misused or used in combination with alcohol or other central nervous system depressants.

Finally, we victimize our elderly when we do not educate them fully concerning the problems of multiple diseases and polypharmacy. The elderly do not consume these mood-altering drugs *only*; they also consume a variety of other psychoactive medications and other prescription and nonprescription drugs. Most of their conditions are chronic and progressively debilitating. Each physician who treats them must know the "full picture" of diseases and conditions they are presenting to other physicians and the medications, both prescription and nonprescription, they are consuming. The elderly do not always choose to, or even see the need to, disclose this information. However, the person prescribing or dispensing medications *must* appreciate the absolute necessity for knowing all the existing conditions and all the interventions in progress.

CONCLUSION

We have presented data and opinions that would substantiate the following beliefs:

First, the *therapeutic use* of the antianxiety medications, the antidepressant medications, and the antipsychotic medications by the elderly is extensive and increasing. Chemical coping or chemical mood alteration is a prevalent pattern among the elderly, and from their perspective is of significant benefit to them. They would not choose to try to cope without these medications.

Second, the *deviant misuse or abuse* of these mood-altering drugs by the elderly seems to be quite limited. Deliberate noncompliance that would be life-threatening or dangerous to the elderly consumer does not appear to be a real problem. One would anticipate that the prevalence of noncompliance through *under-use* far exceeds that of *over-use*.

Third, the *victimization* of the elderly with these medications seems pervasive and obvious, even to the superficial analyst. Those who would defend or rationalize this victimization based on "good" versus "harm," present superficial and circular arguments. This is especially true when the "harm" dimension of the argument has never been formally or rigidly explored. We haven't tested these medications for use in the elderly, nor have we established their efficacy of them for long-term or maintenance-level use. Not to have done so was wrong—to continue not to do so would be criminal.

REFERENCES

Chambers, C., J. Inciardi, H. Siegal. 1975. *Chemical coping*, Holliswood, N.Y.: Spectrum.

Chambers, C., O. Z. White, J. Lindquist. 1983. Physician attitudes and prescribing practices: A focus on minor tranquilizers. *Psychoactive Drugs* 15(1–2).

National Center for Health Statistics, H. Koch. 1983. Utilization of psychoactive drugs in office-based ambulatory care, National Ambulatory Care Survey, 1098 and 1981. *Advanced data from vital and health statistics*, No. 90. DHHS Pub. No. (PHS) 83–1250. Hyattsville, Md.: Public Service.

National Center for Health Statistics, H. Koch. 1983. Drugs most frequently used in office practice, National Ambulatory Medical Care Survey, 1981. *Advance data from vital and health statistics*, No. 89. DHHS Pub. No. (PHS) 83–1250. Hyattsville, Md.: Public Health Service.

The Statistical Bulletin. 1984. New York: Metropolitian Life Insurance Company.

Medicating the Elderly

ROBERT J. CLUXTON, JR., R.Ph., Pharm.D.

Associate Professor
Clinical Pharmacy
College of Pharmacy
University of Cincinnati

BARBARA HURFORD, R.Ph., Pharm.D.

College of Pharmacy
University of Cincinnati

TIM BIEN, R.Ph.

Adjunct Instructor
Clinical Pharmacy
College of Pharmacy
University of Cincinnati

INTRODUCTION

A great deal of interest in geriatrics exists among the professionals who work with the elderly. However, formal academic programs in the clinical aspects of geriatrics are lacking in the professional schools of medicine, nursing, and pharmacy. Especially deficient are programs dealing with the use and misuse of medications. Less than one-third of the colleges of pharmacy in the United States offer academic courses dealing with the elderly and their use or misuse of medications.

"Elderly" is a term traditionally used for people 65 or older. There is an increasing tendency to subdivide this into the young-old (55 to 64), the old (65 to 75), and the old-old (over 75). The physical, psychological, and sociological changes that occur with the natural aging process are gradual, making it impossible to say at what age these changes become significant. It is important to remember that the elderly population ranges from functional 85-year-olds to infirm individuals who

72

are much younger. Although medication problems increase with age, not everyone over 65 will have them and not everyone under 65 will be free of them. A useful geriatric medicine maxim is that sick old people are sick because they are sick, *not* because they are old.

The number of elderly is increasing; those over 85 are the fastest growing segment of our population. By the year 2030, that number is expected to increase from 11.5 to 20 percent of the total U.S. population (1981 statistics) *(1)*. Statistically, this has several implications for drug therapy.

The elderly are the major consumers of health care, accounting for approximately 30 percent of the $251.4 billion spent annually for health-related expenses (1981 figures) *(1)*. Those 65 and older consume 25 percent of prescription drugs, *(2,3)* yet they constitute only 11.5 percent of the population. By the year 2020 it is estimated that 50 percent of all prescriptions will be for the elderly *(3,4)*. Their expenditures for over-the-counter medications, currently estimated at over $7 billion per year, are expected to increase proportionately. The uncertain impact of increased drug use is of concern to those who prescribe, administer, and provide compensation for medication. Considerable evidence exists about the effectiveness of modern drug therapy in relieving disease symptoms and in palliative or curative therapy. However, past experience has shown a very high degree of association between the increased use of prescription drugs and undesirable side effects.

Clearly the challenge to health professionals and the public is to implement therapeutic regimens that will maximize the benefits from medication while minimizing the inherent risks. Because all medications can cause bothersome, possibly serious side effects, they must be monitored carefully by all persons involved in the care of the elderly, including the elderly themselves. All too often physicians, nurses, pharmacists, and other professionals erroneously assume that the elderly must be cared for and do not sufficiently educate patients so that they can actively participate in their own care. Yet it is the patient who benefits most from this approach, which could be cost-effective and safe.

The factors that make it difficult to achieve cost-effective, safe drug use for the elderly include, but certainly are not limited to:

1. Polypharmacy (the use of multiple drugs to treat a disease)
2. Lack of drug-dosing data in the elderly

3. Compliance with the therapeutic regimen
4. Adverse drug reactions

POLYPHARMACY: THE USE OF MULTIPLE DRUGS

Approximately 30 percent of elderly patients use eight or more medications simultaneously *(4)*. A basic presumption of multiple drug use is that it increases the risk of serious sequelae and creates an excessive economic burden. Sloan reports the incidence of drug interactions is 5.6 percent for two drugs taken concurrently, 50 percent for five, and almost 100 percent for eight or more *(5)*. However, experience has shown that most drug interactions have no long-term detrimental effects, though some are bothersome and on rare occasions they are fatal.

There are legitimate reasons for the elderly to use medications simultaneously. The most significant is that pathological conditions, such as cardiovascular disease and musculo-skeletal disorders, coexist. Table 1 lists some of the common problems that require multiple drug therapy, and Table 2 displays the results of a survey of drug use by therapeutic class in six nursing homes. This survey showed that 62.4 percent of all drug orders were for vitamins, minerals and nutrients (10.5 percent), analgesics and antiinflammatory agents (13.9 percent), laxatives (17.6 percent), dermatologicals (8.8 percent), diuretics (6.0 percent), and antipsychotics (5.7 percent). The average number of drug orders per patient was 7.6, with a range of 6.64 to 9.06. Thus it is clear that most elderly patients have multiple coexistent conditions that require therapy.

Simonson has defined "polypharmacy" as "the *excessive* and *unnecessary* use of medication" and has identified common situations in which detrimental polypharmacy occurs (Tables 3 and 4) *(1)*. The following are actual situations that we have observed.

Use of Medications with No Apparent Indications

An elderly male patient was transferred to a skilled nursing facility (SNF) from a hospital. His drug regimen included the drug Zyloprim (allopurinol), which is usually indicated for treatment of gout, arthri-

TABLE 1
Prevalence of Some Chronic Conditions

Condition	All Ages	65 Years and Over
Neuralgia + neuritis		
specified	1.9	9.0
unspecified	8.2	33.5
Diabetes	20.4	78.5
Sciatica	4.3	11.9
Diseases of urinary system	28.0	60.7
Diseases of kidney and ureter	6.5	10.0
Anemias	14.5	20.9
Thyroid conditions	13.9	19.7
Migraine	21.8	14.7

Rates per 100 persons

tis, or hyperuricema. A review of the history and admission records indicated that none of the normal criteria for using this medication seemed to exist. When questioned about the indication for the drug, the nurse in charge thought it was being used to treat a bothersome skin rash. The SNF house physician agreed that no apparent indication to use Zyloprim was evident, and he discontinued the medication. Followup monitoring of the patient, including blood analysis of uric acid, showed no change in clinical status, but the skin rash (which can be an adverse reaction to this drug) went away shortly after the medication was discontinued.

Use of Duplication Medications

Using duplicate medications in the same patient can arise in two patterns: (1) using more than one drug of the same therapeutic class, or (2) using the same drug in multiple-dose forms.

Using more than one drug of the same therapeutic class

As shown in Table 2, the most frequently used therapeutic class is laxatives. Many factors associated with aging make constipation a common problem. Because of this, and some basic misunderstanding on

TABLE 2
Drug Orders by Therapeutic Class at Six Nursing Homes

Facility	A	B	C	D	E	F	
Type of Licensure	SNF*	ICF+	ICF	SNF	SNF	SNF	
Number of Beds	167	95	70	165	142	100	
Number of Drug Orders Per Patient (Average)	6.6	8.6	6.6	9.1	7.2	7.4	
Therapeutic Class			*% of Drug Orders per Facility*			*Average %*	
Laxatives	15.1	19.5	15.2	22.5	18.9	13.9	17.5
Analgesics and anti-inflamatory agents	10.9	14.6	14.7	14.9	11.9	16.4	13.9
Vitamins, minerals and nutrients	8.9	15.0	9.8	9.2	9.7	10.5	10.5
Dermatologicals	9.1	4.4	10.4	7.6	12.1	9.2	8.8
Diuretics	5.9	6.0	6.3	4.1	5.5	8.1	6.0
Antipsychotic	3.5	2.6	5.8	6.1	1.0	3.3	5.7
Cardiac glycosides	5.8	3.3	4.0	3.4	4.8	4.0	4.2
Opthalmic preps	4.4	5.1	2.5	2.7	3.0	2.7	3.4
Sedative/hypnotic	3.4	4.4	4.1	2.8	3.6	2.1	3.4
Cough, cold, allergy	2.8	2.4	5.7	3.2	1.6	4.3	3.3
Antidiarrheal	2.2	6.9	2.0	1.4	1.8	3.5	3.0
Antianginal	2.8	2.4	2.4	2.3	2.3	3.3	2.6
Antacids	1.9	1.7	3.3	1.6	2.5	2.6	2.3
Antianxiety	1.4	3.2	1.8	2.3	1.9	1.3	2.0
Antihypertensive	2.6	2.6	1.8	0.9	1.7	2.1	2.0
Anti-infective	3.4	1.8	2.3	2.8	1.1	1.0	2.0
Antiemtic	0.9	1.5	0.6	2.8	1.0	2.0	1.5
Antidepressants	2.2	0	1.2	1.7	1.7	1.2	1.3
Antidiabetics	1.1	0.6	1.6	1.4	1.9	0.9	1.3
Anticonvulsants	1.0	1.4	1.4	1.1	0.9	1.0	1.1
Antispasmotic, antichol- energic, and ulcer drugs	2.1	1.2	0.4	0.8	0	2.2	1.1

All others: 1% or less

* SNF = Skilled Nursing Facility
+ ICF = Intermediate Care Facility

TABLE 3
Drug-related Sources of Detrimental Polypharmacy

1. Use of medications with no apparent indications
2. Use of duplicate medications
3. Concurrent use of interacting drugs
4. Use of inappropriate dosage
5. Use of drug therapy to treat adverse drug reaction
6. Inappropriate use of medications

TABLE 4
Nondrug Sources of Detrimental Polypharmacy

1. Poor communication with health care providers
2. Use of more than one physician for different medical problems
3. Self-treatment without medical advice
4. Multiple pathology associated with aging

the necessary frequency of bowel movements, laxative abuse is frequent. For example, an 84-year-old man was using the following medications to try to regulate his bowels:

Drug Brand Name	Drug Generic Name	U.S.P. Therapeutic Class
Cas-Evac	cascara sagrada	cathartic (potent laxative)
Doxidan Capsules	danthron, dioctyl/ sulfosuccinate	laxative
_____	glycerin suppositories	rectal evacuant (potent laxative)
Kondremul (Plain)	mineral oil 55% with irish moss	laxative
_____	soapsuds enema	rectal evacuant (potent laxative)
Fleet Enema	sodium biphosphate	laxative

Normally, two of these medications (agents with different mechanisms of action to attain a synergistic effect) would be used, along with diet, exercise, and proper hydration, to treat chronic constipation. However, there is no standard therapy for chronic constipation in the elderly, and some cases are extremely difficult to manage. In *this* patient, the use of three or more agents to relieve constipation is excessive and exposes the patient to unnecessary expense and the risk of adverse effects, because laxative abuse is common, one of the standards for SNF medication review states that patients receiving more than two concurrent laxatives must be evaluated by the pharmacist.

Using the same drug in multiple-dose forms

Table 2 shows that analgesics represent 13.9 percent of drug use. Multiple drug use in this therapeutic class is more difficult to detect, because different brand-name products may have the same active ingredient. An example case is an 80-year-old female who was using the following medications to treat pain associated with osteoporosis:

Drug Brand Name	Drug Generic Name	U.S.P. Therapeutic Class
Tylenol 325 mg	acetaminophen 650 mg.	analgesic
Anacin #3/Codeine	acetaminophen 300 mg.	analgesic
	codeine phosphate 30 mg.	narcotic
Parafon Forte	acetaminophen 300 mg.	analgesic
	chlorzoxazone 250 mg.	skeletal muscle relaxant

Since the patient had no allergy to aspirin, a more reasonable approach might have been to use aspirin in place of Tylenol or to use a single ingredient agent of each therapeutic class. Excessive doses of acetaminophen had caused irreversible hepatic damage. However, it was easy to inadvertently overdose this patient with "hidden" acetaminophen.

Concurrent Use of Interacting Drugs

Some medications interact, causing an altered action of one or both with the potential for adverse sequelae. An example of this involved a 78-year-old female who had orders for Questran (cholestyramine) and Lanoxin (digoxin). Questran is used to reduce serum cholesterol, and Lanoxin is used for congestive heart failure. When the drugs are given at the same time, Questran can reduce the absorption of Lanoxin and in effect decrease the dose available for systemic action. In this case, Questran and Lanoxin were scheduled to be taken at the same time, and a followup blood level of Lanoxin revealed a serum level much lower than expected. A well-designed dose regimen would schedule the Lanoxin to be taken at least one hour before the Questran. As an alternative, an increased dose of Lanoxin could be prescribed to counteract the decrease in Lanoxin absorption. However, the cost to the patient would increase, and if the Questran were discontinued without the dose of Lanoxin, the patient might experience Digoxin toxicity—a potentially fatal adverse drug reaction.

Use of Inappropriate Dosages

Inappropriate dosing can unintentionally contribute to polypharmacy. If doses are too high, unnecessary expense is incurred and significant morbidity or mortality can occur. Furthermore, additional medication may have to be ordered to combat side effects. Conversely, doses that are too low might lead to "treatment failure." When treatment failure occurs, a second or third medication may be ordered to achieve the desired therapeutic goal.

An example of the second problem occurred in a 74-year-old nursing-home patient with chronic obstructive pulmonary disease as one of her medical problems. Her drug therapy included:

Drug Brand Name	Drug Generic Name	Dose	Frequency	U.S.P. Therapeutic Class
Bricanyl	terbutaline	2.5 mg.	3 times a day	sympathomimetic bronchodilator
Elixophyllin	theophylline 80 mg. per 15 ml. in alcohol 20%	30 ml.	3 times a day	xanthine bronchodilator
Proventil Inhaler	albuterol 90 mcg./puff	2 puffs	every 12 hours	sympathomimetic bronchodilator
Vanceril Inhaler	beclomethasone 42 mcg./puff	2 puffs	4 times a day	corticosteroid
_____	aminophylline suppository	250 mg.	every 16 hours, when needed	xanthine bronchodilator

This patient did not like the taste of Elixophyllin and occasionally refused to take it. She also refused to switch to another xanthine bronchodilator or to a "tasteless" capsule form of Elixophyllin. Not surprisingly, she was not receiving adequate maintenance therapy and required the use of supplementary aminophylline suppositories on an as-needed basis for her frequent shortness of breath. Inappropriate dosing intervals also created the need for additional bronchodilator medications. Proventil inhaler is normally used at 4- to 6-hour intervals to maintain pulmonary bronchodilation. However, in this case, its bronchodilatory effects declined before the prescribed 12-hour interval and additional medication was started to make up for the "therapeutic failure."

Use of Drug Therapy to Treat Adverse Drug Reactions

Often, additional medication is necessary to treat an adverse reaction from a previous medication. One example is a 78-year-old nursing home patient with a diagnosis of severe depression. Her drug therapy included:

Drug Brand Name	Generic Name	Dose	U.S.P. Therapeutic Class
Tofranil	imipramine	100 mg. per day	antidepressant
Haldol	haloperidol	2 mg. per day	antipsychotic
Cogentin	benztropine mesylate	1 mg. per day	antiparkinsonism agent
Surfak	docusate calcium	300 mg. per day	laxative
_____	milk of magnesia	30 ml. when needed for constipation	cathartic (potent laxative)
_____	soap suds enema	when needed for constipation	rectal evacuant (potent laxative)

Initially, Haldol was being used to treat agitation and Tofranil to treat depression. After a time on this regimen, the patient experienced some "Parkinson-like shaking," a common side effect of Haldol, and was placed on Cogentin to treat it. Tofranil, Haldol, and Cogentin can slow intestinal motility and cause chronic constipation, so concurrent Docusate, milk of magnesia, and soapsuds enema were ordered.

As Dr. Simonson states, "A medication that is used to treat a drug-induced side effect or toxicity may have its own side effects, resulting in the use of still more medications, which may have side effects of their own, thus continuing the spiral of polypharmacy" *(1)*.

Inappropriate Use of Medications

Inappropriate use of medication is another source of polypharmacy. An example is the use of a decongestant to treat allergic rhinitis, commonly known as "running nose." Because decongestants and antihistamines both reduce mucous flow, one may erroneously be substituted for the other. Decongestants are vasoconstrictors that reduce mucous flow by decreasing blood flow to secretory sites. Antihistamines reduce inflammatory response of mucous membranes to allergens. If the source of the "running nose" is an allergy, a decongestant will be ineffective; an antihistamine is the correct medication in that case.

Other common examples of inappropriate use include using antibiotics for a shorter or longer time than the physician intended. Using topical antibiotics or antifungals in a sporadic fashion (treatment with no routine or time period specified) is ineffective. The condition is never completely healed and is assumed to be a chronic infection. Thus, sporadic treatment can perpetuate itself and lead to prolonged treatment and significant expense.

LACK OF DRUG DOSING DATA IN THE ELDERLY

Labeling approved by the Food and Drug Administration (FDA) includes very limited information for dosing elderly patients. Recommended doses for most drugs are based on clinical trials in young adults and not specifically in the elderly. Thus, dose regimens for the elderly evolve from anecdotal data, clinical impressions, and trail and error. *(6)*.

The FDA's Division of Drug Advertising and Labeling plans to propose new regulations for geriatic drugs *(7)*. According to Lloyd Millstien, the division's director, the proposed regulations will stipulate:

> **Geriatric Use:** *A specific geriatric indication if any, shall be described under the "indications and usage" section of the labeling, and appropriate dosage for elderly patients shall be stated under*

the "dosage and administration" section of the labeling. If use of a drug in the elderly is associated with a specific hazard, the hazard shall be described in this subsection of the labeling or in the section of the labeling considered to be most appropriate due to the degree of risk or subject matter; e.g. drug interaction or laboratory test that should be obtained because of drug specificity or action in the elderly; and this subsection of the labeling shall refer to it.

In an editorial comment, the Pharmaceutical Manufacturers Association (PMA) concluded that the proposed geriatric labeling information need not be technical or detailed. In fact, the level of information required may not assist the clinician at all. The required information for the phenothiazine class of antipsychotic agents clearly illustrates this:

Age is considered an important determinant of the rates of metabolism and excretion of the phenothiazines. The elderly, the fetus and the infant have diminished capacities to metabolize and excrete these drugs (7).

Although specific drug dosage information is not required, the intent of the proposed labeling requirement is to "motivate" manufacturers to obtain clinical test data on the elderly. *(7).*

The proposed FDA regulations include a pharmacokinetic screen that would require blood-level determinations under defined dosing conditions. The purpose is to display the variability in blood levels. PMA does not agree that pharmacokinetic screening is necessary, contending that such testing would expose large numbers of patients with various conditions, such as hepatic or renal dysfunction, to a new drug to determine if adverse effects occur. The PMA asserts this would be "unacceptably hazardous" *(8).*

The PMA has offered an alternative proposal that would require pharmacokinetic screening tests to identify age-related problems with a drug. *(8).* PMA's approach has three stages:

1. Current drug disposition studies (to determine how a drug is metabolized and excreted).

2. "Special" drug disposition studies in "normal" elderly (to determine if different disposition occurs in the elderly).
3. Inclusion of the elderly in New Drug Application (NDA)–required clinical trials (age is not a factor in the regulations that are used to design required premarketing drug studies).

Neither the proposed FDA regulations nor the PMA counterproposal is acceptable. Data from several studies show an increased risk of adverse drug reactions that is associated with increasing age (9–13). Age-–related adverse effects for heparin (13), nitrazepam (Mogaden) (14), chlordiazepoxide (Librium) (15), diazepam (Valium) (15), and flurazepam (Dalmane) (15) have been clearly demonstrated. Data from these and other intensive monitoring programs illustrate the special therapeutic problems of the elderly but include very limited data for identifying pathophysiological mechanisms involved.

Pharmacokinetics and Aging

Age is closely correlated with an increased incidence and severity of disease. Various anatomical and physiological changes that occur with the natural aging process affect the way the body responds to medication. When we attempt to explain the mechanisms, two principal conceptual approaches emerge: pharmacodynamic and pharmacokinetic (6).

The pharmacodynamic concept holds that a greater drug response occurs in an older person than in a younger one, even when the same drug is present in the same concentration. The pharmacokinetic concept explains altered drug effects on the basis of age-related alterations in drug absorption, distribution, metabolism, and excretion. Data exist to support both the pharmacodynamic and pharmacokinetic concepts. However, the pharmacokinetic approach has been studied more thoroughly and has the potential for wider application.

Pharmacokinetics is a method of mathematical modeling that characterizes the time course of a drug in the body. The three principal functions in pharmacokinetics are drug absorption, distribution, and elimination. Elimination is frequently subdivided into metabolism and excretion. An understanding of pharmacokinetics is essential for the person who prescribes and monitors drug therapy. A detailed discussion is beyond the scope of this chapter. Those who desire to know more about the use of pharmacokinetics are referred to the extensive reviews that have been published. *(16–19).* Our purpose here is to discuss briefly some of the alterations in pharmacokinetics that occur as a result of the pathophysiology of aging.

Specific physiologic changes and their effects on drug therapy in the geriatric patient are summarized in Table 5 *(20).* It should be emphasized that these changes are part of the normal physiologic process of aging in the healthy geriatric patient. The effects become more pronounced if the patient has kidney disease, liver disease, cardiac dysfunction, or other concomitant illnesses. Regardless of the specific pathophysiologic parameter, all pharmacokinetic changes can be categorized into those that affect absorption, distribution, or elimination.

Drug Absorption

For drugs administered orally, absorption is the first pharmacokinetic function. The elderly are reported to have a reduction of gastric parietal cell function leading to decreased acid secretion, elevated gastric pH *(21),* reduced gastric emptying rate *(22),* and impaired nutritional active transport processes *(23).* The effect of these changes on drug absorption is not clear, since most drugs are absorbed by passive diffusion. Little evidence is available to suggest that total drug absorption is altered in old age *(24–26).* In general, the rate of drug absorption is much slower, due to changes in secretory activity, structure, and motility, but the extent of absorption remains the same.

Drug Distribution

Distribution denotes the partitioning of a drug among its numerous locations in the body. The apparent volume of distribution (Vd) is used to quantitate this distribution. Usually measured in liters, Vd is the volume a drug would occupy if uniformly dissolved.

Age-related physiologic and pathologic changes that alter drug distribution are: reduced total body water and extracellular fluid, reduced cardiac output, reduced lean body mass, increased body fat, and reduced plasma proteins. This last change is particularly important, because serum albumin is a major protein for drug binding. The laboratory–determined serum level of a drug reflects the total drug—that

TABLE 5

Physiologic and Pathologic Changes and Their Pharmacokinetic and Therapeutic Consequences in the Geriatric Patients[20]*

Parameter	Physiologic or pathologic change	Organ consequences	Pharmacokinetic consequences	Therapeutic consequences
Body weight	generally reduced, including vital organs	loss of fluid, reduction in heart, kidney and muscle tissue, atrophic tissue	normal adult dose results in higher blood levels, higher drug concentration receptor ratio	overdosing, increase side effects and toxic effects
GI-secretion, GI-tract	reduced secretion reduced GI-motility	higher gastric pH, longer stomach emptying rate, less mixing of GI-contents	altered dissolution rate of tablets and capsules, delayed transition to small intestine; prolonged absorption rate	longer time for onset of effect, lower intensity of effect, prolonged duration of effect
Body fluid	Total body fluid and Intracellular fluid	hypokalemia and hypernatremia	reduced volume of distribution, increased blood levels	overdosing, increased side effects and toxic effects, dehydration
Heart and blood flow	reduced cardiac output, reduced vascular elasticity and permeability, reduced blood flow	possible venous congestion and arterial hypovolemia	slower absorption rate from GI-tract, muscle, skin, rectum, delayed distribution; reduced volume of distribution, increased blood levels	longer time for onset, overdosing, increased side effects and toxic effects, hypoxia

TABLE 5 (continued)

Body composition	reduced lean body mass, increased fat tissue	organ function changed	decrease in volume of distribution in general storage of drugs with high lipid solubility in fat depots and slower elimination	overdosing increased, side effects; reduced response for drugs of high lipid solubility, hangover phenomenon, delayed onset followed by accumulation and overdosing in multiple dosing
Kidney	reduced renal blood flow, reduced glomerular filtration and active secretion	lower creatinine clearance, reduced renal function	increase in biological half-life of drugs eliminated via kidney	overdosing, longer duration of effect, increased side effects and toxic effects
Plasma proteins	reduction in albumin	hypo-albuminemia	saturation of protein binding and increased concentration of free drug, shorter half-life if highly bound	increased intensity of effect, increased side effects and toxic effects, overdosing
Homeostasis	abnormal ability	restricted range or regulatory functions	possible change in volume of distribution	paradoxic drug reactions

* Reproduced with permission of the author.

which is bound to plasma proteins and that which is unbound. For most drugs, only the unbound agent is active and is available for elimination *(27)*. For drugs that are extensively protein-bound, the elderly should have an increased fraction of unbound drug, which increases drug effect without an increase in total serum drug level. To achieve the usual therapeutic levels and avoid drug toxicity, it is necessary to reduce the dose *(27)*.

Drug Elimination

Metabolism and elimination of various drugs may be altered with advancing age. Some drugs are excreted unchanged, while others must be metabolized. The liver is the site of metabolism for most drugs. During the normal aging process, liver function does not change significantly, although the rate of metabolism of some drugs may change. Typically renal function declines with age, so that drugs whose elimination depends primarily on the kidney will be excreted more slowly as age increases. This slower rate can result in drug accumulation in the body.

A mathematical measure of elimination is called the halflife $(t_{1/2})$. In its simplest form, the halflife of the drug is the time (usually in hours) for one-half of the drug to be eliminated from the body. A common error in interpretation of data is to consider the halflife, rather than clearance, as the measure of elimination. Clearance is the hypothetical volume of plasma that the kidney can completely clear of drug per unit time. Halflife is actually a hybrid of clearance and volume of distribution, as seen in Equation 1.

Equation 1

$$Cl = \frac{0.693 \times Vd}{t_{1/2}}$$

$t_{1/2}$ = apparent or observed halflife of drug elimination
Vd = the apparent volume of distribution
Cl = total clearance of the drug from the body

Thus, halflife and clearance are inversely proportional, but only when Vd is not appreciably changed. As we have already discussed, this is not the usual situation in the elderly. To appropriately assess the rate of drug removal, clearance should be evaluated.

Drug Holidays

In an attempt to deal with the aberrant pharmacokinetics of the geriatric population and allow for evaluation of adverse drug effects, a program known as the "drug holiday" has become quite popular. "Drug holiday" refers to the practice of withholding medications for a period of time, usually one or two days a week, to minimize drug accumulation. A common method is to give medication Monday through Friday only. During the "holiday" the patient is closely observed to determine if the medication is really needed and to unmask adverse effects. Guidelines for implementation and parameters for patient evaluation have been published (28) and appear as Appendix I and II of this chapter. Unfortunately, these guidelines and evaluation procedures are not often followed. It has been our experience that a primary, and sometimes exclusive, motivation for a "drug holiday" program is the chance it provides to reduce the number of professional personnel needed for patient care on Saturday and Sunday.

Although theoretically the drug holiday program may have some merit, in practice it is seldom beneficial to the patient. By using drug holidays, health care professionals may convince themselves that they are doing all they can to minimize overmedication of patients. But drug holidays may encourage patients to feel that if they do well without medication during the drug holiday, they do not need to take the drugs on other days. It is our opinion that "routine" or "regular" drug holidays can do more harm than good if they are not properly planned and implemented. Within a matter of weeks, it becomes acceptable to use "usual adult doses," which may be higher than the patient needs, because the facility has a policy declaring Saturday and Sunday as drug holidays. For a drug-holiday program to be effective, careful patient evaluation by highly specialized personnel is required. Such expertise is usually well beyond that found in a typical long-term care facility and may require hospitalization for successful implementation.

COMPLIANCE WITH THE THERAPEUTIC REGIMEN

A major factor contributing to unexpected or adverse drug effects in the elderly is lack of compliance with the medication regimen. "Noncompliance" is loosely defined as failure of the patient to follow instructions for use of the medications. The reported rate of noncompliance within the elderly population ranges from 2 to 95 percent, depending on the criteria used for defining noncompliance, the population sampled, and the methods used. Simonson estimates that on the average, between one-fourth and one-third of the population are noncompliant *(1)*. Eraker et al. estimate that noncompliance for chronic disease therapy averages about 50 percent *(29)*.

Failure to take medication is the most common form of noncompliance, accounting for about half of all cases. Patients often forget to take their medication, especially if the dosing regimen is complicated or consists of multiple doses during the day. If the patient cannot remember whether or not he has taken the medication, he may elect to skip the dose rather than take a double dose. Some patients may deliberately skip doses for financial reasons; it lengthens the time interval between prescription refills and decreases costs. However, most patients do not realize the hidden costs or consequences of noncompliance, such as increased physician visits for resolution of symptoms due to inadequate therapy. Another problem is that some patients may not be able to get to a pharmacy to have their prescriptions filled or refilled before the medication runs out. This is especially prevalent in those elderly persons who live alone and have no transportation.

Other patients may knowingly skip doses on a routine or scheduled basis as a means of reducing or tolerating adverse reactions or exaggerated responses to the medication. Weintraub refers to this as "intelligent" noncompliance, especially when it is followed by a report to the physician or other professional involved in the patient's therapy *(30)*. About 5 percent of prescriptions that are written are not filled because the patient cannot afford the medication, lacks transportation, feels that the medication is not needed, or feels that the risk involved is too great *(29)*.

Although failure to take the medication is the most common form of noncompliance, several other types exist. Taking medication at the wrong time of the day can have potentially serious consequences. For example, when a medication is ordered to be taken once a day, the patient may think this means *once any time during the day*, while the physician and pharmacist intend it to mean *once every 24 hours*. The patient takes the medication at 9 A.M. on the first day, 9 P.M. on the second day, and 9 A.M. on the third, resulting in a dosage interval ranging from 36 to 12 hours. Such variation can lead to relatively long periods of subtherapeutic effects or to toxicity. This is especially important in drugs such as digoxin, warfarin, and theophylline, which have a very narrow therapeutic range—between the therapeutic dose and the toxic dose. Other dosing terms that are frequently misinterpreted are "every six hours," "with meals," and "every P.M."

Another form of noncompliance is excessive consumption. The old maxim that "if one is good, two is better" does *not* apply to medications. Increased consumption can occur in the patient who cannot remember whether or not he has taken a medication and so takes a second or third dose. Inability to remember may be directly due to actual memory loss or to a blunting of mental function by central nervous system depressant drugs, including alcohol. Some patients lay out the entire day's supply to help them remember. Some patients even take the entire daily supply at one time. Thus, the patient is in double jeopardy, taking too much medication at once and by missing the remaining doses.

Premature discontinuation of medication or poor compliance occurs frequently in the "symptomless" diseases, such as hypertension and diabetes. Eraker et al. report that up to 50 percent of patients with hypertension fail to follow referral advice, over 50 percent drop out of care within one year, and only about two thirds of those who remain under care consume enough medication to control their blood pressure adequately (29).

Failure of the health care provider to communicate changes in drug therapy can inadvertently lead to excessive medication consumption by the patient. The physician may prescribe a different drug in the same chemical class to obtain better therapeutic effects or to minimize side effects, but may forget to tell the patient to discontinue taking the previous medication.

Prematurely discontinuing the medication without the physician's authorization can be considered another form of noncompliance. The patient may think that he no longer needs the prescribed medication and stop the drug on his own, or he may stop the medication early and save the remainder to be used when a similar episode occurs. This is especially common with antibiotics. After a few days of therapy, the patient begins to feel better and stops the antibiotics on his own. Unfortunately, the infection may not be resolved, resulting in additional days of antibiotic therapy and additional costs.

Taking medications that have not been prescribed is a common practice in the elderly and can lead to serious adverse drug reactions. This includes taking medications that have been saved from prior illnesses and sharing medications with a friend or family member. Selection of the proper medication and dose is highly specific to patient and disease and should not be attempted without medical supervision.

Understanding Noncompliance

Compliance to a medication regimen decreases when the regimen is lengthy, complex, dependent on an alteration of the patient's lifestyle, inconvenient, or expensive (29, 31–32). The patient's noncompliance may be reasonable, in light of these factors.

Health care professionals tend to think that treatment outcome is based solely on whether or not the patient follows the recommended therapy. Faithful adherence to the therapeutic regimen may not always produce the desired outcome. Treatment failures can occur in some patients, even though the right diagnosis was made and the correct therapy was prescribed. Unfortunately, there is no way to predict these treatment failures beforehand. In addition, some conditions may improve in spite of poor compliance. This is especially true when the outcome of the disease without treatment is uncertain (29).

The patient's perspective on compliance is influenced by his own health-related beliefs, which have several origins—cultural standards, parents' and families' beliefs, previous experience with illnesses and medications, misinterpretation of factual information, and acceptance of information from nonmedical sources (29). In addition, patients are continually exposed to the controversies, contradictions, and advancements of the medical field through newspapers, television, radio, and other media. These forces all play a part in determining the patient's willingness to seek and accept medical treatment.

Physical disabilities associated with aging may also limit the ability to communicate with health care providers and have a direct effect on compliance. Persons suffering from arthritis and other degenerative joint diseases may have difficulty opening child-resistant containers and need to be informed that nonchildproof containers are available on request. Other persons suffer from presbycusis, a hearing loss associated with aging in which low tones are heard but high tones are indistinguishable. Words become distorted and hard to understand. Also, as the optic lens loses elasticity visual acuity diminishes. Then too, the lens of the eye also tends to yellow with age, making color discrimination, especially between blue and green, difficult (33). A recent study indicates that elderly patients have difficulty distinguishing between blue and green tablets and between yellow and white ones (34).

The ability of the elderly to comprehend medication information also influences compliance. Elderly persons can learn as well as younger people, but at a much slower rate (35). The elderly appear to have good short-term memory but diminished long-term memory (36). Important drug information about dosing and side effects needs to be reinforced with each prescription refill, not only with the initial prescription. Short, simple, easy-to-read printed information that can be taken home and assimilated slowly may also help (37). The elderly should be given specific guidelines for taking "as-needed" medications. These can include physical markers (pains, discomfort), time limits (four times daily; four hours between doses) or other information (maximum doses within 24 hours) (37).

Individual patients are usually reluctant to reveal their noncompliance. Consequently, special efforts are required to detect it. Unfortunately, there are no readily observable characteristics that can accurately predict which patients will be noncompliers (38). Table 6 summarizes some traits to look for when noncompliance is suspected (1).

TABLE 6
Traits of Noncompliant Individuals

1. Illness fails to respond to therapy.
2. Patient is socially isolated.
3. Patient is forgetful or confused.
4. Sensory deficits are present.
5. Drug therapy is complex.
6. Patient fails to keep appointments.
7. Drug therapy is inexpensive.
8. Patient fails to obtain timely prescription refills.

Source: W. Simonson, Medications and the Elderly: A Guide for Promoting Proper Use (Rockville, Md.: Aspen, 1984).

IMPROVING COMPLIANCE: INVOLVING THE PATIENT AS A MEMBER OF THE HEALTH CARE TEAM

Appropriate prescribing of multiple drugs demands a careful titration of medication needs with the patient's ability to adhere to and tolerate the effects of therapy. Demographic and lifestyle factors, which may be easier to ignore than to cope with, must also be considered. While many tend to place the blame for misuse or abuse of drugs on the elderly patient, others attempt to fix responsibility on the providers. It should be apparent that the responsibility and the blame are shared *(39, 40)*.

As much as possible, the patient should be included in decisions regarding therapy, for misinformation and false or negative health beliefs contribute to the patient's compliance and overall health behavior. Providing effective communication about the nature of the disease state, drug therapy, and consequences of neglect or inadequate treatment can contribute to improved compliance and adoption of appropriate health behaviors *(37, 39)*.

Health-care professionals dealing with the elderly are often afflicted with ageism, the tendency to think sick old people are sick because they are old, not because they are sick. There is growing evidence that elderly patients suffer from communication discrimination. Moore et al. conducted a randomized telephone survey of 1,223 subjects, including 267 elderly, representing a cross-section of the national population. The survey dealt with communications between patients and health professionals about prescribed medications. The results indicate that a substantial amount of information is not being communicated by the provider or is not being absorbed by the elderly. When receiving a prescription at a pharmacy, 80 percent of the elderly reported receiving no verbal information. Information was restricted to directions for drug use, while the younger population reported getting information about drug use and side effects. The elderly reportedly received written information (pamphlets, auxiliary labels, etc.) at one-third the rate of the younger population. Seventy-five percent of the elderly reported receiving drug information from the physician, primarily about the purpose of the drug and directions for its use. Younger patients received additional information regarding side effects from the physician at four times the rate of the elderly *(37)*.

Health care professionals need to become more cognizant of providing medication information to their patients and of using techniques to ensure that the patient understands and is retaining the information. Fedder has proposed an index for establishing a priority list for patients at an increased risk for medication problems and require special attention *(39)*. This index is summarized in Table 7.

Health professionals can encourage their patients to comply with the therapeutic regimen in a number of ways.

1. *Involve the patient as a member of the health care team.* As discussed earlier, understanding the disease state and drug therapy enhances patient compliance. Involving the patient in the decision can help produce a regimen that has minimal impact on the patient's lifestyle.

2. *Simplify complex regimens.* The patient's drug regimens should use the fewest medications and number of dosing intervals possible. The regimen should be tailored to the patient's lifestyle. When possible, use of routine nonessential medications should be avoided. If necessary, the regimen should be prioritized, emphasizing the critical aspects of the drug therapy.

3. *Patient education.* Drug information should be clearly presented and should avoid the use of technical terms that are difficult for the patient to understand or interpret (e.g., "sublingually," "topically," "every six hours," "with meals"). Any visual, auditory, or physical disabilities the patient may have should be considered when presenting information. The patient should be asked to repeat essential information to test his or her comprehension of it. Both benefits and risks should be presented.

4. *Special medication packaging and labeling techniques.* For those with visual defects, large type on prescription labels will improve readability. Some pharmacies offer prescription labels typed in Braille. Auxiliary labels attached to the prescription bottle can be used to reinforce medication instructions or warnings. Placing the label lengthwise on the vial, rather than around the circumference, eliminates constant turning to read the instructions. Color coding the label to correspond to either the medication or the dosage interval may also be helpful. Also nonchildproof containers are available for those who have difficulty opening childproof caps, and specially designed "day-of-the-week" containers or other memory aids are available. However, cau-

TABLE 7
Risk Index for Medication Problems

Risk Factor	Problem	Solution
Age	As age increases, ability to adjust to changes in drug therapy decreases. Those 85 years and older are especially at risk.	Adjust therapy slowly. Inform patient of warning signs and symptoms and how to report them.
Sex	Females are more prone to adverse reactions. (2/3 of those less than 85 years old are female.)	Be cautious and more alert for side effects.
Socioeconomic status	Indigent Marginally poor—may not be able to buy food and medications.	Refer to appropriate agencies. Provide help in establishing priorities for meeting nutritional and therapeutic needs.
Living arrangements/ support systems	Elderly living alone have increased potential for medication errors.	Simplify drug therapy as much as possible. Know availability of family, friends, health professionals frequently in touch with patient. Ask them to help as needed.
Multiple pathology	May present with conflicting therapy needs. May be seeing more than one physician.	Secure complete, accurate drug history to avert problems.
Multiple drugs/ complicated drug regimen	Increased potential for medication errors and drug interactions.	Design simplest drug regimen possible, taking into account sensory/ physical impairments. Maintenance of medication profile by family pharmacists facilitates appropriate drug utilization.

Source: D.O. Fedder, *Drug Use in the Elderly: Issues of Noncompliance* (1984).

tion must be used when using them, because they do not contain the labeling instructions and identification of the original container.

Improving the quality of health care for the elderly can be facilitated through educational programs for both health care practitioners and the elderly themselves. The National Council on Patient Information and Education (NCPIE) is developing a comprehensive collection of materials on health promotion. NCPIE is sponsored by several professional organizations, including the American Pharmaceutical Association.

In July 1984 the U.S. Department of Health and Human Services (HHS) announced the results of a new market-research survey of older Americans, entitled "Aging and Health Promotion" *(41)*. In part HHS concluded that:

1. Enhancement of appropriate drug use by the aging would be a significant health promotion achievement.
2. The use of multiple channels of communication to reinforce medication messages may be advantageous.

HHS was cautious, however, pointing out that *just* providing better education to the elderly will be insufficient unless it can be shown to improve patient adherence to medication regimens. HHS found some new methods of communication an excellent way to reach the elderly. Television and radio talk shows and a daily newspaper column appear to be highly favored. Regarding printed instructions, most respondents wanted more brochures and pamphlets, especially in pharmacies "right up next to the drug counter where you can't miss them." These brochures should be "plain and large size."

Many pharmaceutical firms are also concerned with improving professional communication with the elderly. One leader is the Parke Davis Elder Care Project. Parke Davis has produced and distributed a 30-minute videotape entitled "The Medicated Generation," which depicts a radio talk show and several "real life" encounters between the elderly and pharmacists *(42)*. Another program, started by the Dallas County (Texas) Pharmaceutical Society, involves hosting "brown bag" Seminars. The public are invited to come and bring their medication in a paper sack for review by a group of pharmacy practitioners *(43)*. To maximize attendance, the seminars are held in different locations.

ADVERSE DRUG REACTIONS:

"All substances are poisons; there is none which is not a poison. The right dose differentiates a poison from a remedy."

—*Paracelsus (1493–1541)*

Drug therapy provides the most cost-beneficial approach to managing many acute and chronic conditions that affect the elderly. Unfortunately, drug-induced side effects and adverse reactions present a real problem for the geriatric patient. Adverse drug reactions occur two to three times more frequently in the 70- to 80-year-old group than in the younger population (*1*) and can have serious medical and economic repercussions. One-sixth of all hospital admissions for those over 70 are drug-related, compared with 1 in 35 admissions for the general population (*44*).

The risk of adverse drug reactions in the geriatric population is compounded by several factors (Table 8). The elderly tend to have multiple, chronic diseases, requiring multiple drugs. As mentioned previously, the probability of incurring a drug-related problem increases as the number of medications used increases. The physiological changes associated with aging diminish the body's ability to distribute or metabolize medications and may increase the risks of drug therapy. Age-related hepatic or renal impairment can interfere with the normal mechanisms for breaking down and clearing drugs from the body and may lead to drug accumulation and toxicity.

Sociodemographic factors (age, sex, income, education, living conditions) may also contribute to the increased incidence of adverse drug reactions. For example, such reactions are more prevalent in females than in males. Elderly females outnumber males 2 to 1 (3 to 1 in institutions) and also are more likely to live alone (*1*). Those living alone are less likely to comply with medication therapy and more likely to make medication errors. Thus, the problem of adverse drug effects is magnified in the elderly female population.

Due to their widespread use, diuretics are more commonly associated with adverse reactions and subsequent hospitalizations in the general elderly population than are any other drug groups (*46*). The Boston Collaborative Drug Surveillance Program found that in hospitalized patients, 37 percent of the diuretic furosemide was prescribed for patients over 70 and 64 percent for patients over 60 (*47*). Although

TABLE 8
Factors That Increase Risk of Undesirable Drug Effects[45]

1. A physician with limited knowledge of pharmacogeriatrics
2. Multiple drug therapy
3. Previous history of allergies or adverse drug reactions
4. Concurrent diseases—especially renal and severe liver insufficiency
5. Impairments—mental, visual, auditory, locomotive
6. Late senescence—very limited homeostasis
7. Self-medication
8. Multiple physicians
9. Multiple pharmacies
10. Small body size
11. Living alone
12. Lack of community support services
13. Socioeconomic problems resulting in inadequate followup.

Source: J. A. Jernigan, "Update on Drugs and the Elderly" (1983).

diuretics are the most common cause of adverse reactions, the side effects of antihypertensives, anticholinergics (including many anti-Parkinson's agents), digoxin, psychotropics, and central nervous system depressants pose the greatest risk of serious adverse reactions in the geriatric patient (*9*).

Toxicity from digoxin (Lanoxin), which is used for certain cardiac dysfunctions, occurs frequently because there is a very narrow margin between its therapeutic dose and toxic dose. It has been estimated that 15 to 20 percent of institutionalized patients on maintenance digoxin therapy exhibit an intolerance to or toxicity from the drug (*48, 49*). Several factors make the geriatric population particularly susceptible to digoxin toxicity: (*50*)

1. Reduced digoxin dosage requirements due to age- or disease-related alterations in pharmacokinetics.
2. Concurrent administration of other medications that may predispose digoxin toxicity (e.g., quinidine, diuretics).
3. Concomitant disorders that may result in electrolyte disorders and other metabolic derangements that may increase susceptibility to digoxin toxicity.
4. Initiation and maintenance of digoxin therapy for inappropriate or uncertain indications.
5. Failure to recognize early symptoms of digoxin toxicity.

6. Compliance problems—confusion about dose, inappropriate use, or accidental overdose.

Prudent use of digoxin and subsequent monitoring of therapy are necessary to minimize these risks.

Psychotropics and sedative-hypnotic agents are among the drugs most often prescribed to the elderly. In this age of polypharmacy, it is not unusual to encounter a patient taking two or more drugs with psychotropic or sedative properties. The effects of these drugs tend to be cumulative or additive. Furthermore, the use of alcohol with such agents is dangerous (5). Ironically, psychotropic drugs account for abnormal behavior in a large percentage of hospitalized patients (2). Additionally, digoxin, antihistamines, levodopa, antidepressants and beta-blockers (including those used topically for glucoma) have all been reported to produce depression and dementia.

Several physiologic mechanisms are partially responsible for the elderly's increased susceptibility to adverse reactions from the psychotropic agents and central nervous system depressants. Generalized psychomotor slowing and prolonged reaction time appear to be a consequence of aging. Loss of nerve cells in the brain, as well as plaque formation in the cells, may contribute to this. The elderly tend to have a higher proportion of fat tissue in their bodies, which results in increased retention of fat-soluble drugs such as the psychotropics. This, coupled with any diminished liver or renal capacity, can lead to increased drug concentrations in the body and possible toxicity. Finally, the senescent brain seems to be especially sensitive to the direct neuronal effects of these drugs (1).

Nonprescription drugs can also cause adverse and even fatal reactions in the elderly. Excessive amounts of aspirin and other salicylates, acetaminophen, antacids, alcohol, vitamins and minerals have been implicated most frequently (44). Unfortunately, many people believe that nonprescription medications have no potential for harm, even with indiscriminate use.

Drug Interaction

A subtype of potential adverse reaction is a drug interaction. This occurs when a drug, food, or nutrient alters an individual's response to another drug. Drug interactions have been implicated in about 7 percent of all reported adverse reactions. As stated previously, the potential for an interaction increases with the number of medications being taken, the risk rising from 5.6 percent when two drugs are taken, to 100 percent in patients receiving eight or more drugs (5). Therefore a key to reducing drug interactions may be to reduce or minimize the number of drugs taken concurrently.

Drug interactions occur frequently in the elderly population, because of the numbers of types of medication consumed. The same factors that predispose the geriatric patient to an adverse drug reaction increase the likelihood that a *significant* drug interaction will occur. Several hundred drug interactions are described in the literature. Many of these are poorly documented, and determining which are clinically significant is a difficult task. The health care practitioner should have a thorough understanding of the basic mechanisms of drug interactions to be able to anticipate and recognize their occurrence and minimize their consequences. An indepth discussion of the mechanisms of drug interaction is beyond the scope of this chapter. Thorough reviews of the subject are available for those who desire more detail (*51, 52*).

Fortunately most drug interactions are manageable and pose little risk to the patient. Usually two drugs with a known interaction can still be used concurrently if appropriate dosage adjustments or other modifications in the therapeutic regimen are made. In a patient receiving two or more drugs, health care practitioners should be alert for any new signs or symptoms that can be temporarily related to the initiation of the second drug. Although most drug interactions are not inherently dangerous, on rare occasions they can be serious if not recognized. Possible consequences of some unrecognized drug interactions are listed in Table 9 (5).

Drug interactions may result from altered pharmacokinetics, such as altered drug absorption from the gastrointestinal tract, changes in protein binding of the drugs involved, or modifications in the metabolism and elimination of drugs from the body. (See also the section on pharmacokinetics.) Another common type of drug interaction may occur when two or more drugs with similar pharmacological properties, taken concurrently, result in cumulative or additive effects. This often occurs with the central nervous system depressants, especially if alcohol is taken with them.

TABLE 9
Possible Consequences of Unrecognized Drug Interactions

Sign/Symptom	Interacting Drugs
Hemorrhage	Warfarin (Coumadin) + chloral hydrate (Noctec)
Hypoglycemia	Tolazamide (Tolinase) + phenylbutazone (Butazolidin)
Hypotension	Nifedipine (Procardia) + nitrates
Hypertensive crisis	Epinephrine + propranolol (Inderal)
Arrhythmia	Digoxin + quinidine
Excessive drug accumulation of theophylline	Theophylline + erythromycin

Drug interactions can have beneficial as well as adverse effects. The use of probenecid with procaine penicillin is an example of a well-known drug interaction that is used beneficially. Probenecid and procaine penicillin both use the same transport system in the kidney for excretion. Probenecid slows the removal of penicillin from the body, resulting in higher penicillin levels and a more prolonged antibacterial effect. Clinical situations exist where the effect of one drug can minimize or prevent toxicities of another drug. Treatment of overdoses and poisonings with specific antidotes utilizes the concept of beneficial drug interactions.

Summary on Adverse Drug Reactions

Health care practitioners are becoming increasingly aware of drug-induced adverse reactions in the geriatric population. The risk of adverse reactions and drug interactions can be minimized if medications are prescribed and used wisely. Guidelines for avoiding toxicity and minimizing the risks of drug-induced illness are summarized in Table 10 (45, 53). As long as the special problems of the elderly are kept in mind, essential drug treatment should not be withheld from older patients.

CONCLUSION

To avoid misuse of medications in the elderly, the following procedures should be followed:

✓ TABLE 10
Reducing the Risk-Benefit Ratio in the Elderly Patient[44,53]

1. Know the patient's background of drug use, drug reactions, and pathophysiology.
2. Know the basic pharmacology of the drugs being used and the possible interactions.
3. Use drug therapy only when the benefit outweighs the risk.
4. Start with less than the usual adult dosage and increase the dosage slowly until a therapeutic response is noted or side effects develop.
5. Keep the dosage schedule as simple as possible.
6. Keep the number of capsules or tablets to a minimum, but try to avoid combination drugs. Combinations may be used only after the benefit and tolerance to each drug, given separately in the same dose as in the combination preparation, have been established.
7. Discontinue or reduce the dosage of the drug if side effects are unacceptable. Try another drug from the same class using the same procedure of dosage titration.
8. Discontinue the drug if there is no therapeutic result.
9. If in doubt about a drug's benefits, discontinue it.
10. Adverse drug reactions may result from taking over-the-counter drugs or drugs prescribed for others in the household in addition to those prescribed for the patient. Have the patient or a family member bring in all medications the patient may be taking.
11. Remember that the effects of sedative–hypnotics persist much longer in the elderly and may produce confusion. Avoid this class of drugs whenever possible. Ask the patient about alcoholic beverage use.
12. While pharmacokinetics can provide a scientific basis for dose selection and for predicting clinical outcome, do not substitute academic knowledge for clinical judgement.

Source: "Congressional Hearing Probes Drug Misuse in the Aged," *American Pharmacist* (1983, pp. 5-6). L. Z. Feigenbaum, "The Frail Elderly and the Five I's," *Current Medical Diagnosis and Treatment* (Lange, 1984).

1. Use as few drugs as possible. This includes combination products and over-the-counter medication. To avoid common undesirable pharmacologic effects, drugs that must be taken concurrently should be reviewed. Use of multiple agents within a given therapeutic class must be justified on the basis of synergistic therapeutic effect. Usually this synergy will be obtained by combining agents with different mechanisms of action. It is important to be certain that every prescribed drug has a clear and appropriate indication.

2. Check the patient frequently. Because of the lack of information on dosing for the geriatric patient, frequent observation is required to

achieve maximal therapeutic effects with minimal side effects. Dosage regimens should be individualized; there is no "standard dose" for all geriatric patients. Patient-specific pharmacokinetic data are needed to develop general dosing guides for subgroups of geriatric patients.

3. Make it as easy as possible. To improve compliance and minimize over- and undercompliance, it is important to choose a dose form that can be easily administered, use as few medications as possible, and choose single daily doses over multiple doses. The patient should be fully informed about the drug prescribed. In particular patients should be given verbal and written explanations of the purpose of the medication, precautions to take before using it, precautions to take while using it, side effects and how to obtain more information. The patient should understand what to do if a dose is missed and when to stop taking the medication. This same information should be given to someone who cares for the patient. Noncompliance should be suspected when the patient does not respond to therapy or has none of the common side effects of the medication. Remember that there are no common behavior patterns for patients who are noncompliant.

4. Review the therapy regularly. For geriatric patients in a long-term care facility, the pharmacist, medical director, chief administrator, and head nurse must establish policies and procedures for regular, periodic drug therapy review. An initial evaluation should be conducted within 7 days of admission, after the first 30 days, and at least every 90 days thereafter. Survey procedures should be in accord with Section 3160ff, Survey Procedure for Pharmaceutical Services in Long Term Care Facility (54); Section 3161, Indicators for Survey or Assessment of the Performance of Drug Regimen Reviews (54); and Section 3160, Survey or Procedures for Pharmaceutical Service Requirements in Long Term Care Facilities (55).

Appendix I: Drug Holiday Programs

GUIDELINES FOR IMPLEMENTATION

The goal of a drug holiday program is to optimize the patient's drug regimen. The patient's safety and well-being are the most important considerations. Detailed planning and conscientious administration of a drug holiday program will ensure that benefits to the patient are maximized. The following guidelines have been developed to assist health professionals in implementing safe and effective drug holiday programs:

1. Secure the cooperation and support of administration, medical staff, and nursing staff. This is best accomplished through the facility's pharmaceutical committee, which may adopt a policy statement supportive of the drug holiday concept.
2. Develop information for physicians and nurses explaining drug holiday and its goals. Encourage the pharmaceutical committee to develop standards prior to drug holiday implementation.
3. Conduct drug holidays under the direction of the patient's attending physician. Designation of which drugs to withhold and for how long is ultimately the physician's responsibility.
4. Develop parameters for patient monitoring. Attending physicians will want assurance of adequate and consistent patient monitoring.
5. Schedule educational programs before establishment of the drug holiday program so that professional personnel involved in patient monitoring are knowledgeable concerning disease states and pharmacology of the drugs to be withheld.

Appendix II:
Drug Holiday Evaluation

PARAMETERS FOR PATIENT EVALUATION

Close evaluation of the patient's condition is an essential component of the drug holiday and is the responsibility of the professional nurse. Changes in any of the following parameters should be noted and considered when reviewing the patient's medication regimen. Frequency of such notations may be predetermined and flow sheets used to standardize and expedite documentation of observations.

EVALUATION PARAMETERS

1. Mentation
   a. Orientation to time, place, person.
   b. Recognition of familiar stimuli (persons, places).
   c. Memory, recent and remote.
   d. Ability to perform activities of daily living.
   e. Hallucinations, delusions, ideas of influence or reference.
2. Sleep Needs
   a. Number of hours spent sleeping and times of sleep.
   b. Difficulty falling asleep, middle of night or early morning awakening.
   c. Response to traditional comfort measures: back rub, milk and crackers, quiet talking, music.
   d. Specific evidence of sleepy behavior or fatigue when awake.
   e. Increased or decreased dreaming, nightmares, sleep-walking.
3. Appetite/Eating Habits
   a. Specific amount of food consumed.
   b. Changes in taste, dry mouth, difficulty swallowing, poor appetite.
   c. Daily weights.
4. Elimination
   a. Hydration: Complaints of thirst or extra requests for fluids, frequency of urination. (*Note:* Patients receive some hydration with administration of medications. Offer liquids routinely to compensate for decreased intake as a result of drug holiday.)
   b. Color and specific gravity of urine, presence of glucose.
   c. Complaints of pain, itching, burning, incontinence, urgency.
   d. Bowel status: constipation; diarrhea; color, formation and frequency of stools; presence of blood, pain, mucus; continence.
5. Central Nervous System
   a. Presence of tremors (fine or coarse), changes in gait, spinal or nuchal rigidity, any weakness, changes in balance.
   b. Complaints of lack of feeling in limbs, dizziness, changes in vision or hearing.
   c. Level of consciousness, response to increased environmental stimuli.
6. Physical Assessment Parameters

    a. Temperature, pulse, respiration, BP sitting and standing.
    b. Lung sounds.
    c. Heart sounds.
    d. Bowel sounds.
    e. Skin changes.
    f. Edema (measure, don't guess).
    g. Shortness of breath (use of pillows to sleep, ability to lie flat).
7. Socialization
    a. Increase or decrease in irritability.
    b. Initiation or participation in social interactions with others (how many others?).
    c. Mode of interactions: friendly, complaining, dependent, angry/threatening, flat affect.
8. Energy level
    a. Interest and enthusiasm for living.
    b. Sexual interest (if observed): includes attention to opposite or same sex, improved grooming, masturbation, sexual intercourse.
9. Patient's Own Assessment of Status
    a. Pain: present/absent, describe.
    b. Other discomfort: itching, nervousness, inability to keep still, nausea, anything else.
    c. Feelings and opinions about medications.

REFERENCES

1. Simonson, W. 1984. *Medications and the elderly: A guide for promoting proper use.* Rockville, Md.: Aspen.
2. Pies, R. 1983. Geriatric psychopharmacotherapy. *Am. Fam. Physician* 28:171–76.
3. 1983. Problems with prescription drugs highest among the elderly. *Am. Fam. Physician* 28:236.
4. 1983. Problems with prescription drugs highest among the elderly. *Am. Fam. Physician* 28:236.
5. Sloan, R. W. 1983. Drug interactions. *Am. Fam. Physician* 27:229–38.
6. Greenblatt, D. J., E. M. Sellers, R. I. Shader. 1983. Drug disposition in old age. *N. Engl. J. Med.* 1081–83.
7. 1984. FDA proposes geriatric labeling. *Am. J. Pharmacy* NS24:14.
8. FDC Reports. 1984. Geriatric drug testing: PMA suggests targeted drug disposition studies. June 25, p. T&G 4.
9. Seidl, L. G., G. F. Thornton, J. W. Smith, L. E. Cluff. 1966. Studies on the epide-

miology of adverse drug reactions III. Reactions in patients on a general medical service. *Bull. Johns Hopkins Hosp.* 119:299–315.

10. Steel, K., P. M. Gertman, C. Crescenzi, J. Anderson. 1981. Iatrogenic illness on a general medical service at a university hospital. *N. Engl. J. Med.* 304:638–42.

11. Hurivity, N. 1969. Predisposing factors in adverse reactions to drugs. *Br. Med. J.* 1:536–39.

12. Miller, R. R. 1973. Drug surveillance utilizing epidemiologic methods: A report from the Boston collaborative drug surveillance program. *Am. J. Hosp. Pharmacy* 30:584–92.

13. Jick, H., D. Slone, I. T. Border, S. Shapiro. 1968. Efficacy and toxicity of heparin in relation to age and sex. *N. Engl. J. Med.* 279:284–86.

14. Greenblatt, D. J., M. D. Allen. 1978. Toxicity of nitrazepam in the elderly: A report from the Boston collaborative drug surveillance program. *Br. J. Clin. Pharmacol.* 5:407–13.

15. Greenblatt, D. J., M. D. Allen, R. I. Shader. 1977. Toxicity of high dose flurazepam in the elderly. *Clin. Pharmacol. Ther.* 21:355–61.

16. Atkinson, A. J., W. Kusher. 1979. Clinical pharmacokinetics. *Ann. Rev. Pharmacol. Toxicol.* 19:105–27.

17. Benet, L. Z., L. B. Sheiner. 1980. Design and optimization of dosage regimens; pharmacokinetic data. In A. G. Gilman, L. S. Goodman, and A. Gilman (eds.), *The Pharmacological basis of therapeutics*, 6th ed. New York: MacMillan.

18. Greenblatt, D. J., J. Koch-Weser. 1975. Clinical pharmacokinetics. *N. Engl. J. Med.* 294:702–5, 964–70.

19. Winter, M. E. 1983. General principles: Clinical pharmacokinetics. In B. S. Kacther, L. Y. Young, M. A. Koda-Kimble (eds.), Applied therapeutics, 3rd ed. San Francisco: Applied Therapeutics.

20. Ritschel, W. A. 1977. Drug action and interaction in the geriatric patient. *Scientia Pharmaceutica* 45:304–10.

21. Geokas, M. C., B. J. Haverback. 1969. The aging gastrointestinal tract. *Am. J. Surg.* 117:881–92.

22. Evans, M. A., E. J. Tiggs, M. Checing, et al. 1981. Gastric emptying rate in elderly: Implication for drug therapy. *J. Am. Geriatic Soc.* 29:201–5.

23. Montgomery, R., M. R. Haeney, I. N. Ross, et al. 1978. The aging gut: A study of intestinal absorption in relation to nutrition in the elderly. *Q. J. Med.* 47:197–211.

24. Kramer, P. A., D. J. Chapron, J. Benson, S. A. Mercik. 1978. Tetracycline absorption in elderly patients with achlorhydria. *Clin. Pharmacol Ther.* 23:467–72.

25. Ochs, H. R., D. J. Greenblatt, M. D. Allen, et al. 1979. Effects of age and billroth-gastrectomy on absorption of desmethyldiazepam from clorazepate. *Clin. Pharmacol Ther.* 26:449–56.

26. Ochs, H. R., H. Otten, D. J. Greenblatt, et al. 1982. Diazepam absorption: Effects of age, sex and billrothgastrectomy. *Dig. Dis. Sci.* 27:225–30.

27. Koch-Weser, J., E. M. Sellers. 1976. Binding of drugs to serum albumin. *N. Engl. J. Med.* 294:311–6, 526–31.

28. Salzer, L. B., R. A. Plant, P. K. Wilson. 1982. Drug holiday in long term care facilities. *Am. Soc. Consultant. Pharmacist. Newsletter Special Inset*, September.

29. Eraker, S. A., J. R. Kirscht, M. H. Becker, 1984. Understanding and improving patient compliance. *Ann. Int. Med.* 100:258–68.
30. Weintraub, M. 1981. Intelligent noncompliance with special emphasis on the elderly. *Contemp. Pharm. Pract.* 4:8–11.
31. Becker, M. H., L. A. Maiman. 1980. Strategies for enhancing patient compliance. *J. Community Health.* 6:113–35.
32. Matthews, D., T. Hinhdon. 1977. Improving patients compliance: A guide for physicians. *Med. Clin. North Am.* 61:879–89.
33. Gilbert, J. 1957. Age changes in color matching. *J. Gerontol.* 12:210–15.
34. 1984. Elderly may fail to detect color differences in pills. *Am. Fam. Physician* 29:242.
35. Schonfield, D., B. A. Robertson. 1966. Memory storage and aging. *Can. J. Psych.* 20:228–36.
36. Caneteaki, R. E. 1966. Paced and self-paced learning in young and elderly adults. *J. Gerontol.* 18:165–68.
37. Moore, S. R. 1983. Cognitive variants in the elderly: An integral part of medication counseling. *Drug Intell. Clin. Pharm.* 17:840–42.
38. Haynes, R. B., D. L. Sackett, D. W. Taylor. 1980. How to detect and manage low patient compliance in chronic illness. *Geriatrics* 35:91–97.
39. Fedder, D. O. 1984. Drug use in the elderly: Issues of noncompliance. *Drug Intell. Clin. Pharm.* 18:158–62.
40. Lamy, P. P. 1980. Misuse and abuse of drugs by the elderly: Another view. *Am. Pharm.* NS20:14–17.
41. 1984. Elderly eager for pharmacists information. *Apharmacy Weekly* 23:115.
42. 1984. The medicated generation. Parke Davis Elder Care Project.
43. 1984. Pharmacy Practice, August.
44. 1983. Congressional hearing probes drug misuse in the aged. *Amer. Pharm.* NS 23(9):5–6.
45. Jernigan, J. A. 1984. Update on drugs and the elderly. *Am. Fam. Physician* 29:238–47.
46. Smith, W. E., T. H. Steele. 1983. Avoiding diuretic-related complications in older patients. *Geriatrics* 38:117–25.
47. Greenblatt, D. J., D. W. Duhme, M. D. Allen, et al. 1977. Clinical toxicity of furosemide in hospitalized patients. *Am. Heart J.* 94:6–13.
48. Carter, B. L., R. G. Small, M. R. Garrett. Monitoring digoxin therapy in two long-term facilities. *J. Am. Geriatr. Soc.* 29:263–68.
49. Merry, D. A., J. M. Lowe, D. A. Larson, et al. 1981. The changing pattern of toxicity of digoxin. *Postgrad. Med. J.* 57:358–62.
50. Algeo, S., P. E. Fenster, F. I. Marcus. 1983. Digitalis therapy in the elderly. *Geriatrics* 38:93–101.
51. Hansten, P. D. 1984. Drug Interactions, 5th ed. Philadelphia: Lea & Fibiger.
52. 1984. American Pharmaceutical Association Evaluation of Drug Interactions, 3rd ed.
53. Feigenbaum, L. Z. 1984. The frail elderly and the five I's: "Iatrogenic" drug reactions. In *Current medical diagnosis and treatment*, Lange Medical Publications.

54. 1982. State operations manual provide certification. *Am. Soc. Consultant Pharmacists, Special Bulletin Transmittal* No. 149, January.
55. 1984. Medication error survey procedure, effective July 1, 1984. *Am. Soc. Consultant Pharmacists, Special Bulletin, Transmittal* No. 165, May.

Using Tranquilizing Medications in Nursing Homes for Symptom Relief and Behavior Control

CARL D. CHAMBERS, Ph.D.

Professor
School of Health and Sport Sciences
College of Health and Human Services
Ohio University
Athens, Ohio

MICHAEL T. HARTER, Ph.D.

Professor
School of Health and Sport Sciences
College of Health and Human Services
Ohio University
Athens, Ohio

KATHRYN S. FELTON PRIBBLE, M.HSA

Health Services Administration Program
School of Health and Sport Sciences
College of Health and Human Services
Ohio University
Athens, Ohio

Why, then, are phenothiazines used at all? Simply, their benefits outweigh their disadvantages. They, more than any other advance in psychiatry, have enabled many highly disturbed people to lead relatively normal lives. *It is when such patients get old that the undesirable effects are apt to show up.*

—Poe and Malloway, 1980

INTRODUCTION

It is widely held that the necessity for managing patients with significant behavioral problems in nursing homes is *increasing* (Zimmer, et

110

al., 1984). Most often, this increased necessity is presumed to be the result of: (1) the increased number of the "very old," who are more likely to have accumulated those physical and mental conditions that produce both direct and indirect behavioral disturbances and (2) the number of deinstitutionalized patients from public mental health institutions who have become elderly and physically debilitated and who now bring both their physical and mental impairments into the nursing home.

While we acknowledge that these assertions have merit, we are also concerned about the possibility that the increase in chemical behavioral control may be the result of several other influences.

We have come to suspect that one such influence is purely economic. As reimbursement becomes more restricted, it becomes more "economical" to manage some patients chemically; any facility would require fewer staff resources if patients were being heavily tranquilized or sedated. We have also come to suspect that some nursing staff within facilities recognize that significantly less nursing skill and experience are required to "service" heavily tranquilized or sedated patients. Finally, we have come to suspect a *contagion effect* in prescribing these medications: "successful" use might simply breed further use. If attending physicians and nurses were spending less time and effort with patients, the nurses might request even greater utilization, and physicians would be able to reduce their own time commitments to specific patients and to the facility generally.

During 1983 and 1984 Ohio University secured research and training site agreements with a number of skilled nursing facilities (SNFs) and intermediate care facilities (ICFs). These new cooperative agreements set the stage for formal inquiry into the roles that the tranquilizing and sedating medications were playing in symptom relief, behavior control, and facility management. This report summarizes one such collaborative inquiry.

STUDY

In 1984, as part of a continuous assessment of patient care, the owner-administrator of a 100-bed SNF requested the research team to: (1) assess the role that the "major" and "minor" tranquilizers were playing in symptom relief and patient behavior control in the facility, (2) determine the extent to which these medications were being "used" by nursing service to "manage" wards, nursing shifts, and the facility, and (3) make any needed recommendations regarding the use of tranquilizing medications in providing quality care to patients.

The research team undertook this effort with the full cooperation and collaboration of the administrator and director of nursing. For each patient treated in the nursing home during 1980 and during 1983, a review of the complete medical record was made. In addition to comparing the prescribing situation within the same facility for two different time periods, this study compared the 1983 situation in this SNF with the prescribing situation in an ICF located in the same region of the state.

All record reviews and data abstractions were accomplished by baccalaureate-prepared registered nurses. In a meeting of all the data collectors, data from each patient's record were then discussed before being synthesized.

This inquiry was designed to answer the following questions:

- What was the baseline (1980) prevalence with which tranquilizing medications were prescribed to relieve symptoms of emotional distress and to control behavior?
- What is the current (1983) prevalence with which tranquilizing medications are prescribed to relieve symptoms of emotional distress and control behavior?
- What changes, if any, have occurred between the two study periods?
- What differences, if any, exist between the SNF and the ICF nursing homes in the contemporary use of tranquilizing medications?

The Study Settings

Before presenting the results of the inquiry, it seems appropriate to review the definition of a skilled nursing facility, especially as it would be relevant to patient care and behavior control.

A *Skilled nursing facility* is a specially qualified facility providing 24-hour nursing care by or under the supervision of licensed nurses. The skilled nursing facility accommodates individuals who no longer require hospital care but still need extensive nursing care. Quality skilled nursing care means those procedures commonly employed in providing for the physical, emotional, and rehabilitative needs of the ill or otherwise incapacitated— including without limitations procedures such as irrigations, catheterizations, dressing applications, and supervision of special diets; objective observation of change in patient condition as a means of analyzing and determining nursing care required and further medical diagnosis and treatment needed; special procedures contributing to the rehabilitation of the patients; and administration of medication by any method ordered by a physician. Quality skilled nursing care also means carrying out other treatments prescribed by a physician that involve a similar level of complexity and skill in administration (Buttaro, 1983, and Ohio Department of Health, 1983).

An *Intermediate care facility* is an institution equipped and maintained to accommodate individuals who are unable to care for themselves but are not acutely ill and whose chronic conditions do not require hospitalization or skilled nursing care. Supervised nursing care is provided with licensed personnel in accordance with various state regulations and codes. Rehabilitation and other related services are generally provided at a much lesser degree than those available in a skilled nursing facility (Buttaro, 1983, and Ohio Department of Health, 1983).

In addition to such general statements about level of care, the "quality of care" provided by a skilled facility includes requirements that:

- All skilled nursing care shall be provided by a nurse.
- No medication or treatment shall be given a patient unless ordered by a physician. If orders are given by telephone, they shall be recorded by the nurse on duty with the physician's name and the order shall be signed by the physician on his next visit.
- All patients will be seen by a physician not less than once each month.
- Physician-directed emergency medical care must be available at all times.
- Drugs shall not be used as a means of restraint or control unless ordered by a physician, and this order must be in writing and include the date ordered, means to be employed, reason for restraint, and the duration of the restraint.
- No form of restraint or control shall be used or applied in such a manner as to cause injury to the patient (Buttaro, 1983, and Ohio Department of Health, 1983).

Study Results

The independent review of each patient's medical record did permit the research group to answer each of the research questions. This review included documentation of each medical diagnosis recorded for each patient, the medications being ordered that would relate to symptom reduction or maintenance relief for the specified conditions, and the actual dispensing of these medications. The principal focus for the inquiry was use of the tranquilizing medications.

Tranquilizers are pharmacologically divided into two general groups, "major" and "minor." The major tranquilizers, drugs such as Thorazine (chlorpromazine), Mellaril (thioridazine), Compazine (prochlorperazine), Stelazine (trifluoperazine), and Haldol (haloperidol), are most often prescribed to reduce, alleviate, or control the symptoms of psychoses. The minor tranquilizers, drugs such as Valium (diazepam), Librium (chlordiazepoxide), Serax (oxazepam), Tranxene (chlorazepate), and Vistaril (hydroxyzine) were developed and marketed for the short-term management of anxiety.

Tranquilizers are among the most widely prescribed pharmaceutical products. Until quite recently, for example, Valium was the most prescribed drug in the United States and is still the most prescribed of the psychoactive drugs. This only confirms that society in general has long accepted the fact that millions of noninstitutionalized people cope with transient emotional distress with minor tranquilizers. However, we are just beginning to appreciate how easily physicians and nurses can manipulate, manage, and control institutionalized "patients" with these medications.

The major tranquilizers have been used primarily to address both acute and chronic psychotic symptoms. Used for this antipsychotic purpose, they reduce panic, fear, hostility, agitation, and reactions to hallucinations and delusions. The development of these medications to ameliorate such symptoms was as important in the treatment of mental illness as was the development of the antibiotics in the treatment of physical illness.

In recent years, however, the major tranquilizers have been prescribed and dispensed to regularize thinking and ameliorate disorganized behavior. It is in this latter area that we believe the nursing home patient is most vulnerable to victimization. Indeed, it was this concern that led to the current research effort.

Research Question #1. **What was the baseline (1980) prevalence with which tranquilizing medications were prescribed to relieve symptoms of emotional distress and control behavior?**

During calendar year 1980, 106 patient records were available for medication review. Of these, 34 (32 percent) had been prescribed one of the major tranquilizers and 26 (25 percent) had been prescribed a minor tranquilizer.

Major tranquilizer only	19	18%
Minor tranquilizer only	9	9%
Both tranquilizers	32	30%
Neither tranquilizers	46	43%
Total patients reviewed	106	100%

Thus in 1980, some 57 percent of the patients in this skilled nursing facility were receiving one or both of the tranquilizing medications.

Among those who were receiving a major tranquilizer, 35 percent (N=12) were getting Mellaril (thioridazine), 29 percent (N=10) were getting Haldol (haloperidol), and 24 percent (N=8) were getting Thorazine (chlorpromazine). The remaining 13 percent (N=4) were being dispensed a variety of the other major tranquilizers.

Among those who were receiving a minor tranquilizer, 31 percent (N=16) were getting Valium (diazepam), with the others being almost equally distributed among Vistaril (hydroxyzine), Serax (oxazepam), Tranxene (chlorazepate), and Librium (chlordiazepoxide).

In addition to these tranquilizing medications, 28 percent (N=30) were being given a sedative/hypnotic. Virtually all were being given Dalmane (flurazepam), which is quite often prescribed as an anxiety-reducing tranquilizer in place of one of the other minor tranquilizers.

Finally, only 7 percent (N=8) of the 106 patients were being prescribed a clinical antidepressant such as Elavil (amitriptyline) or Tofranil (imipramine).

Research Question #2. **What is the current (1983) prevalence with which tranquilizing medications were prescribed to relieve symptoms of emotional distress and control behavior?**

During calendar year 1983, a total of 110 patient medical records were available for review. Of these 110 patients, 71 (65 percent) had been receiving one of the major tranquilizers, and 12 patients (11 percent) had been receiving one of the minor tranquilizers.

Major tranquilizer only	61	55%
Minor tranquilizer only	2	2%
Both tranquilizers	10	9%
Neither tranquilizers	37	34%

Thus in 1983 some two-thirds of the patients were receiving antianxiety and/or antipsychotic tranquilizing medications.

Virtually all the patients who were receiving a *major* tranquilizer were receiving either Haldol (haloperidol), Mellaril (thioridazine), or Thorazine (chlorpromazine); 68 patients—or 96 percent of all patients who were given a major tranquilizer—had one of these three. During 1983, fully one-third of the total facility population (N=37 patients) had been receiving Haldol, an antipsychotic tranquilizer, as one of their prescribed medications.

At the same time, virtually all the patients receiving a *minor* tranquilizer were being given Vistaril (hydroxyzine), a sedating antihistamine. Eighty-three percent of those receiving a minor tranquilizer got this one drug.

In addition to these tranquilizing medications, 14 patients (13 percent) were being given a prescription sedative/hypnotic, either Dalmane (flurazepam) or phenobarbital. Dalmane is also commonly prescribed as an anxiety-reducing minor tranquilizer, and in this situation it was not always clear whether the physician wanted to reduce anxiety with this medication or provide some sedation for sleeping.

Interestingly, only one patient in the total population of 110 had received a clinical antidepressant during the 1983 study period.

Research Question #3. *What changes, if any, have occurred between the two study periods?*

Prior to making any comparison between the situation in 1980 and 1983, the researchers ascertained the comparability of the two study groups in the facility. Interviews with the owner-administrator, the director of nursing, and the assistant director of nursing indicated that during the study period:

- The sex ratio had remained fairly stable (3 to 1 female to male).
- The median age of the patients had remained fairly stable (in the late 70s).
- The type of patient (e.g., the presenting health status) had remained about the same. Certainly there had been no significant increase in the number of patients with primary or secondary diagnoses of mental disturbances.
- The owner, administrator, senior nursing staff, and principal attending physician were the same.

However, there were some significant differences in prescribing and dispensing of psychoactive medications between the two study periods. These differences were found, even though the mean number of psychoactive drugs (1.5) being used by each patient in the two study groups remained the same.

The principal difference between the two study periods had two dimensions. First, the prescribing and dispensing of the "minor" tranquilizers had *decreased* by 56 percent, while use of the "major" tranquilizers had *increased* by 51 percent.

Drug Group	1980		1983	
	N	%	N	%
Any use of the minor tranquilizers	26	25	12	11
Any use of the major tranquilizers	34	32	71	65

In 1980 the principal pattern of use was *no* use. Forty-three percent of the patients received neither type of tranquilizer. In 1983, however, the principal pattern was to use major tranquilizers by themselves. Fifty-five percent were being given major tranquilizers alone and only one-third of the patients were receiving *no* tranquilizing medications.

	1980 N=106	1983 N=110
Major tranquilizers only	19%	55%
Minor tranquilizers only	8%	2%
Both tranquilizers	30%	9%
Neither tranquilizers	43%	34%

The specific tranquilizing medication being prescribed and dispensed had undergone some "market share shifts," although the medications being utilized had remained the same. Only three major tranquilizers—Mellaril, Haldol, and Thorazine—were being prescribed and dispensed during both periods. In 1980, Mellaril was the most frequently used, but Haldol was most frequently used in 1983.

Patients Receiving Major Tranquilizers

Major Tranquilizer	1980		1983	
	N	%	N	%
Mellaril	12	35	16	23
Haldol	10	29	37	52
Thorazine	8	24	15	21
All others	4	12	3	4
Total	34	100	71	100

While Valium was the most used minor tranquilizer in 1980, it had been replaced by Vistaril by 1983.

With regard to the other psychoactive drugs, the use of the sedative/ hypnotics was *down* from 28 percent to 13 percent; the use of the clinical antidepressants was down from 8 percent to less than 1 percent and the use of both narcotic analgesics and prescription nonnarcotic analgesics had remained stable, at about 5 percent and 20 percent respectively.

Controlling for those patients receiving one or more of the tranquilizing medications, the majority did *not* have a specific diagnosis in their records that would make an antianxiety or antipsychotic medication a predicted "order." This situation had not changed between the two study periods.

| Had a specific diagnosis or behavioral disturbance requiring tranquilizers | Patients Receiving Major/Minor Tranquilizers | | | |
| | 1980 | | 1983 | |
	N	%	N	%
Yes	26	43	30	41
No	34	57	43	59
Total	60	100	73	100

Virtually all those who were being tranquilized *and* who had an appropriate diagnosis in their medical records justifying this medication had been diagnosed as organic brain syndrome (93 percent, or 28 of 30 patients in 1983).

> *Research Question #5. **What differences, if any, exist between the SNF and the ICF nursing homes in the contemporary use of tranquilizing medications?***

One would expect that patients in an intermediate care facility would be receiving fewer psychoactive medications than patients being treated in a skilled nursing facility. However, in the two facilities compared in this study, this was not the case.

- In the SNF (1983 data), 102 of 110 patients (92 percent) were receiving one or more psychoactive drugs, whereas in the ICF, 37 of 42 (88 percent) were using one or more.
- The mean number of psychoactive drugs being used by these two patient populations—1.5 in the SNF and 1.6 in the ICF—also was virtually the same.
- In both types of facilities, the prescribing and dispensing of the clinical antidepressants, sedative/hypnotics, narcotics, and prescription nonnarcotic analgesics was essentially the same.

Drugs	SNF	ICF
Antidepressants	less than 1%	2%
Sedatives/hypnotics	13%	12%
Narcotic analgesics	5%	10%
Nonnarcotic analgesics	23%	26%

The differences in medicating in these nursing homes centered around the tranquilizing medications. The use of the major tranquilizers was almost twice as prevalent in the SNF (65 percent) as in the ICF (29 percent). The use pattern with the minor tranquilizers, however, was reversed, with the prevalence of use in the ICF (26 percent) more than twice that in the SNF (11 percent). The major tranquilizer of choice was Haldol (58 percent of all use). Other patients received Mellaril. The minor tranquilizer most used was Atarax, a hydroxyzine identical to Vistaril. A comparative distribution of tranquilizer use is presented below:

	SNF (N=110)	ICF (N=42)
Any major tranquilizer use	65%	29%
Any minor tranquilizer use	11%	26%
Major tranquilizer only	55%	17%
Minor tranquilizer only	2%	14%
Both tranquilizers	9%	12%
Neither tranquilizers	34%	57%

The tranquilizer medicating differences could *not* be explained by differences in psychiatric diagnosis or documented behavioral disturbances. Twenty-seven percent of those in the SNF and 31 percent in the ICF carried these formal labels. The prevalence of diagnostic labels was the same, but prescribing for such symptom relief or control of aberrant behavior was some 35 percent higher in the skilled nursing facility (66 percent versus 43 percent).

CONCLUSIONS, CONCERNS AND IMPLICATIONS

The data are conclusive. The use of the major tranquilizers in the SNF nursing home increased significantly. This increase appears to have occurred in the absence of any comparable increase in diagnosed psychoses or documented increases in aberrant behaviors such as agitation, wandering, belligerence, and assaultiveness. Nursing staff do *not* believe that the patient population changed appreciably enough to account for the significant increase. In fact, senior nursing administrators expressed surprise at both the increase and the high rate of contemporary use.

The prescribing and dispensing of tranquilizing medications, both major and minor, was also found to be very prevalent in the ICF nursing home. While antianxiety medicating is understandable, antipsychotic medicating does not appear to be warranted. In neither the SNF nor the ICF was the tranquilizer use rate documented as needed in the patient records. In most cases these medications were being prescribed and dispensed without a diagnosis of psychosis or a full elaboration of the behavioral problems that caused the medications to be ordered. The major tranquilizer most often prescribed and dispensed, both in the SNF and the ICF during 1983, was Haldol.

Pharmacologists and pharmacologically trained clinical users of psychotherapeutic drugs have known for years that the major tranquilizers prescribed and dispensed most frequently in these nursing homes—Thorazine, Mellaril, and Haldol—are essentially "peer" drugs (Hollister, 1975). If these drugs are essentially equal in terms of overall efficacy, there seems little reason to switch from Thorazine or Mellaril to Haldol. "The patient's past experience is quite a reliable guide. If he has done well previously on some drug . . . one would be foolhardy to change drugs or to reinstitute lapsed treatment with a different drug" (Hollister, 1975).

In point of fact, there is convincing data to suggest that such a switch was inappropriate. For example, published clinicians and researchers were reporting in 1980 that Mellaril was the *most* useful of the major tranquilizers for the agitated or unruly elderly patient (Poe and Holloway, 1980). These researchers suggested that Haldol is more appropriate only if the nursing home patient is hallucinating or exhibiting the most disturbing of psychotic symptoms. *We found no evidence that the patients in either the skilled nursing facility or the intermediate care facility met these criteria.* And yet, the physicians were switching existing patients to, and placing new patients on, Haldol. When the researchers asked the physician and the nursing staff why the switch was made so obviously to Haldol, they were unable to explain. When pressed, the only reason they seemed to give was that Haldol required a smaller dose. *No* mention was made of better sedation or more effective psychotic behavior control. Equally important, there was *no* mention of fewer adverse side effects.

"*All neuroleptic drugs are equally effective in controlling disordered thinking and behavior*. Moreover, they differ in side effects. Selection of the appropriate neuroleptic for each elderly patient depends more on the knowledge of differential toxicity than on differential clinical efficacy" (Salzman, 1982). If this is the appropriate procedure for selecting a drug of choice for *each* patient independently, two data sets would exist. First, there would be evidence of the prescribing and dispensing of a wide variety of the available tranquilizing medications. Obviously, this was not the case in the nursing homes we studied, because there was a significant "clustering" in the prescribing and dispensing of Haldol. Second, if there were any reason for such prevalent clustering with Haldol, it would be because one had documented that Haldol produced fewer or the others produced more undesirable side effects. This was not the situation either.

During a routine probing with regard to monitoring for side effects, the director and assistant director of nursing in the SNF indicated that they suspected Haldol, and perhaps other major tranquilizers as well, were producing intestinal bleeding leading to death in a number of patients. They indicated the cases "stood out" because the onset of the bleeding was both unexpected (not related to an existing or emerging physical condition) and occurred shortly after the patient was placed on regular or maintenance doses of the tranquilizing medications. When asked if they had shared this observation with the attending physician, they indicated that they had done so but that their concerns had been dismissed as not supportable in the literature. *In spite of these professional observations and concerns, prescribing behavior had not been altered.*

In this SNF the average length of stay was approximately 18 months. As a result, the nursing staff became quite familiar with the patients. Relying on this knowledge, the research group asked the nurse administrators if they could identify those patients whom they suspected had developed intestinal bleeding as a side effect to being placed on a major tranquilizer. In response they produced a previously prepared list of 25 names that they had been compiling over a three-year period (1980–1983). The research group secured the medical records for each of these cases. Eight of them were men and 17 were women. All had died in the nursing home or had been transferred to an acute care hospital where they had died.

Based on the medical records, the only thing these 25 elderly patients had in common was their use of the major tranquilizers *and* almost all had been given Haldol.

1980–1983
Suspect Cases
(N=25)

Haldol only	16	64%
Haldol plus Thorazine	5	20%
Haldol plus Mellaril	2	8%
Mellaril only	2	8%
Total	25	100%

If Haldol was precipitating the intestinal bleeding, the effect was emerging at doses well within the therapeutic range noted in the literature (.5–10 mg). The 23 suspect cases prescribed Haldol were distributed by daily dose as follows:

	.5 mg. h.s.	1
	1.0 mg. h.s.	2
	1.0 mg. b.i.d.	6
	2.0 mg. b.i.d.	3
	2.0 mg. p.r.n.	9
greater than	2.0 mg. t.i.d.	2
	Total haldol users	23

It is interesting to note that almost 40 percent of all orders for this tranquilizer were written "as needed," leaving it up to the nursing staff to decide when and if to dispense. While this is not uncommon in nursing homes where physician contact is infrequent and abbreviated, it does permit the nursing staff great control over when and how a patient will be managed with chemicals rather than by staff.

In conclusion, we believe that there is an immediate need to review the widespread use of the tranquilizing medications being prescribed and dispensed in nursing homes. The documented level of "serious behavioral problems" in the SNFs does not warrant the utilization rates for these tranquilizers that we discovered. If these medications are needed to relieve symptoms (e.g., hallucinations, aberrant behavior, assaultiveness, agitation, or belligerence) this fact needs to be completely documented. The personal medical record must contain full details on the nature of the problem behaviors, including whether patients are endangering themselves or others, or are merely bothersome to the staff. In addition, the personal medical record should contain a detailed chronology or history of behavior problems, including relevant *diagnoses* that correspond to the chemical intervention being applied. Finally, the personal medical record should note what precise side-effects monitoring is being done and with what results. In the absence of these three interrelated sets of data, one must assume that patients are being victimized.

While we are not in the position to suggest the elimination of Haldol as a drug of choice in the tranquilizing of the frail elderly, we strongly suggest that sufficient data exist to cause us to be concerned about the use of this drug in this patient population. We also believe that suspicions held by both clinical researchers and nursing home staffs warrant an immediate inquiry that should include extensive clinical trials and monitoring of long-term side effects. Until these trials are completed, we would question the continued reliance upon Haldol when other "peer" medications are not under the same cloud of suspicion.

Studies by the General Accounting Office for the House Selection Committee on Aging have shown about 82 percent of nursing home patients were under drug regimens that are not adequately supervised and that up to 25 percent of the drugs being administered may be administered in error (Editorial, G.A.O. Study Findings, 1980). Our study would certainly confirm the high level of inadequate supervision of drug prescribing and dispensing in nursing homes.

REFERENCES

1. Buttaro, P. J. 1983. *Principles of long term health care administration*, rev. ed. Aberdeen, S.D.: Health Care Facility Consultants.
2. Editorial, G.A.O. Study Findings. 1980. "Drug regimens poorly supervised." *Contemporary Administrator*, August, pp. 8, 38.
3. Hollister, L. E. 1975. *Clinical use of psychotherapeutic drugs*. Springfield: Charles Thomas.
4. Ohio Department of Health, Public Health Council. 1983. *Nursing and rest home law and rules*, 6352.12, rev.
5. Poe, W. D., and D. A. Holloway. 1980. *Drugs and the aged*. New York: McGraw-Hill.

6. Salzman, C. 1982. A primer on geriatric pharmacology. *American Journal Psychiatry* 139(1): 67–74.
7. Zimmer, J. G., N. Watson, and A. Treat. 1984. Behavioral problems among patients in skilled nursing facilities. *American Journal of Public Health* 74(10): 1118–21.

Elderly Victims of Domestic Violence

SUZANNE K. STEINMETZ

Professor
Individual and Family Studies
University of Delaware
Newark, Delaware 19716

INTRODUCTION

The autonomy and private nature of the family provides an environment that has allowed, and in many instances encouraged, abuse of its
members. We were made aware of child abuse during the 1960s, and in
the 1970s wife beating attracted public attention. Now, during the first
half of the 1980s, abuse of the elderly has gained national attention. All
these forms of family violence have existed throughout recorded history, but only recently has the public demanded protection for individuals considered to be economically dependent, politically weak, and
lacking in adequate legal protection.

Strong economic motives encourage society to provide help for
abused children and spouses: we need to protect them so that they may
become, or remain, productive adults. The aged, however, are at the
end of their economically productive lives, and productivity is the basis
on which our culture values individuals, shows them deference, and
gives them status, respect, and rewards. Given the cost of providing
humane, alternative care for the elderly—especially when such care is
subjected to cost-benefit analysis and compared to other social service
needs—selective inattention can be politically expedient. Although
numerous states have passed laws to protect the elderly against abuse,
money for helping them or reducing the risk of abuse by caregivers is
still virtually nonexistent.

According to mythology, past societies coped adequately with the

Author gratefully acknowledges the assistance of Cathy Sullivan in technical editing
and manuscript preparation.

126

problems of the aged. However, part of their "success" was due to the average life expectancy, which in the eighteenth century was only 35, in 1900 was 50, and today is in the early to mid 70s. Not only was life expectancy shorter; one was permitted to work as long as one was physically able. Today, advanced life-sustaining medical technology and miracle medicines have assured survival in quantity—if not in quality—of life for the elderly.

By the close of the century, 1 in 5 citizens will be 65 or older, and the greatest increase (53 percent) will be among those 75 and older. This group is most vulnerable to physical, mental, and financial crisis requiring the care by their family and society (U.S. Bureau of the Census, 1977; Brody, 1978).

The increasing number of vulnerable elderly is a distinctive concern of this decade. However, it is not only their increased numbers that is a critical issue. We must also recognize that those in their seventh, eighth, or ninth decade have caregiving children who are or soon will be elderly. A sizable number of persons over 65 have one or more living parents. Furthermore, about 1 in 10 older persons are parents of a child over 65 (Butler and Lewis, 1977; Townsend, 1968). About one-half of all persons over 65 who have living children are members of a four-generation family. This is the century not only of old age, but of multi-generational families, often several generations of near elderly, elderly, and frail elderly women. Townsend's prediction that the family of the future could conceivably include a generation of frail elderly has become a reality.

Unfortunately caregivers are often emotionally and financially unprepared to assume responsibility for their elderly family members. Families face increased expense for their children's college educations and weddings, and women want to fulfill their own educational and occupational goals. Since caretaking responsibility will most likely be assumed by a woman, she may resent this further interruption of her personal goals. The responsibility of caring for an elderly parent, when one wants to concentrate on spouse and children, results in additional frustration and stress, producing an environment conducive to battering.

While those born in the early 1900s have experienced increased longevity, the smaller family size during the 1920s and 1930s has resulted in fewer younger kin available to provide support for their elders (Treas, 1977).

Currently the birth rate is declining; women are putting off child-birth until later in life and having fewer children. Thus, there will be fewer members of the younger generation (Brody, 1978; Treas, 1977). These declining birth rates restrict the older generation's access to younger kin on whom they can count for assistance (Treas, 1977). In addition to the declining birth rates, later marriages restrict and narrow the average span of years between generations. Thus, we find families in which several members live into advanced age and relatively few members of the child and grandchild generations are available to provide assistance. Divorces, remarriage, and blended families increase the number of elderly that one may feel responsible for.

HISTORICAL OVERVIEW

To understand our care and treatment of the elderly in the past, a number of myths need to be explored.

The three-generational family that was idealized in the television series *The Waltons* was not the prevailing family pattern. Those who moved west in earlier times were the young and the healthy; the elderly stayed at home. Geographic patterns of settlement and the high mobility of families throughout the immigration and westward expansion periods must also be examined. For the first time in history, almost all children are growing up with grandparents, and many have great-grandparents. When the early settlers came to this country, they came as relatively young individuals, leaving their own parents behind. Today society is highly mobile (1 out of 5 persons moves each year), yet it is becoming a society of four-generation families. When considering a job move, families must consider appropriate housing, occupational opportunities for the spouse, educational facilities, *and* residential and nursing home facilities for elderly family members.

The myth of the family's total devotion to the ill or dying elder is another one that often contrasts with reality. The image of yesteryear includes vignettes in which Granddad worked in the fields on Monday, became ill on Tuesday, and—following two days of round-the-clock vigil—died on Friday and was laid to rest on Saturday. Today the dying process has been prolonged to months or years in expensive nursing homes or hospitals. The price often strips families of emotional and financial resources.

Our view of the past is often rose-colored because of the way it has been related to us. Even today, many of our oldest citizens are first-generation immigrants who left their own families behind. They were following a persistent pattern: the young and adventurous move to the frontier; the elderly remain at home. The only care that many of these immigrants provided to their elderly kin in the old country was emotional support through letters and small amounts of money. The very different circumstances of family life do not allow anyone to say, "In an earlier time we cared for our elders and today we are unwilling to do so," because the contemporary family situation cannot be compared to that of an earlier era.

Another myth concerns the belief that in the good old days, the family willingly provided excellent, self-sacrificing care of the elderly. The evidence to refute this position is found in diary and court accounts of abuse, in property transfers requiring provisions for elderly parents, and in frontier migration patterns.

Old age was venerated in early America; however, veneration was construed to mean reverence, respect, worship—not affection or love (Fischer, 1977). The Fourth Commandment required respect of one's parents, but this veneration did not automatically come with aging. The special powers assumed to be held by elders might be in the form of God's grace or the devil's. Aging brought a mixed blessing: elders were venerated and respected, but also feared, isolated, and despised.

These elderly poor were treated badly and brutally. Colonial court records are replete with examples of attempts to bar the elderly from entering a town, because they would increase the population of the almshouses. A 1772 New Jersey law actually required justices of the peace to search arriving ships for old persons and other undesirables and to send them away in order to prevent the growth of pauperism (Smith, 1980: 61). Neighbors often drove out poor widows, who were "warned out" and forced to wander from town to town.

At a meeting of the Boston City Selectman on April 15, 1737, it was reported: "Whereas One Nicholas Buddy an Idle and Poor Man has resided in this Town for Several Years past, and is in danger of becoming a Charge to the Town in a Short time, if not Transported. And There being now an Offer made by some of his friends of Sending him to Jersey (his Native Countrey) Provided they might be Allowed the Sume of Five Pounds towards defraying the Charges of his Passage thither."

If the elderly were native to a community or had served the community in an exemplary fashion, they were provided with aid. For example, the September 28, 1737 entry of the selectmen's meeting states: "Richard Watford, a Disbanded Soldier from Pemaquad, being weak in Body and extream Poor, sent to the almshouse Recommended to the Overseers of the Poor, there to be kept at the Province Charge."

The status of being poor and aged fell most heavily on women, and for widows the effects were often devastating. When the assessors and collectors gave their account to the December 14, 1742, meeting of the Boston Selectman, they noted, "We also Apprehend there is about 1,200 Widows included in the above numbers of Souls One Thousand whereof are in low Circumstances and a great Number of other Persons so poor that they are not Taxed."

As we know, mistreatment of the elderly was not practiced only by Justices of Peace who were carrying out the law. There is evidence that children often neglected their aged parents and that in many cases, actual abuse occurred. Increase Mather in *Dignity and Duty* complains that "there were children who were apt to despise an Aged Mother." And, Landon Carter in 1771 writes, "It is a pity that old Age which everybody who lives must come to should be so contemptible in the eyes of the world" (Smith, 1980: 275).

A father's use of economic means to control his adult children often produced conflicts. In one family, 32-year-old Robert Carter was to spend an additional 20 years under his father's authority because he lacked the financial ability necessary to secure his independence. Bitter arguments, mostly resulting from the middle-aged son's continued dependence on his father, almost resulted in physical blows. Landon Carter, the father, feared for his life and went around armed with a pistol. He noted, "Surely it is happy our laws prevent patricide or the devil that moves to this treatment would move to put his father out of the way. Good God, that such a monster is descended from my loin" (Greene, as cited by Fischer, 1977).

Conflicts such as this apparently occurred throughout American history. In 1868 a bill for boarding a poor, sick old man was brought to the board of commissioners of Brown County, Minnesota. Oliver Mather, son of the old man, had driven his father off and did not want to support him (Fischer, 1977: 152–53).

Property transfers, both through inheritance and deeds of gifts, provide insights into parents' attempts to use economic control as a hedge against maltreatment in their old age. An examination of wills, property transfers, and deeds of gift reveals a tug of war over control between parent and child. Often, these documents included elaborate instructions for a surviving wife's care, requiring the child who inherited the property to furnish food, clothing, shelter, and services or risk forfeiture of the inheritance.

Henry Holt, by a deed of gift, gave his unmarried son the original homestead when he reached 30 years of age. The deed required him to "take ye sole care of his father Henry Holt" for the rest of his days and to provide for all his needs, which were carefully detailed. Failure to supply any of the required articles would result in forfeiture of the property. Joseph Winslow left all his movable properties to his wife for her to distribute after death according to the performance of filial duties (Mayflower Descendants XXXIV: 34, as cited by Demos, 1970: 75).

It is obvious that these precautions would not have been deemed necessary unless maltreatment of elders by their children, after property had been transferred, were known to exist. By incorporating these requirements, elders maintained the ability to revoke a property transfer and regain the economic ability to pay others for their care.

PRECURSORS TO ABUSE AND NEGLECT

Today, a number of stresses seem to be related to dependence of the elderly on their children. As the needs of the elderly increase, the stress experienced by the caregiving family can result in abuse of both caregiver and elder, unless adequate resources are available (Blenkner, 1965, 1969).

The increased amount of time required to care for a dependent elder often leaves little time for fulfilling the caregiver's own needs. Furthermore, the elder may view the caregiver's attempts to reserve personal time as rejection.

Control over one's environment and lack of privacy are other causes of conflict (Foulke, 1980). It is often difficult for an old person who has been transplanted from his or her home to find an appropriate role in the new setting.

Economic dependency produces a loss of self-esteem, and thus a loss of power and prestige. Furthermore, the caregiving family experiences economic drain and conflict over competing goals for the use of limited resources (Silverstone and Hyman, 1976; Steinmetz, 1984).

Caregivers must also resolve problems resulting from the elder's physical dependence as physical deterioration adds new burdens.

Medical costs frequently are not compensated or at best may be undercompensated by public and private health insurance. The stress of meeting the elderly parent's physical needs is intensified because the caregiver realizes that inadequate care could produce a life-threatening situation. Social, emotional, and mental-health dependencies are particularly stressful because of the increased amount of personal time spent in social interaction with a dependent elder. As one grows older, the physical areas that define one's social life decrease. Thus the caregiver and family often become the only social life an older person has, and this can cause resentment on the part of the family.

Foulke (1980), in her analysis of the support provided by caregiving families, describes their sense of burden as a complex of issues that involves the family, the elder, and the family's situation. This perception may reflect "coping abilities" and therefore alternative strategies to violence. Steinmetz and Amsden (1983) found that the degree of dependence, which is an objective measure of additional tasks and responsibilities provided by the caregivers, was not related to a sense of burden, a subjective expression of caregivers' feelings about these tasks and responsibilities. Since a person's perception of a situation is often a better predictor of behavior than are objective criteria (Steinmetz, 1977), caregivers who report a sense of burden may have a greater potential for being abusive or neglectful.

FREQUENCY OF ABUSE

Research has shown that the most frequent abusers of the elderly are family members (Block and Sinnott, 1979; Douglas, 1979; Steinmetz, 1978; 1980). Thirteen percent of the service providers who responded to a mail survey reported abuse; however, 88 percent were aware of the problem, even if they had no cases to report (Block and Sinnott, 1979). Seventeen percent of respondents from a mail survey of professionals reported physical abuse of an elder, and 44 percent reported verbal and emotional abuse (Douglas, Hickey and Noel, 1980).

A mail survey, sent to over 1,000 medical people, social service professionals, and paraprofessionals, was conducted by the Legal Research and Services for the Elderly in Boston, Massachusetts (O'Malley et al., 1979). These researchers note that although 183 reports of elder abuse were received, it is possible that different professionals were reporting the same case. They found that in 70 percent of the reports, the abuse occurred at least twice; in 75 percent, the victim lived with the abuser; and in over 80 percent, the abuser was a relative. These researchers suggested that abuse, like charity, begins at home. Nearly three-fourths were experiencing some form of stress, such as alcoholism, drug addiction, medical problems, or long-term financial problems. However, it was also noted that the elderly victim was a source of stress to the abuser primarily because of the physical, emotional, or financial care required. Most studies found that although abuse occurred in all age groups, it tended to be concentrated among those 75 or older. Furthermore, a greater proportion of the victims (80 percent in the O'Malley study) were women. Therefore, it may be the elders' frailty that results in abuse acts producing visible, serious injury.

Family Services Association of greater Lawrence, Massachusetts, also collected data through a specialized program funded by Title III of the Older American Act. During a 12-month period (March 1, 1978 to February 28, 1979), 82 cases were referred to this project. Clients' ages ranged from 60 to 99, with about half between 80 and 99. In one three-month period, December 1978 to February 1979, 50 cases were handled. Of these, 8 were cases of suspected abuse by a family member, 4 were cases of suspected abuse by a nonrelative, and 3 were referred for possible neglect by a family member. However, a followup of all the cases revealed that 21 of the elderly were experiencing, or were seriously threatened with, harm by individuals on whom they were dependent (Langdon, 1979).

During a single year in 1978, the Baltimore City Police Department reported 149 assaults against individuals 60 or older. Nearly two-thirds (62.7 percent) of these assaults were committed by relatives other than spouses (Block and Sinnott, 1980).

In the first eight months after passage of the Connecticut Elderly Protective Service Law (June 1978 to January 1979), 87 cases of physical abuse, 314 cases of neglect, 65 cases of exploitation, and 8 cases of abandonment were reported (Block and Sinnott, 1980). By April 1979 the total number of reported cases was 1,065 involving 937 separate persons, including 651 neglect cases (both self-neglect and neglect by caretakers), 166 cases of physical abuse (a majority of which had been inflicted by grown children of the abused victim or by a spouse), 127 cases of exploitation, 32 cases of abandonment, and 89 cases needing other kinds of assistance. Law and Kosberg (1978) found that over three-fourths of their abused elderly cases involved physical abuse and over half involved psychological abuse. Data from the above studies were obtained from third parties—for example, social service delivery professionals, police, and protective or social workers.

A broad-based but nonrandom sample of caregivers was conducted by Steinmetz (1981, 1984) and Steinmetz and Amsden (1983) using a snowball technique (Bailey, 1978). In all, 104 caregivers, 14 of whom cared for two elders, met the following criteria:

1. The family and the elder shared a residence, and the elder was not a house guest or visitor.
2. The adult child performed some tasks for the elder, indicating that the elder was to some degree dependent.
3. The elder was over 55 years of age.
4. The caregiver was the adult responsible for the household.
5. If the elder was deceased, death had occurred within the preceding three years.

Because the health status, level of dependency, and interaction between the caregivers and elders might differ in families caring for two people, the elders in these instances were treated as separate cases, yielding 118 sets of interviews.

Ninety-four percent of the elders were cared for by female caregivers. Three-quarters of the caregivers were married, and in more than half of these families children still lived at home. The majority (45 percent) of the caregivers were in their 50s, about one-fourth were in their 40s, 11 percent were under 40, and nearly 20 percent were 60 or older. Thus, nearly two-thirds of the sample were elderly (by census definition) or approaching that stage.

Eighty-five percent of the elders were women; 91 percent were 70 years or older, and 20 percent were in the ninth or tenth decade of life. The average age of the elderly was just over 82, although the ages ranged from 59 to 103. About 85 percent experienced diminished physical functioning, and 38 percent had been hospitalized during the last year. While 85 percent of the adult children reported talking out problems, many noted that this talking was often done with a raised voice or loud tone. Screaming also was frequently reported (see Table 1).

The technique caregivers reported that elders used most frequently as a control mechanism was pouting or withdrawing. Sixty percent of the elders used this method as a means of dealing with conflict. Other methods included manipulation, especially pitting one family member against another (43 percent), crying (38 percent), using their disabilities to gain sympathy (33 percent), or imposing guilt (50 percent). Since 16 percent of the elders refused food and 13 percent refused medication, it is not surprising that 4 percent of the children resorted to forcing food and 14 percent to forcing medication on an elder. Four percent withheld food, but it tended to be done for dietary reasons (for example, keeping sweets from a diabetic).

TABLE 1
Percent of Adult Children and Elderly Parents
Using Various Conflict-Resolution Techniques

Methods	Child to Parent	Parent to child
Talked	85	—
Sought advice	65	—
Considered alternative housing	20	—
Threatened nursing home	7	—
Pouted/withdrew	—	61
Confined to room	1	—
Manipulated others	—	43
Imposed guilt	—	54
Used disability to gain sympathy	—	33
Forced food	3	—
Refused food	—	16
Withheld food	4	—
Forced medication	14	—
Refused medication	—	15
Screamed and yelled	40	36
Cried	—	37
Called police	—	5
Physically restrained	8	—
Threatened physical force	5	—
Slapped, hit with object, shook	1	18

As a result of conflicting demands, abusive and neglectful methods often become the method of last resort. Many of the negative methods of control were used to keep the elder from danger. Physical restraint was used by 8 percent of the caregivers; physical force was threatened by 4 percent and used by 1 percent. This violence is not unidirectional; 19 percent of the elders slapped, hit with an object, or threw something at their caregiver. Some of the methods used by elders in their attempts to maintain control were perceived by the caregivers as incidents that precipitated the decision to arrange for alternative caregiving.

FACTORS LEADING TO ABUSE

In many of the families, the elders maintained a high degree of independence and autonomy, while in other families almost all tasks had to be performed for them. Housekeeping tasks were the most frequently performed tasks. When all household items were considered, 99 percent of the caregivers provided this help. In fact, only one family reported that they did not do any of the housekeeping for the elderly.

Over 98 percent of caregivers provided social and emotional support (two families provided no support), and 92 percent helped with mental health tasks (six families were not performing these services). Ninety percent provided some form of help with financial management; 74 percent provided help with health care; 67 percent helped with personal grooming; and 72 percent helped to maintain family interaction. The least frequently observed type of dependency, mobility, was still provided in some degree by 61 percent of the families.

While 64 percent of the caregivers reported a sense of burden, those who did and did not differed significantly only on two items: "bathing the elder" and "helping with decision making." However, when the stress resulting from these tasks was compared for burdened and non-burdened caregivers, burdened caregivers tended to report a greater degree of stress as a result of the elder's dependence.

The correlation matrix (Table 2) shows the relationship between stress, dependency, feeling burdened, and abuse. Out of 154 possible relationships between conflict-resolution techniques used by elders and stress reported by caregiver, 51 percent (N=78) were significant, and these relationships tended to be stronger than those exhibited between caregivers and conflict resolution techniques.

One of the most interesting relationships is that between the elders' level of mental health dependency (totmen) and the use of verbal and physical abuse by elders and caregivers. For caregivers, the correlations were .46 for screaming/yelling and .18 for hitting/slapping; for elders, the correlations were .21 and .49 respectively. In fact, the variable "elder hits/slap/throws" produced high, significant correlations with all the dependency variables except household management (tothous) and mobility (totmob). This might reflect the elders' loss of other means to gain control (lack of money, loss of ability to maintain social life, dependency on caregiver for health and grooming), as well as the mental health variable, which measures nonrational and explosive behavior.

The interviews revealed that social, emotional, and mental health variables were frequently performed (only household management tasks were performed more frequently) and were reported to be the most stressful. But the interviews also differentiated burdened from nonburdened caregivers and found the distinction to be strongly and significantly correlated with abusive interactions. Apparently an overall sense of burden increases the likelihood of abusive and disruptive family interaction.

CONCLUSION

Elder abuse in generationally inversed families has only recently gained public awareness. Yet our knowledge about factors contributing to other forms of family violence and demographic trends predicts an increased number of abused elderly unless, as a society, we are willing to commit resources to prevent this. Women predominate not only as vulnerable elders but also as caregivers. However, in the near future, women caregivers are likely to be working women—working until 70 years of age to maintain an adequate standard of living and fulfill occupational goals.

If the goal of society is to deinstitutionalize the elderly, alternatives must be developed that enable women to maintain their standard of living while providing care, often 24-hour care, to an elderly relative. Adult day care; respite care; homemaker, nursing, housekeeping services must be provided. Top incentives as well as cash payments must be available.

TABLE 2

CAREGIVER	Findep	Gromdep	Emodep	Physdep	Mobsen	Noteat	Dietned	Lonely	Demand	Houseman	Transp	Prirae	Rolnain	Disrupt	Tohouse	Totperh	ToFin	Totmob	Totemot.	Totemen	Totdep	BURDEN
	DEPENDENCY														STRESS							
1. Talked	07	-12	11	22*	-08	-12	12	-07	19*	01	-12	-06	02	08	0	04	-09	11	11	-02	04	-22*
2. Screamed/yellec	05	25*	34*	24*	44*	18	-03	11	12	19*	20*	18*	-03	-13	10	20*	14	06	12	46*	25*	09
3. Phys. restraint	03	12	24*	20*	32*	06	0	29*	22*	33*	11	05	02	-02	05	13	26*	21*	16*	27*	24*	15
4. Forced Feed	-10	02	11	0	16	36*	-08	07	-05	18*	-04	-13	-05	-07	07	25*	04	28*	-06	16*	17*	13
5. Withheld food	-10	-05	17	24*	13	-03	-11	10	-04	-07	-06	-14	-05	-07	04	06	11	04	-07	03	05	06
6. Threat/Nursing Home	03	17	17	10	20	11	-01	10	16	07	10	04	-08	-11	17*	06	12	16*	16*	18*	20*	04
7. Threat phys. force	-06	21*	17	03	19	-06	-01	09	20*	07	08	03	04	-01	03	-03	02	05	01	07	03	05
8. Confine/room	39*	08	07	-02	04	04	—	02	03	01	- 0	-07	-04	-05	05	-01	07	17*	-05	10	07	-08
9. But/slap	—	12	-01	04	04	09	—	—	03	05	11	04	-03	-04	08	12	04	12	03	18*	13	07
10. Give medication	23*	15	38*	32*	40*	18	-04	08	17*	08	17*	00	-08	0	04	29*	21*	20*	24*	44*	33*	16*
11. Seek, advice	16	30*	19	16	30*	27*	11	25*	32*	31*	18*	01	11	03	07	20*	11	06	18*	38*	23*	30*
12. Alt. housing	25*	10	28*	17	29*	05	-10	27*	10	07	01	27*	-05	18*	19*	04	-06	-01	02	33*	12	02
ELDER																						
1. Screamed/yell	12	21*	28*	04	16	24*	0	34*	37*	21*	18*	14	09	08	-13	-01	12	05	09	21*	06	10
2. Pout/withdraw	23*	17*	15	18	17	-03	14	26*	40*	04	25*	13	-05	05	-03	-01	09	12	11	19*	10	05
3. Refuse to eat	46*	21*	25*	03	37*	50*	01	03	20*	04	20*	06	-07	-02	17*	18*	22*	05	24*	33*	28*	-05
4. Refuse med. treat.	24*	06	10	14	05	24*	-01	11	12	16*	23*	09	-03	11	03	03	-01	06	15*	24*	11	08
5. Manipulate	36*	10	28*	17	16	06	51*	17*	54*	23*	42*	29*	11	-07	-11	-14	02	-02	-08	05	-08	20*
6. Cry	39*	12	14	07	05	07	20*	13	25*	-01	45*	02	0	06	-07	08	16*	10	24*	30*	18*	02
7. Hit/slap/throw	33*	32*	34*	12	48*	29*	09	21*	21*	19*	29*	33*	05	-07	15	29*	29*	09	30*	49*	38*	11
8. Use disability	40*	14	10	07	08	13	31*	23*	51*	09	44*	20*	06	18*	-01	08	21*	15*	28*	26*	22*	15
9. Call police	42*	26*	29*	06	35*	23*	15	11	26*	23*	27*	29*	-06	-09	09	14	19*	-01	25*	33*	24*	16*
10. Impose guilt	42*	24*	14	07	12*	07	22*	27*	54*	19*	27*	26*	09	13	-10	-09	14	-04	24*	22*	07	13
11. Doesn't respect priv.	24*	15	08	03	08	06	23*	29*	42*	26*	39*	35*	18*	23*								

TABLE 2 (continued)

Stresses:
  Findep—elder financially dependent
  Gromdep—elder needs help with personal grooming
  Emotdep—elder has severe emotional/mental disability
  Physdep—elder has severe physical disability
  Mobsen—elder is mobile but senile
  Noteat—elder won't eat
  Dietned—elder has special dietary needs
  Lonely—elder is lonely
  Demand—elder makes excessive demands
  Houseman—household management
  Transp—elder needs transportation
  Privac—privacy
  Rolmain—maintain authority role in family
  Disrupt—elder is disruptive to family lifestyle

Dependency:
  Tothous—total score for all household tasks
  Totperh—total score for all personal grooming/health
    care tasks
  Totfin—total score for all financial tasks
  Totmob—total score for all mobility tasks
  Totmot—total score for all emotional/social tasks
  Totmen—total score for all mental health tasks

*Significant at $\leqslant .05$.

We must educate our children about the needs and responsibilities inherent in care for our elders, so that they can make informed choices about the best care. Affordable nursing facilities must be available so that family care is *chosen*, not turned to as the only option or a last resort. If we as a society believe that family care is truly the best care, we must be certain that we do not penalize families who take on this responsibility. Finally, we must recognize that for some families, family care may not be the best choice for either caregiver or elder.

REFERENCES

Bailey, K. D. 1978. *Methods of social research.* New York: Free Press.
Blenkner, M. 1965. Social work and the family relationships in later life with some thoughts of filial Maturity. In E. Shanas and G. Streib (eds.), *Social structure and the family.* Englewood Cliffs, N.J.: Prentice Hall.
———. 1969. The normal dependencies of aging. In R. Kalish (ed.), *The dependencies of old people.* Ann Arbor: University of Michigan Institute of Gerontology.

Block, M. and J. P. Sinnott. 1979. *The battered elder syndrome: An exploratory study.* College Park, Md.: Center on Aging, University of Maryland.

———. 1980. Prepared statement. *Elder abuse: The hidden problem.* Briefing by the Select Committee on Aging, U.S. House of Representatives. (96) June 23, 1979. (unpublished)

Brody, E. 1978. The Aging of the family. *Annals AAPSS* 438, (July): 13–26.

———. 1979. Women's changing roles, the aging family and long-term care of older people. *National Journal* 11 (October): 1828–33.

Butler and Lewis. 1977. *Aging and mental health.* St. Louis: Mosby.

Demos, J. 1970. *A little commonwealth.* New York: Oxford University Press.

Douglas, R. 1979. *A study of neglect and abuse of the elderly in Michigan.* Paper presented to the Thirty-second Annual Meeting of Gerontological Society. Washington, D.C., November.

Douglas, R., T. Hickey, and C. Noel. 1980. *A study of neglect and abuse of the elderly and other vulnerable adults.* Final report to the U.S. Administration on Aging and the Michigan Department of Social Services, Ann Arbor, November.

Fischer, D. H. 1977. *Growing old in America.* New York: Oxford University Press.

Foulke, S. R. 1980. *Caring for the parental generation: An analysis of family resources and support.* Unpublished Thesis, University of Delaware, Newark.

Langdon, B. 1980. Statement presented to the House of Representatives Select Committee on Aging (96) June 23, 1979. (unpublished)

Law, E., and J. Kosberg. 1978. "Abuse of the elderly by informed care providers: Practice research issues. Paper presented at the 31st Annual Meeting of the Gerontological Society, Dallas, Texas, November.

O'Malley, H., J. Bergman, and H. Segars. 1979. *Elder abuse in Massachusetts: A survey of professionals and paraprofessionals.* Boston: Legal Research and Services for the Elderly.

Silverstone, B. and H. K. Hyman. 1976. *You and your aging parent.* New York: Partheon Books.

Smith, D. B. 1980. *Inside the great house: Planter family life in the eighteenth century Chesapeake Society.* Ithaca: Cornell University Press.

Steinmetz, S. K. 1978. The politics of aging, battered parents. *Society,* July–August: 54–55.

———. 1979. Prepared Statements. *Elder abuse: The hidden problem.* Briefing by the Select Committee on Aging, U.S. House of Representatives. (96) June 23. (unpublished)

———. 1981. Elder abuse. *Aging* (January-February) 6–10.

———. 1982. Dependency, stress and violence between middle-aged caregivers and their elderly parents. In J. I. Kosberg, *Abuse and maltreatment of the elderly.* Littleton, Mass,: John-Wright.

———. 1984. Family violence towards elders. In S. Saunders, A. Anderson, C. Hart, and G. Rubenstein (eds.), Violence, individuals and families, A handbook for practitioners. Springfield, ILL.: Charles C. Thomas.

———. and D. J. Amsden. 1983. Dependent elders, family stress and abuse. In T. H. Brubaker (ed.), *Family relationships in later life.* Beverly Hills: Sage.

Townsend, P. 1968. "The emergence of the four-generation family in industrial so-
ciety." In B. L. Neugarten, (ed.), *Middle age and aging*. University of Chicago
Press.
Treas, J. 1977. "Family support systems for the aged: Some social and demographic
considerations. *The Gerontologist* 17 (6):486–91.
U.S. Burau of Census, 1977. *Current population reports*, p. 25, no. 643, Tables 2 and 5.

Issues in the Criminal Victimization of the Elderly

JOHN H. LINDQUIST, D. Soc. Sci.

Professor
Department of Sociology
Trinity University
San Antonio, Texas

INTRODUCTION

The subject of elderly criminal victimization has produced a vast literature within a very short period of time. Unfortunately, the results of
these efforts are scattered among dozens of journals and books. Others
(for example, Lawton 1980–1981) have sought to summarize the research findings, but no one has examined the literature in terms of the
issues raised by the various researchers. Unless and until the issues are
clearly understood, research efforts are one-dimensional and lack
cohesion. The focus of this paper, therefore, is on the issues and their
implications for further research and other efforts.

As Fischer points out (cited in Barron and Smith, 1979), the process
of growing old in America, has elicited different responses from the
American public. Prior to 1820 the aged were more honored and
obeyed than hated and feared. As the nation rapidly expanded its population through the immigration of youthful males and the large
number of children born to each family, the young came to be glorified.
The aged were more often victims than victimizers, feared rather than
revered. Around the turn of this century, the elderly came to be seen as
a social problem requiring an elaborate network of social services and
agencies to provide these services. Victimization in the workplace,
housing, medical care, income, and recreation was seen as rampant. In
addition, the term "ageism" was invented to refer to negative stereotyping of the elderly. But only within the past decades have criminal vic-

timization and the fear of criminal victimization become manifest among the elderly and recognized by researchers as a topic worthy of study.

Public and scholarly awareness of the nature and extent of the fears of aged Americans is of recent origin. The now-famous Louis Harris poll of over 1,600 elderly Americans (1975) brought these fears into sharp focus. This poll destroyed the myth that older Americans feared loneliness, financial instability, empty lives, worthlessness, and all the other stereotyped notions that marked conventional wisdom. Instead they told their interviewers over and over again that what frightens them the most is crime. They are afraid of the streets, of young people who are potential purse-snatchers, of dark hallways in apartment buildings, of unlit streets, and all the other factors associated with crime. Over 1 in 5 (22.6 percent) regarded crime as a "very serious problem." This translates into over 5 million aged Americans fearfully trying to protect themselves from the predators of the streets and the stealthy intruders of the night. What is true for the nation is also true for various locales within the nation. Bild and Havighurst (1976) replicated the Harris poll in Chicago, as a part of a larger study of various ethnic and neighborhood groups of elderly in that city. For the persons they interviewed, fear of crime was the overwhelming concern.

DEVELOPING DATA SOURCES ON ELDERLY VICTIMS

The fears of the elderly regarding crime parallel those of Americans in general. Throughout the 1960s and into the 1970s, Gallup and other pollsters routinely included questions regarding fear of crime as a part of their polls. By the end of the 1960s, crime had moved into the top position on the list of problems that concerned Americans (Erskine, 1974).

This fear of crime came as a surprise to professionals serving the elderly. In 1959 the Senate Subcommittee on Problems of the Aged and Aging asked "all organizations concerned with problems of older persons" the following questions:

1. What are the major problems of the aged?
2. How well are public and private agencies dealing with these problems?

3. Is the present federal role adequate or is there a need to increase it?
4. What new ideas in the field would benefit the aged?
5. What should be the role of management, labor, health, and educational groups in dealing with the problems of the aged?

"All organizations" included every state and every major private
agency serving the aged in the nation. The subcommittee published a
volume of replies, not one of which mentioned crime or the fear of
crime as a major problem facing the elderly. The respondents discussed
the standard litany of needs typically serviced by public and private
social service agencies: health, housing, diet, income, etc. If nothing
else, the survey underscores the need to speak to elderly relatives about
their needs and concerns; professionals have demonstrated that *they*
cannot speak for the aged.

At the same time that public concern regarding crime became a major issue, criminologists (whose major emphasis had been on crime and
the accused rather than on the victim) were proposing surveys to determine the nature and extent of criminal victimization in the nation
(Ennis; 1967; Biderman et al.; 1967). This recent interest has not gone
unnoticed by those whose orientation has been toward providing services to victims of crime. McDonald rebuked the criminologists for
their lack of interest, writing: "The entire criminal justice establishment, including legal scholars and criminologists, have largely ignored
the victim . . . there are no schools of victimiology and no textbooks
on how victims are treated by the criminal justice system and what
happens to them," (1976:19).

The paucity of empirical analyses of victims was related directly to a
lack of data. From their inception in the early nineteenth century, criminal statistics were focused on the crime, the defendant, and the incarcerated (Allen, et al., 1981). The emphasis has been on explaining
crime, to reduce or even eliminate it. When we read those who criticize
the lack of scholarly and legal interest in the *victim*, we must remember
that until the mid-nineteenth century, victims could sue offenders for
restitution (see, for example, Hall, 1952). Only recently has the modern
state substituted *itself* for the victim in this regard. In fact, many offenses now prosecuted under criminal codes were once pursued entirely within the framework of the civil law by the victim or by those
acting in the victim's name. The legal system underwent a major

change in the nineteenth century, but there was no corresponding re-orientation by those responsible for gathering crime statistics. The most comprehensive statistics in the United States, the Uniform Crime Reports, are published annually by the Federal Bureau of Investigation from data provided by local law-enforcement agencies. These data are presented and analyzed in many ways; geographically, ethnically, and so on. But they are not analyzed by the victim's age, though most reporting agencies do gather this information (U.S. Congress, Subcommittee on Housing and Consumer Interests, 1977).

When by the mid-1960s, crime had come to be a major concern of the American public (Erskine, 1974:131), only a few victim surveys had been conducted. These were small-scale studies by a few criminologists, using high school and college students as subjects (Biderman, et al., 1967:26). No studies had been conducted that could generate estimates of the nature and extent of victimization for the population of the United States. The interest was there, but the enormous cost associated with drawing and interviewing samples large enough had so far precluded the research (Ennis, 1967: iii). As is often the case, rising public concern with crime generated political interest; in this instance, the President appointed a Commission on Law Enforcement and the Administration of Justice. Those interested in exploring unreported crime, the "dark side of crime," convinced the commission to sponsor victimization studies using very large samples (Biderman, et al., 1967). In the 1970s these surveys were institutionalized by the newly created Law Enforcement Assistance Administration (LEAA) as annual surveys, conducted by the U.S. Bureau of the Census.

The LEAA surveys (and others conducted to answer questions raised by the LEAA data) have provided students of victimization with the bulk of the information they have used in analyzing the criminal victimization of the elderly, as well as other selected population groups. There are also a few nonsurvey data sources available. For example, the Midwest Research Institute made a detailed study of 1,831 elderly criminal victims, interviewing some victims and others involved in the criminal justice process (Midwest Research Institute, 1977; Cunningham, 1976). The surviving sister of a murder victim (herself a criminologist) carried out extensive interviews with crime victims and surviving relatives and friends of victims. Her focus was not on the elderly, however, but on victims, per se (Barkas, 1978). Another published study reports the experiences of those involved in the Crime Victim Service Center in the Bronx. This study focused on victims in general, not elderly victims (Reiff, 1979).

As yet, no one has conducted lengthy, indepth interviews with elderly victims and nonvictims of crime. The survey data have been very useful in informing us about unreported crimes and providing a data base for secondary analyses; but we can only draw inferences from the statistical manipulation of the variables in the survey data regarding the fears of the elderly, their experiences with crime, the impact of crime and fear of crime on their way of life, and the nature of their fears. No studies of the elderly, victims and nonvictims alike, address these issues. Only recently have we begun to see phenomenological studies of victims (Fischer, 1984) but none of elderly victims per se.

ELDERLY CRIMINAL VICTIMIZATION: THE ISSUES RAISED

Criminologists as well as those concerned specifically with criminal victimization of the elderly were stunned by the conclusions of the President's Commission on Law Enforcement and the Administration of Justice. The surveys showed that elderly victims ranked behind, sometimes far behind, other age groups for the various crime categories defined by the Uniform Crime Report. The volume of victimization and the rate of victimization (computed as the number of victimizations per 100,000 people) were both low compared to other age groups, with only one exception—aged females, who were ranked first as victims of malicious mischief and arson (Ennis, 1967; Biderman, et al., 1967). These findings have been reaffirmed by succeeding surveys (Bureau of Justice Statistics, 1981).

These conclusions, however, have not gone unchallenged. The reported undervictimization of the elderly has been questioned by some criminologists, but primarily by advocates of services to the elderly. As a result of these challenges and the responses they have generated, we are confronted with several unresolved issues that make difficult our comprehension of the impact crime and the fear of crime have upon the elderly. At the core of most of these issues is a debate over public policy—the engine driving public funding of services designed to prevent victimization and to assist those victimized.

Some criminologists have suggested that reported elderly victimization, either officially or through surveys, may be suppressed by the elderly, who, in effect, reduce their "risk" by removing themselves from situations of potential victimization. The suggestion is that if these adaptations were not made, the rate of victimization, as well as the absolute number of victimizations, would be greater than reported in the surveys (Balkin, 1979; Cohen, Kluegel, and Land, 1981; Conklin, 1976; Hindelang, Gottfredson, and Garofalo, 1978; Lindquist and Duke, 1982; Block and Block, 1984).

Criminologists, however, have contributed little to the debate over elderly criminal victimization. Their interest continues to remain focused on crime and the criminal. The bulk of the victimization research regarding the elderly has been conducted by two groups of advocates: those who seek funding of services designed to reduce elderly victimization and its effects, and those who argue that the "real" victims of crime are young, poor, black males, who therefore should be the focus of public policy attention.

These advocates have raised five substantive issues over which they are sharply divided: (1) which age group is most victimized by crime, (2) which crime category or categories should be the appropriate unit of analysis, (3) what data source is appropriate for use in analyzing victimization, (4) which group suffers the most from victimization, and (5) is the fear of crime by the aged rational or irrational? Our understanding of elderly criminal victimization is also clouded by three methodological issues: (1) the salience of victimization for the victim, (2) potential underreporting of some crimes to interviewers, and (3) survey deficiencies that may lead to nonreporting of some crimes.

The first issue in the literature that debate between the two advocacy groups developed went to the core of the subject of elderly victimization: whether or not the elderly were indeed over- or undervictimized.

National Crime Panel Survey findings notwithstanding, one of the most prominent advocates of the elderly, using a different data source, stated, "Old people are victims of violent crime more than any other age group" (Butler, 1975:300). He then went on to make explicit the policy implications of this assertion: "Specific programs to reduce crime against the elderly and to assist them after a crime has been committed are in order as long as crime remains a major threat to their well-being" (Butler, 1975:307). The suggested programs include (1) emergency shelters for elderly crime victims; (2) 24-hour social services, including protective services and public guardianship; (3) compensation for medical expenses and court costs; (4) increased police observation to prevent reprisals against those who report victimization; (5) self-defense and survivor education; (6) provisions for security in the home—secure locks, buzzer systems, guards, doormen, and television monitoring (in public housing); (7) improved street lighting; and (8) community escort service (Butler, 1975: 307).

The more dramatic of the advocates for the elderly stated: "*We are well into a crisis situation concerning the criminal victimization of the elderly who live in or near the higher crime areas of cities*" (Cunningham, 1975: 32; emphasis in the original).

The claim that the elderly are the most victimized by violent crime was rejected by analysts of the National Crime Panel Surveys and other national surveys of large population samples. They claim that "the elderly . . . are least likely to be the victims of most classes of crime" (Cook and Cook, 1976: 636). They also make clear their policy concerns (p. 644):

> It is a fact of policy life that a variety of social problems compete for a finite quantity of attention and funds. Claims that victimization of the elderly has reached crisis proportions may serve to mobilize public attention and support behind the elderly. But at what cost? Our fear is that, if the plight of elderly crime victims becomes even more visible nationally, more resources will be devoted to them at the cost of poor, black males, who are in fact the most likely victims (and perpetrators) of crime in the United States.

Advocates of the elderly quickly attacked this interpretation of the data, but were unable to refute it.

> Some recent victimization surveys, and especially the mammoth National Crime Panel Surveys, have led to urgings that more attention be directed toward that age group *most* often victimized by crime, and less toward the over-65 age group which is the *least* often victimized. The most insidious of these statements are made by those having vested interests in programs, and who see some of the finite resources being siphoned off for the elderly (Sunderland, 1978: 32).

Thus the second issue in this debate, the unit of analysis, is introduced in terms of the *category* of crime to be used to determine degrees of victimization. Advocates of poor, young, black males argue that reported elderly victimization is much less than that of other age groups when crime is categorized *broadly*. The unit of analysis they favor is a single index of crime—robbery, burglary, rape, arson, assault, homicide, and auto theft—the major crimes defined by the FBI Uniform Crime Report. According to their analysis, "The elderly are the least likely age group to be victimized in many serious crime categories (including burglary, theft, rape, robbery, and assault) and are no more likely than other age groups to be victimized in the crime category of personal thefts (i.e., picked pockets and snatched purses" (Cook, et al., 1978: 338).

Advocates for the elderly, however, seek to emphasize crimes that are subsumed under the broad categories preferred by their opponents. They argue, "Although general statements about crime can serve a purpose, they often result in erroneous conclusions and misconceptions. We must begin to talk about *specific* crimes, *specific* locations, and other specific factors" (Sunderland, 1978: 32). These advocates concede that the elderly are less victimized when the unit of analysis remains at the broad-category level but argue that the elderly are over-victimized in specific areas within these broad categories, particularly purse snatching, strong-arm robbery, and bunco games (Sunderland, 1978).

The third issue was also introduced by the advocates of the elderly, who sought to shift the debate from analyses of data collected at the national level to examination of data gathered from smaller geographic areas. National survey data, they argued, "may mask some important differences in the risks which crime presents to the elderly within different parts of the nation or the city" (Jaycox, 1978: 329). Malinchak and Wright (1978), seeking to make this very point, reviewed criminal victimization studies for various cities across the country. Their data indicated that the elderly were more victimized than younger persons for specific crimes within specific cities. Examples they cited included personal injury requiring hospital treatment in Boston; robbery, swindling, and purse snatching in a Houston model neighborhood; fraud and confidence games in Los Angeles and San Francisco; robbery in Oakland, California; street crime in Wilmington, Delaware; robbery in Kansas City, Missouri; and purse snatching and pocket picking in Miami, Florida. Their conclusion was that: "the elderly are being victimized. We can and must work to alleviate this problem" (Malinchak and Wright, 1978: 16).

Advocates who oppose policy decisions favoring victim services for the elderly at the expense of other (they argue more needful) age groups steadfastly maintain their position that the national scene is the proper focus of attention. This position is most clearly articulated by the acting director of the Bureau of Justice Statistics, Benjamin H. Renshaw III), in his introduction to a review of eight years of National Crime Surveys: "Using data from the National Crime Survey, the Bureau of Justice Statistics has examined crime against the elderly in several studies. From our early report dealing with 'Myths and Realities About Crime' to our recent White House briefing materials, the finding has been the same—the elderly are less likely than other age groups in American society to be victims of crime" (Bureau of Justice Statistics, 1981).

The fourth issue raised by policy advocates is the extent to which the elderly suffer physically, financially, and psychologically as a result of criminal victimization. Once again we are presented with two diametrically opposed viewpoints.

The Midwest Research Institute made a study of criminal victimization in Kansas City, Missouri, for the period 1972–1974. Their conclusions represent the broadest possible support of those who advocate on the side of the elderly crime victim: "The elderly are particularly impacted by criminal victimization. Although crime rates against older Americans are generally lower than those of other age groups, the elderly tend to suffer the greatest *relative* deprivation financially, physically and psychologically as a result of the crimes which do occur" (Midwest Research Institute, 1977, S-1).

Advocates for the elderly cite specific studies to support their contention that the elderly suffer greater physical injury than do younger victims of crime. A Boston study, for example, found that "Criminals are more likely to use violence on older persons." Only 25.2 percent of victims under 60 years of age were injured (19.7 percent required hospital treatment) while 41.9 percent of the over-60 victims were injured and 27.5 percent needed hospital treatment" (Malinchak and Wright, 1978: 15).

Additional support for their viewpoint is found in a Chicago study of criminal victimization which concluded: "The percentage of homicide which results from robbery clearly increases with the age of the victim" (Block; 1977: 56).

This viewpoint is rejected by those who do not support policy decisions favorable to the elderly. They acknowledge the popular belief that the elderly are more devastated economically, physically, and psychologically than younger persons by criminal victimization (Hochstedler, 1981:1). But they argue that this belief is not supported by the National Crime Panel Survey data. It is their contention that a careful reading of these surveys leads one to conclude that "The elderly not only suffer the fewest attacks but also the fewest injuries. Forty-six percent of the elderly who were physically attacked escaped injury, whereas only 35 percent of those between 35 and 64 and 40 percent of those between 12 and 34 escaped a physical attack uninjured" (Hochstedler, 1981: 11).

Another statistical analysis of the National Crime Panel Surveys came to a similar conclusion regarding the likelihood of being attacked, but differed in its interpretation of the likelihood of injury. The researchers noted that while the elderly are not the most likely to be injured in an attack, only one other age group (40–49) is more likely to be injured when attacked (Cook, et al., 1978: 345). This caveat notwithstanding, they concluded: "The data reported here offer scant systematic support to persons who believe that, when elderly Americans are victimized by criminals, they suffer more severe financial or physical hardship than younger persons" (Cook, et al., 1978: 346).

Financial losses, say advocates, are a particularly difficult burden for the elderly to bear. As an example they cite the story of an older woman whose apartment was burglarized. Her Social Security check was too small to both pay her living expenses and to repair the broken lock. "I've either got to stop eating for the next two weeks or live in constant fear" (Bard and Sangrey, 1979: 143). Friedman makes much the same point, arguing that even small financial losses are extremely serious. Replacing items lost in a burglary, such as a television set, represents a severe financial hardship (1976: 111–12).

This view is disputed by those who make statistical analyses of the National Crime Panel Surveys. They contend that financial losses for the elderly are no greater, in absolute or relative terms, than those of younger victims (Cook, et al., 1978: 343).

The psychological impact of crime is often emphasized by advocates of the elderly, but ignored by their critics. This results in a one-sided debate in which advocates seek to portray the elderly as living in constant fear for their safety and, if victimized, suffering psychological trauma which may last indefinitely (Barkas, 1978; Stein, 1981). They critique their silent opponents for what they see as their obdurate refusal to acknowledge this reality: "The hard fact is that crime is devastating the lives of thousands of relatively defenseless older Americans. Harder, and even sadder, facts are that many public officials and private citizens are unaware that a special problem exists, or they choose not to believe the evidence of its existence" (Cunningham, 1976: 31).

The fifth substantive issue concerns whether fear of crime by the elderly is rational or irrational. The view of the advocates is that these fears are rational. Their opponents, who believe the elderly are little victimized, assert that such fears are irrational.

Advocates for the elderly make three arguments in support of their view. First, they assert that the elderly are most fearful of the crimes for which they are the most victimized—purse-snatching and pocket-picking—and the least fearful of crimes, such as rape, that affect them very little. This, they say, suggests that the elderly are making an accurate, rational assessment of their risk of criminal victimization (McPherson, 1978: 323). Second, they say that the elderly fear crime because they know they may not be capable of recovering from physical violence. "Perhaps, then, our fearful elderly are no more or less irrational than their younger neighbors. The majority are quite concerned about crime and a great many of them have good reason to be" (Jaycox, 1978: 333). Buttressing this argument with data showing that the elderly are more likely than younger persons to be injured during a robbery, Block argues, "The old person's fear of street crime may not be as irrational as base statistics would indicate" (1977: 57). The third point they make is that while some of the fears of some elderly may indeed be more imagined than real, those living in high-crime areas (low-income, inner-city) have good cause to be fearful, because they are frequently victimized (Faris, 1978: 1).

Opponents, however, dismiss this assertion (Atunes, et al., 1977; Cook, et al., 1978). Having done so, they offer two explanations. The first is that the elderly do not fear crime as much as they fear young, black, male strangers, who fit "the profile of persons who usually attack the elderly" (Atunes, et al., 1977: 325). This fear is therefore irrational, they claim, because the young black may be perfectly innocent. Second, opponents argue that the elderly do not suffer greater financial loss and physical harm than other age groups. They contend that while the elderly suffer less than the youngest adults, they do suffer more than those next to them in the age pyramid. "It seems reasonable to assume that when seniors do compare themselves to others, (a) they will tend to choose persons of middle age rather than adolescents and persons in their early 20s and (b) they will restrict their comparisons to a limited set of consequences where they do suffer more. If they do, comparisons could lead to a special dread of crime" (Cook, et al., 1978: 347).

There are even those who accept *as fact* the irrationality of fear of crime by the elder, just as they accept as fact a low rate of victimization for this age group. For them, these conditions are reality (Clemente and Kleiman, 1976: 207): the elderly merely need an educational program, to explain the facts to them and a service program for those few who are victimized. The director of the Los Angeles Area Agency on Aging, during his appearance before the House Subcommittee on Housing and Consumer Interests of the Select Committee on Aging, testified that:

> The data in Los Angeles show that the percentage of seniors who are victimized is generally less than that of the population as a whole, except for purse snatches. This has led me to wonder if our efforts to warn the elderly about crime do not increase their fears, and all the deleterious effects that these fears generate. If the assumption that fear may have more harmful effects than crime itself is correct—because many seniors are fearful, but only a few are victims—then the response should be a program which allays fears and assists the victims of crimes. This approach may be more effective than crime prevention efforts in some ways, because preventive education may increase fear (U.S. Congress, 1976: 5).

This issue has also attracted the attention of criminologists, who have come to no definitive conclusion. Some of their research findings tend to support the view that fear of crime is generally irrational, whether expressed by elderly or other population groups (Brooks, 1974: 241). Other research findings support the view that fear of victimization is entirely consistent with the fact that the elderly are unable to protect themselves (Thomas and Hyman, 1977; Hindelang, Gottfredson, and Garofalo, 1978). "Unsettled times" is the theme of another approach taken by criminologists, who argue that fear of crime per se is actually fear of young people identified with criminal acts such as drug use and violence (Poveda, 1972). Finally, a reduced crime victimization rate (specifically for women and the elderly) is considered to be a function of fear of victimization—fear creates precautionary behaviors, which, in turn, reduce the rate of victimization (Baumer, 1978).

In addition to these substantive issues, three methodological issues have been raised. The first addresses the significance of criminal victimization. Those who conduct surveys using carefully drawn samples and forced-choice questions conclude that crime is not "salient" (significant) to those interviewed. The respondents do not readily recall incidents of victimization, which suggests that "most criminal incidents were not among the most salient events in the lives of victims—as compared, say with births, deaths, illnesses, marriages, job changes, draft calls, auto accidents and a myriad other happenings that fill lives" (Biderman, et al., 1967: 158–59). Albert Reiss, who directed the other survey sponsored by the President's Commission on Law Enforcement and the Administration of Justice, came to the same conclusion (1967: 142–48). This low "salience" was found even for victimizations that are serious *legally* (Biderman, et al., 1967: 33).

Providers of victim services and researchers who use indepth interviews rather than forced-choice questionnaires, on the other hand, find that victimization has a lasting and often profound effect on victims. This is said to be the case even if they are unharmed and suffer only minor financial loss. "They feel violated and become wary and suspicious of strangers" (Barkas, 1978: 149). Fischer and her associates interviewed 50 victims of assault, seeking to understand the impact of victimization on the victim. She concluded "the trauma of victimization is not only deeper than distress over physical loss, but deeper even than fearfulness of further victimization. Most radically traumatized is the victim's sense of community. The social order of one's immediate world has been disrupted. Everyday faith in shared values, continuity, and control over one's life has been undercut. Reciprocity among citizens is no longer taken for granted" (1984: 167–68).

The second methodological issue is that survey methodology, while uncovering much previously unreported crime, will itself produce underreporting when (1) disclosure would act to embarrass the victim, (2) victimization involves a relative or acquaintance, (3) the victim contributes to the victimization, and (4) the event is not clearly defined as criminal (Skogan, 1976: 135–36).

A third methodological issue is raised by advocates for the elderly, who consider the surveys defective because they fail to include questions about crimes that they believe affect the elderly more than other age groups—crimes such as fraud, confidence games, medical quackery, and harrassment by teenagers (Malinchak and Wright, 1978: 14).

DISCUSSION AND SUGGESTIONS FOR FURTHER RESEARCH

While not saying so in print, the advocates for both sides tend to agree more than they disagree regarding the issues that appear to divide them. They take positions that remind one of the blind men placed at different points around an elephant and asked to guess what it was. Understanderably, they came to different conclusions. Like the blind men, the advocates in this debate, who seek to gain, maintain, or shift funds from one service program to another, emphasize interpretations of the data that support their position and denigrate or ignore those that don't.

To the neutral observer, however, the research leads to several conclusions:

1. Elderly victimization rates, while low in most categories of crime, are higher in some.
2. Victimization rates vary for different age groups by locale within the United States.
3. Elderly victimization, as a proportion of all criminal victimization, is less than that for other age groups.
4. Elderly fears of victimization may be irrational, but there is a high probability that they are based on realistic interpretations of the likelihood of victimization for certain crimes.

The recent work of Stafford and Galle (1984) lends credence to this view. In their study of personal-property crime in Chicago, they created an adjusted exposure to risk rate of victimization (measured as weekday hours spent away from home). Two of their conclusions are pertinent here: (1) fear of crime parallels the rate of victimization when adjusted for exposure, and (2) victimization declines with age, except for black males. This pioneering study will undoubtedly be replicated and the measure of exposure to risk refined. Advocates for the elderly will most certainly engage in such research to bolster their claims that fear of victimization among the elderly is rational and that victimization is greater than the raw data suggest.

Our data sources do not allow us to come to any firm conclusions regarding the other issues reviewed—for example, the impact of crime and the fear of crime. Too few studies regarding the effects of victimization have been done to warrant any definitive statements and the information available is not specific to this research need. That is, the research methodologies have not gathered data regarding several variables, such as health, that would help us understand their behaviors. Surveys tell us that the elderly—more than other age group—do not go out at night, but they don't provide enough information to determine why. The elderly may restrict their movements because of fear of crime, but also because of poor health or the desire to spend more time at home.

We do not know the extent to which victims recover medical costs and property losses through insurance and replacement by private persons and social service agencies, which would help in assessing the relative cost of victimization by various social categories. There are few studies, such as Fischer's, of the psychological impact of victimization. Most data come in the form of anecdotal information gathered during interviews with victims. We have no information regarding the way in which the elderly (victims and nonvictims alike) seek to protect themselves from crime, other than the standard survey questions asking if they have installed dead-bolt locks or bought a gun. There is nothing in the literature that expressly traces the path between fear of crime and the behaviors of the elderly. Phenomenological research has yet to gain the same acceptance as survey research.

The three methodological issues have not been addressed and need to be examined. Our society tends to focus on violent crime and burglary, and thus we know little about such crimes as fraud and confidence games. We do not know if the survey type of interview is capable of determining the salience of crime. The interview setting may not be appropriate. That is, victims may prefer to conceal their states of mind regarding victimization from strangers. Alternatively, the event may have been so traumatic that the victim prefers to keep it buried, rather than chance the emotional effect continued examination might produce. The brief survey interview may not provide sufficient time to explore the emotional content of victimization.

The victimization of the elderly by relatives is a vast unchartered field. What little information we have in this regard comes from some few surveys of agencies that serve the elderly. This particular victimization is not readily revealed by the methodologies so far employed. That is, surveys that interview elderly respondents in their homes, with the rest of the family present, are not conducive to the disclosure that the son is physically abusing the father or stealing from the mother's purse. The extant research has one additional flaw: it ignores one of the largest and fastest growing minorities in the United States, Mexican-Americans.

There is, in addition, one further issue not explicitly discussed, though implicit in much of the literature reviewed: the level of elderly criminal victimization society will tolerate. That is, the degree of victimization acceptable as "normal" has not been established. It is an issue embedded in one's value system, much like toleration of unemployment, poverty, and other indicators of social inequality. Geis argues that *any* criminal victimization of the elderly is too much: "I think the old have earned and do deserve special protection. I think they ought to be left alone by exploiters and by people who set out to hurt them. . . . They need to be allowed to muster and to retain as much dignity as they can achieve in their last years" (1977: 7–8).

A reduction in elderly criminal victimization can be achieved in a number of ways. The level of crime itself may be reduced, which would benefit the elderly as well as all other categories of society. This, however, is no easy task. "Law and order" has been a popular political issue throughout history. Attempts to reduce crime in the United States have not been noticeably successful. Billions of dollars spent on all aspects of the judicial system under the auspices of the LEAA had less impact on the crime rate than the passage of the baby-boom generation from youth to middle age.

Victimization can also be reduced to some extent by the potential victims themselves. This is the approach typically taken by the police and others who urge individuals to install dead-bolt locks and stay away from dark streets at night. This approach is consistent with the American ideology of individualism and individual responsibility for one's fate, exemplified by the "blaming the victim" thesis.

A third approach to the reduction of victimization is supported by Butler (1975) and other activists for the elderly, who urge that government and public alike create an environment that is safe for the elderly. Their approach pits them against reformers who argue that crime, particularly property crime, is a function of poverty and that elimination of the underlying causes of property crime will result in the reduction of criminal victimization of the elderly *and* blacks. Geis's plea is clearly not being heard or, if heard, ignored.

One final note. No one has as yet sat down and discussed these issues with the elderly in a systematic way—devoting the time necessary to allow them to fully develop their thoughts about crime. The issues reviewed are too complex to be examined through the standard forced-choice questionnaire and too sensitive to be explored in an interview that lasts only minutes. Existing studies of victims are also defective, because crime and the fear of crime affect nonvictims as well. Both need to be allowed to express themselves. However, only the elderly can explain how crime affects their lives. Surrogates cannot respond for the elderly, nor tell us their thoughts, feelings, and behaviors. The time has come to let the elderly speak for themselves, within a research framework that allows full and complete discussion of the impact crime and the fear of crime have on their lives.

REFERENCES

Allen, H. E. et al. 1981. *Crime and punishment: An introduction to criminology.* New York: Free Press.

Atunes, et al. 1977. Patterns of personal crime against the elderly. *Gerontologist* 17:321–27.

Balkin, S. 1979. Victimization rates, safety and fear of crime. *Social Problems* 26:343–58.

Bard, M., and D. Sangrey. 1979. *The crime victims.* New York: Basic Books.

Barkas, J. L. 1978. *Victims.* New York: Charles Scribner's Sons.

Barrow, G. M., and P. A. Smith. 1979. *Aging, agism, and society.* New York: West Publishing.

Baumer, T. 1978. Research on fear of crime in the U.S. *Victimology* 3:254–64.

Biderman, A. D. et al. 1967. *Report on a pilot study in the District of Columbia on victimization and attitudes toward law enforcement.* Washington, D.C.: Bureau of Social Science Research.

Bild, B., and R. Havighurst. 1976. Senior citizens in great cities: The case of Chicago. *Gerontologist* 16: part 2.

Block, R. 1977. *Violent crime: Environment, interaction, and death.* Lexington, Mass.: Lexington Books.

Block, C. R., and R. Block. 1984. Crime definition, crime measurement, and victim surveys. *Journal of Social Issues* 40 (1): 137–60.

Brooks, J. 1974. The fear of crime in the United States. *Crime and Delinquency* 20: 241–44.

Butler, R. 1975. *Why survive? Being old in America.* New York: Harper & Row.

Clemente, F., and M. B. Kleiman. 1976. Fear of crime among the aged. *Gerontologist* 16:207–10.

Cohen, L. E., R. K. Kluegel, and K. C. Land. 1981. Social inequality and criminal victimization. *American Sociological Review* 46:505–24.

Cocklin, J. E. 1976. Robbery, the elderly, and fear: An urban problem in search of solution. In J. and S. S. Goldsmith (eds.), *Crime and the elderly.* Lexington, Mass.: Lexington Books.

Cook, F. L., and T. D. Cook. 1976. Evaluating the rhetoric of crisis: A case study of criminal victimization of the elderly. *Social Service Review* 50:632–46.

Cook, et al. 1978. Criminal victimization of the elderly: The physical and economic consequences. *Gerontologist* 18:338–49.

Cunningham, C. L. 1976. Pattern and effect of crime against the aging: The Kansas City study. In J. and S. S. Goldsmith (eds.) *Crime and the elderly.* Lexington, Mass.: Lexington Books.

Ennis, P. H. 1967. Criminal victimization in the United States: A report of a national survey. President's Commission on Law Enforcement and the Administration of Justice. Field Surveys II. Washington, D.C.: Government Printing Office.

Erskine, H. 1974. The polls: Fear of violence and crime. *Public Opinion Quarterly* 38:131–45.

Faris, J. B. 1978. Introduction. *Aging,* March–April facing p. 1.

Fischer, C. T. 1984. A phenomenological study of being criminally victimized: Contributions and constraints of qualitative research. *Journal of Social Issues* 40 (1):161–78.

Friedman, D. M. 1976. A service model for elderly crime victims. In J. and S. S. Goldsmith (eds.). *Crime and the elderly.* Lexington, Mass.: Lexington Books.

Geis, G. 1977. The terrible indignity: Crime against the elderly. In M. A. Y. Rifai (ed.), *Justice and the older Americans.* Lexington, Mass.: Lexington Books.

Hall, J. 1952. *Theft, law, and society.* Indianapolis: Bobbs-Merrill.

Harris, L. et al. 1975. *The myth and reality of aging in America.* Washington, D.C.: National Council on Aging.

Hindelang, M. J., M. R. Gottfredson, and J. Garofalo. 1978. *Victims of personal crime: An empirical foundation for a theory of personal victimization.* Cambridge, Mass.: Ballinger Publishing Co.

Hochstedler, E. 1981. *Crime against the elderly in 26 cities.* U.S. Department of Justice, Bureau of Justice Statistics. Washington, D.C.: Government Printing Office.

Jaycox, V. 1978. The elderly's fear of crime: Rational or irrational? *Victimology* 3:329–34.

Lawton, M. P. 1980–81. Crime, victimization, and the fortitude of the aged. *Aged Care and Services Review* 2:20–31.

Lindquist, J. H., and J. M. Duke. 1982. The elderly victim at risk: Explaining the fear-victimization paradox. *Criminology* 20:115–26.
Malinchak, A. A., and D. Wright. 1978. The scope of elderly victimization. *Aging*, March–April: 11–16.
McDonald, W. F. 1976. Criminal justice and the victim: An introduction. In W. F. McDonald (ed.), *Criminal justice and the victim*. Beverly Hills, Ca.: Sage Publications.
McPherson, M. 1978. Realities and perceptions of crime at the neighborhood level. *Victimology* 3: 319–28.
Midwest Research Institute. 1977. *Crimes against the aging: Patterns and prevention*. Kansas City, Mo.
Poveda, T. G. 1972. The fear of crime in a small town. *Crime and Delinquency* 18:147–53.
Reiff, R. 1979. *The invisible victim: The criminal justice system's forgotten responsibility*. New York: Basic Books.
Reiss, A. J., Jr. 1967. *Studies in crime and law enforcement in major metropolitan areas*. President's Commission on Law Enforcement and the Administration of Justice. Washington, D.C.: Government Printing Office.
Skogan, W. G. 1976. The victims of crime: Some national survey findings. In A. L. Guenther (ed.), *Criminal behavior and social systems: Contributions of American sociology*, 2nd ed. Chicago: Rand McNally.
Stafford, M. C., and O. R. Galle. 1984. Victimization rates, exposure to risk, and fear of crime. *Criminology* 22:173–85.
Stein, J. H. 1981. Victim crisis intervention: An evaluation proposal. In S. E. Salasin (ed.), *Evaluating victim services*. Beverly Hills, Cal.: Sage Publications.
Sunderland, G. 1978. National organizations launch crime prevention programs. *Aging*, March–April:32–34.
Thomas, C. W., and J. M. Hyman. 1977. Perceptions of crime, fear of victimization, and public perceptions of police performance. *Journal of Police Science and Administration* 5:305–17.
U.S. Department of Justice. 1981. Bureau of Justice Statistics. Bulletin, Crime and the Elderly. Washington, D.C.: Government Printing Office.
U.S. Congress. 1976. Subcommittee on Housing and Consumer Interests of the Select Committee on Aging. House of Representatives, Ninety-Fourth Congress. Second Session. *Elderly crime victims: Personal accounts of fear and attacks*. Held September 18, 1976, in Los Angeles. Washington, D.C.: Government Printing Office.
———. 1977. Subcommittee on Housing and Consumer Interests of the Select Committee on Aging, House of Representatives, Ninety-Fifth Congress, First Session. *In search of security: A national perspective on elderly crime victimization*. Washington, D.C.: Government Printing Office.
———. 1959. Subcommittee on Problems of the Aged and Aging of the Committee on Labor and Public Welfare. United States Senate, 86th Congress. First Session. *A survey of major problems and solutions in the field of aged and aging*. Washington, D.C.: Government Printing Office.

Elderly Felons: Dispositions of Arrests

JOHN H. LINDQUIST, D. Soc. Sci.

Professor
Department of Sociology
Trinity University
San Antonio, Texas

O. Z. WHITE, Ph.D.
Professor
Department of Sociology
Trinity University
San Antonio, Texas

CARL D. CHAMBERS, Ph.D.

Professor
Health Services Administration
School of Health and Sport Sciences
College of Health and Human Services
Ohio University
Athens, Ohio

INTRODUCTION

In this chapter we present an examination of the disposition of arrested felony offenders categorized as "elderly" and "nonelderly." We use what many see as the now-conventional definition of "elderly offenders," those 55 and over, as suggested by Shichor and Kobrin (1978).

We were not suprised that we found only one research paper and no published reports dealing with the processing of elderly offenders by prosecutors and courts. Given the lack of research (see Newman and Newman, 1984) on other aspects of elderly offenders, we had no reason to believe that this area would be more heavily researched. There is, however, an additional reason why we expected to find few published research reports: the data necessary for such analyses are extremely difficult to obtain. Given the small amount of crime by the elderly that is reported (Shichor, 1984), one needs large numbers of cases in order to do anything more than a very superficial analysis. Research on prisoners or arrestees is relatively easy to conduct because data are more or less readily available. That is, a fairly small number of state and federal prisons and their centralized bureaucracies collect and disseminate fairly detailed statistical information that researchers can use in their studies of prisoners. Since 1964 (Keller and Vedder, 1968), the Uniform Crime Report has broken down its previously collapsed older-age categories, which had hitherto presented data on all older offenders in a single category (age 50 and over), into five-year categories to age 65. This has facilitated the use of the data contained in these reports.

It is much more difficult to examine the disposition of cases by both the criminal prosecutors and the courts. Our criminal justice system, notorious for lacking organization, divides processing and record keeping among its constituent elements and among the political units into which the United States is divided. Thus, while data regarding arrests and prisoners are available prosecutorial and judicial decisions are not. No single agency collects information on the way prosecutors or trial courts dispose of cases. To conduct research regarding these portions of the criminal justice system, one must examine the files contained in the office of each prosecutor and each court. This situation is made even more difficult because data needed for analysis are normally available only as judicial files, maintained on the bases of individual case folders, stored away in the offices of judges (in those cases in which the offender has been sentenced to probation) or in dead storage. In either event one must examine each file individually in order to reconstruct the events that make up each case. Such reconstructions are extremely time-consuming.

Computerized record-keeping systems specifically designed for various political jurisdictions of the criminal justice systems of the United States are few and far between. Fortunately for us, a Law Enforcement Administration Agency grant supported the development of a computerized record-keeping system for the Bexar County (Texas) Criminal Justice System. These computer files represent a complete record of every event (arrest, warrant, motion, etc.) that takes place as an arrested person moves through the system. Input is provided by the San Antonio Police Department (the largest metropolitan area in Bexar

County), the Bexar County Sheriff's Department, the Bexar County District Attorney (prosecuting attorney), and the Bexar County District Courts (trial courts). Thus, the entire judicial record for each person arrested in or in any way processed by the various elements of the Bexar County Criminal Justice System is available on computer tape. Each event in a case is physically recorded (required papers are filed in a record jacket) and the event is simultaneously entered into the computer system. Without this computerized system, we could never have been able to undertake the research reported here.

The only other research similar to ours that we discovered was conducted by Donald Bachand (1983), who examined the dismissals of Part I offenses by the police and prosecutors of Detroit, Michigan. His research covered all persons arrested by the police in 1981, those whose cases were forwarded to the prosecutor by the police, and those whose cases were terminated by the police within their own department. (He did not do a separate analysis for police and prosecutor dismissals.) Bachand concluded that the elderly are treated more leniently than are younger arrestees, because they have their cases dismissed at a statistically higher rate. Our research differs from his; we examined the disposition process by the prosecutors and the courts, but not by the police. We examined all cases that reached the district attorney's office but none of the cases the police themselves dismissed.

DATA AND METHOD

In the judicial files of the Bexar County District Courts for the period between September 1975 and August 1977, we examined all cases for which prosecution was being considered by the district attorney. During this two-year period, 3,923 offenses were processed, of which 85 were committed by persons 55 and over (2.2 percent of the total). The oldest offender was 81. In this research we examined only Part I offenses; a later paper will examine misdemeanors.

We used age as the independent variable, dichotomized as "under 55" and "55 and over," and each aspect of the dispositional process as dependent variables. The dependent variables were therefore: (1) type of Part I offense (dichotomized as violent and nonviolent); (2) case rejected by the prosecutor; (3) case no-billed by the grand jury; (4) case dismissed by the prosecutor; (5) trial result; (6) sentence length; and (7) sentence type (probation or prison term). The numbers found in the tables vary as a result of missing data.

FINDINGS

Elderly offenders processed by the Bexar County Criminal Justice System are typically more violent than are younger offenders. Their Part I offenses are almost evenly divided between violent (40) and nonviolent (45) offenses. Younger offenders are much more likely to be arrested for a nonviolent than a violent crime. Only about 1 in 4 of the younger, but nearly one-half the elderly arrestees are charged with a violent crime. This is a statistically significant difference.

TABLE 1
Age and Type of Offense

Type of Offense	Under 55		55 and Over		
	No.	%	No.	%	Totals
Violent	965	25.1	40	47.1	1005
Nonviolent	2873	74.9	45	52.9	2918
Totals	3838	100.0	85	100.0	3923

X^2 = 20.96 with 1df, p < .05

*All tables are for the Bexar County (Texas) Criminal Justice System, 1973–1978.

At most of the steps in the prosecutorial and judicial processes, elderly offenders are treated differently. We examined three aspects of the process controlled by the district attorney: outright rejection of the case (refusal to carry forward a case presented for prosecution); being no-billed by the grand jury; and having the case dismissed by a formal motion to the court of jurisdiction for a particular case. Dismissals are sought for a variety of reasons: refusal of complainant to come forward; death of a major actor in the case; plea bargaining (dismissal of the present case and the entering of a guilty plea to a lesser-included offense); refusal of a jurisdiction seeking the arrest and extradition of an individual to transport the offender back to the jurisdiction holding the warrant; and transferral to another jurisdiction (dismissal of a charge in order that the individual may be prosecuted by another jurisdiction). We examined three events that take place within the jurisdiction of the courts: the trial outcomes, length of sentence of those convicted, and type of sentence (probation or prison).

TABLE 2
Age by Disposition by District Attorney (D. A.) and Courts

Dispositions	Under 55		55 and Over		Totals
	No.	%	No.	%	
Rejected by D. A.	1088	28.3	32	37.6	1125
No-billed	245	6.4	12	14.1	257
Dismissed by court	391	10.2	8	9.4	399
Tried, not guilty	41	1.1	3	3.5	44
Tried, guilty	1662	43.3	19	22.4	1681
Pending	411	10.7	11	13.0	422
Totals	3838	100.0	85	100.0	3923

In two of these processes within the prosecutors' jurisdiction, elderly arrestees received favorable treatment (were not prosecuted) when we compare their outcomes with those of persons under 55. The elderly had a one-third greater chance of having their case rejected by the prosecutors—that is, of having the prosecutors refuse to present the case to the grand jury. Also, the elderly, compared to those under 55, have twice the chance of having their cases no-billed by the grand jury. The third process within the jurisdiction of the prosecutors—dismissals—shows very little difference between those under and over 55. The nonelderly arrestees have an 8 percent greater chance of having their cases dismissed than do the elderly.

There is a public perception that the criminal justice system is "soft" on persons brought before the courts. If one means by "soft" that every person tried does not get a long prison term or the death penalty, perhaps the courts can be said to be "soft" on offenders. However, if "soft" means that the person tried typically walks out of the court a free person, the courts of Bexar County, Texas, are far from soft. During the period we examined, 1,725 persons were tried in these courts. Of these, 1,681 were found guilty of the crime for which they were charged. Only 44 persons were found not guilty; 41 were under 55 and three were 55 and over. Though we have very few cases for comparison, the elderly are more likely to walk out of the court free than are younger defendants. However, we cannot overlook the fact that elderly *and* younger defendants are more likely to be found guilty than not guilty once they go to trial.

TABLE 3
Age by Cases Rejected, No-Billed and Dismissed
and Tried before Court

Dispositions	Under 55		55 and Over		
	No.	%	No.	%	Totals
Rejected, No-billed Dismissed	1724	50.3	52	70.3	1776
Trial before court	1703	49.7	22	29.7	1725
Totals	3427	100.0	74	100.0	3501

X^2 = 11.55 with ldf, p <.05

*Excludes cases still pending.

Younger defendants (98 percent) are almost certain to be found guilty (as is well known, the bulk of these verdicts are prearranged pleas) while the elderly have a 1 in 6 chance of going free. In this examination of two of the constituent parts of the criminal justice system, prosecution and adjudication, we found that the elderly fared much better at the hands of prosecutors than at the hands of judges. The public courtroom is a more dangerous place for the elderly than are the not-so-public offices inhabited by prosecutors. Over 70 percent of the cases involving elderly defendants never see the courtroom, compared to less than 55 percent of the cases in which the defendant is under age 55. This is a statistically significant difference.

If we add "not guilty" verdicts to previously discussed actions that resulted in the freeing of the defendants, the elderly obtain "lenient" treatment (to use Bachand's term) nearly 75 percent of the time their cases get past the police and into the prosecutors' and judges' hands, while younger defendants receive "lenient" treatment only 51 percent of the time. That is, in 75 percent of the cases, elderly defendants have their cases rejected by the district attorney, are no-billed by the grand jury, have their cases dismissed by court order, or are found not guilty by the courts, while only half the younger defendants attain these results.

Following a guilty verdict, the court (judge or jury) must decide length of sentence to be served and whether the sentence will be served under supervision of a probation office or a corrections officer.

TABLE 4
Age by Length of Sentence

Sentence in Years	Under 55		55 and Over		Totals
	No.	%	No.	%	
1–10	1448	90.2	12	80.0	1460
11–20	126	7.8	3	20.0	129
21–30	21	1.4	0	0	21
31–40	7	0.4	0	0	7
41–99	4	0.2	0	0	4
Totals	1606	100.0	15	100.0	1621

*When collapsed into 2×2 table, i.e., 1–10 and 11 + years, X^2 = .02 with ldf, p>.05.

There are some notable differences between the length of sentence assessed against the elderly and the nonelderly, but they are not statistically significant. We discovered that elderly felons received fewer sentences in the 1- to 10-year category than did the nonelderly (10 years is the maximum sentence one can receive in Texas and still be placed on probation) and more in the 11- to 20-year range. Only 32 defendants received sentences in excess of 20 years; none of them were elderly. We have too few cases to analyze these data, unless the data are collapsed into a two-by-two table—age by sentences of 1 to 10 years and sentences of 11 and more years. When this is done, the differences are found to be statistically nonsignificant. The fact remains, however, that elderly defendants receive shorter sentences than younger defendants.

The last aspect of the dispositional process we examined was the type of sentence served. Here the differences are even less noticeable. Nine of the elderly (60 percent) and 863 of the younger defendants (53.2 percent) were sentenced to serve their time in prison. Six of the elderly (40 percent) and 758 of the younger felons (46.8 percent) were given probation by the courts. These differences were not statistically significant.

TABLE 5
Age and Type of Sentence

Type of Sentence	Under 55		55 and Over		
	No.	%	No.	%	Totals
Prison	863	53.2	9	60.0	872
Probation	758	46.8	6	40.0	764
Totals	1621	100.0	15	100.0	1636

X^2 = .03 with 1df, p <.05

DISCUSSION

Two fundamental problems confront those who seek to conduct research on elderly criminal offenders. There is the paucity of research, both published and unpublished, and little agreement as to just what age should be used to define the elderly offender.

Little has changed regarding research into elderly criminality since Pollak wrote: "Old criminals offer an ugly picture and it seems as if scientists do not like to look at it for any considerable amount of time. . . . Criminologists have touched the problem of old age criminality only occasionally and if so, very briefly" (1941:213).

The problems created by the lack of research are confounded by a lack of agreement as to just what ages the term "elderly" represents. While we and others (e.g., Shichor and Kobrin, 1978; Shichor, 1984: Goetting, 1984; Bachand, 1983; Newman and Newman, 1984; Cohen, 1984) accept age 55 as the dividing line, there is no unanimity in this regard. Shichor and Kobrin originally suggested 55 as the appropriate age to define the "elderly" criminal, based on the sharp decline in criminal behavior at this age, as indicated by the FBI Uniform Crime Report (Shichor and Kobrin, 1978; Rubenstein, 1984). Other researchers, examining other issues and other data sources, have come to use an age other than 55.

These differences both precede and follow Shichor and Kobrin's 1978 attempt to bring rationality to the definition of the elderly criminal. This suggests that factors inherent within the research process are at work to produce varying definitions. If this is the case, we will be plagued with these differences and the problems they impose for the foreseeable future. Research on prisoners, the relationship between the police and citizens, a study of homicide, and a general study of crime and the elderly illustrate this problem.

With the exception of Goetting, researchers often use ages other than 55. Schroeder (1936), studying prisoners in the Illinois state prison, used the median age (40) as the watershed dividing elderly from nonelderly. Teller and Howell (1981) examined prisoners in the Utah state prison, using 50 as the age when prisoners became "older." Vedder and Keller (1968) also used age 50 in their study of Illinois state prison to define the "older offender." They argued that previous criminological research and the 1964 Uniform Crime Report, which showed a decline in crime after that age, made this the appropriate age. Vedder (Adams and Vedder, 1961) previously had published results of a 12-year study of the Florida state prison population, in which age 50 was used to divide the older from the younger prisoners.

Studies of police contacts with citizens, published by Smith and Visher (1981) and Visher (1983), who made use of the same data base, set age categories of under 19, 19 to 35, and over 35. While they provided no particular rationale for this division, an examination of the data suggests that they roughly divided the data into thirds. Malinchak (1980), in his chapter on elderly crime, cited statistics presented by the police department of St. Petersburg and Jacksonville, Florida. Both of these police departments used age 60 when describing crimes of the elderly. Willbanks and Murphy (1984), in their analysis of homicide data, also used age 60 to divide the elderly from the nonelderly. They chose this age because it corresponded to census categories, and they were thus able to use census data in their analysis. In their wide-ranging examination of crime by the aged in Israel, Bergman and Amir (1973) also chose age 60 to define the "aged" criminal.

These differences make straightforward comparisons of results obtained by different researchers impossible. The differences result from research problems inherent in the data or the research methods and techniques. With no theoretically based rationale urging the use of any particular age, these differences will not likely disappear. Even broad comparisons of results are not easy to make. That is, we must ask if it is legitimate to make use of conclusions drawn from a study of age and crime in which the top age group includes all age 35 and older (Smith and Visher, 1981) in a study of the disposition of offenders by prosecutors and courts in which elderly offenders are defined as age 55 and older. Our inability to make comparisons and seek positive or negative evidence from others is also a given when the field of research itself is new and "uncluttered" by numerous research reports. That is, we report here on a subject that has not yet been examined by other researchers in the same fashion that we chose to use for our analysis. Bachand's work (1983) comes the closest to ours, but still reports on a different population and a different, though similar, dispositional set of variables.

Again and again, as we reviewed the research pertaining to elderly felony offenders, we found expressions of surprise, on the part of the writers, at the amount of violent crime committed by elderly offenders (Shichor and Kobrin, 1978: 214; Cohen, 1984: 122). Perhaps this is a function of the literature about elderly criminals and an artifact of our cultural expectations regarding the aged—expectations rooted in the stereotypes of the aged in our society (see Barrow and Smith, 1979, for a discussion of stereotypes of the aged). As Newman and Newman point out in their recent examination of elderly crime as a policy issue (1984: 226): "It is unlikely that elderly crime will ever be seen as a large problem requiring emergency measures and quick solutions." Elderly offenders are not seen as a serious problem, because they represent only a fraction of the felony offenders (Vedder and Keller, 1968: 15) and make up a very small proportion of the prison population (Teller and Howell, 1981: 549). This lack of criminal activity per se is translated into noninvolvement in violent crime by some who are not themselves engaged directly in research involving elderly offenders. In a review of elderly criminals prepared for a medical audience, for example, Rodstein (1975: 639) wrote: "Old people do not usually commit the more violent types of crimes." While this is technically true, it leaves the impression that the crimes of the elderly are usually nonviolent. Some others, while recognizing the fact that the elderly engage in some acts of violence, assert that "in general the pattern of offenses by the aged resembles that of female criminality, the crimes tending to be petty, conniving and passive in type. Exceptions are acts of violence against family members arising out of jealousy or defense of authority or against public officials, especially welfare bureaucrats" (Bergman and Amir, 1973: 152).

The existence of elderly violent crime was both highlighted and obscured by early research in state prisons. This research pointed out that elderly prisoners, more often than younger prisoners, were incarcerated for violent crimes. This did not appear to alert succeeding researchers to the extent of violence that they should expect to find as they began to examine age and crime. This may have been due to the lack of specificity regarding the age of the elderly criminals. For example, Schroeder (1936) clearly states that the elderly are more often than younger prisoners sentenced for violent crimes. But he defined the elderly as age 40 and over. This does not necessarily cause one to expect men 55, 60, and 65 years old to be more violent in their criminal activity than men of 20, 25, or 30. Fox (1946) reported the mean ages of offenders, by offense, of those committed to the Michigan prison. He then categorized offenses according to a statistical test into those that are undifferentiated by the age of the offender, those committed more by older than younger prisoners, and those committed more by younger than older prisoners. Six crimes were committed more by younger persons, 17 were undifferentiated by age, and 12 were committed more by older than younger offenders. But the mean age (with no standard deviation given) of violent offenders does not lead one to expect them to be what one ordinarily thinks of as "elderly." The mean age of those convicted for aggravated assault was 36.8; for homicide, 36.1; and for rape, 35.5 (Fox, 1946: 150). All three of these crimes were among the 12 Fox said were committed more by elderly than nonelderly offenders. Robbery, the fourth crime the Uniform Crime Report includes as a violent offense, was committed more by younger prisoners than by older ones; the mean age for these offenders was 28.7. Fox, in using the median age of 40 as the dividing line between older and younger offenders, does not provide the reader with a firm and stable definition of "elderly." This tends to obscure his findings on the offenses they committed.

The work of Adams and Vedder, using age 50 to define older prisoners, however, made quite explicit what Schroeder and Fox had left unclear. In their report on a study of 12 years of prisoners of the Florida state prison they wrote, "Crimes of violence such as manslaughter, homicide, murder, and sex crimes of all sorts have an incidence in the older group about twice that of the general prison population" (1961: 180).

Our finding—that 47 percent of elderly offenders and 25 percent of younger offenders are arrested for violent crimes—fits into the work previously reported. Perhaps the time has come for us to accept the reality of violence among elderly criminals and to develop explanations of this phenomenon. Some attempts have already been made. Malinchak seeks to explain crime on the part of the elderly as a response to "personal, economic, and psychological pressures which persuade the elderly to engage in criminal behavior" (1980: 152). Some 25 years before, Moberg had suggested much the same thing when he tied crime by the elderly to frustration and emotional tension. They are, he said, (1952, 768): "frustrated socially, economically, and psychologically."

A physiological connection between crime and the elderly was suggested by Pollak, who wrote long before Alzheimer's disease had received any attention. "There is no doubt that the physiological changes in old age have a great deal to do with the criminality of the aged. Changes in the blood vessels and brain cells as well as senile effects upon the sex glands certainly play a role in the causation of many crimes by aged offenders" (1941: 230). The fact that elderly offenders are often first offenders has been known for some time. Pollak pointed out (1941: 231) that German studies of elderly sex offenders (age 70 and over) found that over 70 percent of them were first offenders. Teller and Howell, in their study of prison inmates in Utah, found that the elderly offender "started in crime at a later age than did the young. . . . However, once he did start, he had a greater number of rap entries . . . and was incarcerated more times" (1981: 552). As Newman and Newman argue (1984: 226), we need to produce a public policy response to the challenge of the elderly first offender who, as our data and that of others show, is almost as likely to be as violent as a nonviolent offender. We need also to develop explanations of this phenomenon.

As we examined the various dispositional decisions made by prosecutors and courts, we had to conclude that our criminal justice system seems to prefer not to treat elderly offenders rather than to bring them within the system. There appears to be a pattern in this. Our examination of the decisions made by the prosecutors and judges showed clearly that prosecutors prefer not to carry cases forward to the grand jury when they involve elderly defendants. Nor did they or the grand juries (we cannot tell which) appear to desire to carry cases brought to the grand juries forward to the courts. It is evident that decisions made in the privacy of the district attorney's office and behind the closed doors of the grand jury room tend to favor elderly defendants more than they do their younger counterparts. This same pattern seems to be followed by the police, as reported by researchers. That is, leniency is not unique to prosecutors and grand juries. There is, however, less age-related research regarding police lenience. Visher (1983: 15) found that age produced preferential treatment for females but not males. But she did not specifically study elderly persons who came into contact with police. Rather, she examined three age categories, with 35 and older being used as the elderly group. Bachand argues, "The literature on police discretion supports the hypothesis that the criminal justice system affords the elderly preferential treatment in pre-arrest situations" (1983: 8). On the other hand, Fyfe argues that the police need even more discretion to divert incompetent elderly offenders from the criminal justice system to social welfare agencies. He believes that the pressure of the complainant who seeks an arrest and the "inflexibility of the prescribed arrest process [i.e., fingerprint, book, hold for magistrate decision] may subject elderly offenders to the trauma of detention prior to court appearances that accomplish nothing [e.g., magistrate refuses to process and refers to social agency]. What may be needed is relaxation of the rule that only prosecutors and judges may decline to handle cases involving obviously incompetent defendants" (1984: 107).

The police may find themselves in a difficult position vis-à-vis elderly offenders, partly because they have no specific training as to just how to proceed when confronted by this group. As Fyfe points out, the police of New York City are trained to interact with such groups as drunks, violent demonstrators, minorities, and juveniles but "nowhere does this text [police training manual] discuss police interaction with elderly offenders" (1984: 97). With no training, they are left, as Bachand (1983: 4–5) suggests, to rely on community standards and societal norms. At the same time, this lack of training specific to the elderly offender means that general departmental rules apply when complainants demand an arrest. This suggests to us that when the police are free to use their own discretion when confronted by an elderly offender (i.e., have no vocal complainant present), they will proceed much as the district attorney did in the cases we examined—they will turn loose as many as they can.

We had too few cases to say conclusively that elderly defendants are treated more leniently when tried for their offenses than are younger defendants. But the fact that only 2 percent of younger compared to nearly 14 percent of older defendants are found not guilty suggests leniency. We need to examine this assumption again using a larger data base to make sure that this is not a random event. It is consistent, however, with our findings regarding leniency by the district attorney and what others believe is leniency by police. Most trials are conducted in semiprivate; seldom does anyone other than the family of the defendant and a few courthouse groupies attend. Most cases do not involve a jury. The judge is thus able to dispense justice in relative privacy, using the discretion inherent in the office. The result, as we saw in the data presented, is that while the bulk of the elderly are found guilty, they are more likely than younger defendants to be found nonguilty.

After a guilty verdict is reached, however, the degree of discretion allowed to the actors in the criminal justice system, while still great, is greatly reduced. As we saw in the data on sentencing, elderly offenders receive sentences similar in length to those meted out to younger offenders, with one exception: only younger offenders received sentences of over 20 years. It is not that the elderly do not commit crimes that result in long sentences when committed by younger offenders, but younger offenders pay a higher price for their actions than do the elderly. For example, during the 3½-year period under study, 4 of 5 persons convicted of homicide or manslaughter were 55 and over. All elderly felons convicted of these crimes received sentences of no more than 10 years; 33 of the younger felons received this sentence. But, 9 younger felons were sentenced to serve from 11 to 20 years, and the rest (5) were sentenced to from 21 to 99 years. We need a larger data base to pursue this issue. We simply did not have enough convicted elderly offenders to make conclusive statements about sentence length.

We also lack sufficient cases to warrant definitive conclusions on the imprisonment of elderly offenders. Our data show that there is no statistical difference between them and younger offenders as to whether they receive probation or a prison sentence. However, they do show that the elderly are more likely than younger defendants to be given a prison sentence rather than probation. But, with only 15 elderly convictions, only four more in the probation category would turn this ratio around.

Nearly a decade ago Shichor and Kobrin suggested that, while there was little information available for one to conclude that elderly offenders are treated leniently by the criminal justice system, "there may be good reason to expect that they are differently treated" (1978: 216). Our data and that of Bachand (1983) provide empirical evidence that supports their conclusion. Newman and Newman ask, "Is there something inherently different about elderly offenders that merits special consideration in criminal proceedings?" (1984: 229). We do not know why the elderly receive special treatment, but we are convinced as a result of the data presented here that they do. Leniency by prosecutors is clearly evident. Leniency on the part of the courts is highly possible, but the evidence is less clear. This issue requires more study; in the meantime we need to move on and begin to seek explanations of this lenient treatment.

REFERENCES

Adams, M. E., and C. B. Vedder. 1961. Age and crime, *Geriatrics* 16 (April): 177–81.

Bachand, D. 1983. The elderly offender: A question of leniency in criminal processing. *American Sociological Association Annual Meetings*, Detroit, Mich.: 31 August to 4 September.

Barrow, G. M., and P. A. Smith. 1979. *Aging, agism, and society.* St. Paul: West Publishing Co.

Bergman, S., and A. Menachem. 1973. Crime and delinquency among the aged in Israel. *Geriatrics*, 28 (January): 149–55.

Cohen, F. 1984. Old age as a criminal defense. In E. S. Newman, D. J. Newman, M. L. Gewitz, et al., *Elderly criminals.* Cambridge, Mass.: Oelgeschlager, Gunn, and Hain.

Fox, V. 1946. Intelligence, race, and age as selective factors in crime. *Journal of Criminal Law and Criminology*, 37 (July–August): 141–52.

Fyfe, J. 1984. Police dilemmas in processing elderly offenders. In E. S. Newman, D. J. Newman, M. L. Gewitz, et al., *Elderly criminals*, Cambridge, Mass.: Oelgeschlager, Gunn, and Hain.

Goetting, A. 1984. Prison programs and facilities for elderly inmates. In E. S. Newman, D. J. Newman, M. L. Gewitz, et al., *Elderly criminals.* Cambridge, Mass.: Oelgeschlager, Gunn, and Hain.

Keller, O. J., and C. B. Vedder. 1968. The crimes that old persons commit. *Gerontologist*, 8 (Spring): 43–50.

Malinchak, A. A. 1980. *Crime and gerontology.* Englewood Cliffs, N.J.: Prentice Hall.

Moberg, D. O. 1953. Old age and crime. *Journal of Criminal Law, Criminology, and Police Science*, 43: 764–76.

Newman, E. S., and D. J. Newman. 1984. Public policy implications of elderly crime. In E. S. Newman, D. J. Newman, M. L. Gewitz, et al., *Elderly criminals.* Cambridge, Mass.: Oelgeschlager, Gunn, and Hain.

Pollak, O. 1941. The criminality of old age. *Journal of Criminal Psychopathology*, October: 213–35.

Rodstein, M. 1975. Crime and the aged: The criminals. *Journal of the American Medical Association* 234 (November 10): 639.

Rubenstein, D. 1984. The elderly in prison: A review of the literature. In E. S. New-
    man, D. J. Newman, M. L. Gewitz, et al., *Elderly criminals.* Cambridge, Mass.:
    Oelgeschlager, Gunn, and Hain.

Schroeder, P. L. 1936. Criminal behavior in the later period of life. *American Journal
    of Psychiatry* 92 (January): 915–24.

Shichor, D. 1984. The extent and nature of lawbreaking by the elderly: A review of
    arrest statistics. In E. S. Newman, D. J. Newman, M. L. Gewitz, et al., *Elderly
    criminals.* Cambridge, Mass.: Oelgeschlager, Gunn, and Hain.

Shichor, D., and S. Kobrin. 1978. Note: Criminal behavior among the elderly. *Geron-
    tologist* 18(2):213–18.

Smith, D. A., and C. A. Visher. 1981. Street-level justice: Situational determinants of
    police arrest decisions. *Social Problems* 29 (December): 167–77.

Teller, F. E., and R. J. Howell. 1981. The older prisoner: Criminal and psychological
    characteristics. *Criminology* 18 (February):549–55.

Vedder, C. B., and O. J. Keller. 1968. The elderly offender: Probation and parole.
    Police 13 (September–October):14–16.

Visher, C. A. 1983. Gender, police arrest decisions, and notions of chivalry. *Criminol-
    ogy* 21 (February):5–28.

Willbanks, W. and D. D. Murphy. 1984. The elderly homicide offender. In E. S.
    Newman, D. J. Newman, M. L. Gewitz, et al., *Elderly criminals.* Cambridge,
    Mass.: Oelgeschlager, Gunn, and Hain.

Crime and The Elderly:
A Construction of Official Rates

JAMES A. INCIARDI, Ph.D.

Professor
Division of Criminal Justice
University of Delaware
Newark, Delaware

During the 1970s, public and professional interest in female criminality began to emerge hand in hand with the growth of the women's liberation movement and interest in the general topic of women. Coverage of these phenomena in the mass media fostered the belief that female crime rates were increasing at a rapid rate and that women were committing more and more violent predatory offenses.[1] Moreover, in her widely publicized book *Sisters in Crime*, criminologist Freda Adler strengthened this belief with her comment: "Females . . . are now being found not only robbing banks singlehandedly, but also committing assorted armed robberies, muggings, loan-sharking operations, extortion, murders, and a wide variety of other aggressive, violence-oriented crimes which previously involved only men."[2]

Quite curiously, however, the rise of the new female criminal was in many ways mythical, an outgrowth of incorrect interpretations of official criminal statistics. The various commentators had been examining the increasing number of arrests of women from 1960 through the early 1970s, unmindful of the fact that both the national arrest rate and the size of the female population had also expanded during the same period. By contrast, women had actually accounted for approximately the same share of arrests for violent crimes in the mid-1970s as they had in 1960 and in all the intervening years.[3]

Now, in the 1980s, a similar phenomenon seems to have emerged with respect to senior citizens. A 1982 issue of *U.S. News & World Report* notes, for example, that:

177

- Police and prosecutors across the United States are struggling to deal with a problem that was hardly noticeable a generation ago: Crime by senior citizens.
  Among recent cases:
- A 77-year-old man was jailed for robbing a bank at Kirkersville, Ohio.
- A 62-year-old man died of a heart attack while trying to pull an armed robbery in Los Angeles.
- A 74-year-old man and his 62-year-old wife got 1- to 10-year prison terms in Ohio for selling drugs to minors.[4]

And in *The National Law Journal*: "One of the most publicized and most studied social issues has been crime against elderly victims. But now a flip side of the problem—increases both in the raw numbers and the rate of crime committed *by* the elderly—is raising new concern."[5]

Are these media portrayals accurate? Have rates of crime among the elderly actually risen? Or are these new beliefs about the senior citizen population simply a matter of incorrect interpretations of official criminal statistics, as was the case with violent crime among women a decade ago?

METHOD

To answer these questions, an analysis of national arrest statistics for the period 1964 through 1982 was undertaken. Data on the incidence of arrest were drawn from the FBI's Uniform Crime Reports, and arrest rates for the elderly were constructed for each crime category. The analysis was limited to this 19-year time period because of limitations in the Uniform Crime Reports. Prior to 1964, data on persons 50 and older were reported in aggregate form, and 1982 represents the most recent year for which figures are available.

Although the unreliability of official criminal statistics as measures of the incidence and prevalence of criminal behavior has been well documented, commentaries have suggested, nevertheless, that such data can serve as useful indicators of the changing magnitude and trends of crime.[6] Before continuing, for those unfamiliar with the Uniform Crime Reports, some brief comments on their structure and content seem warranted.

The FBI's Uniform Crime Reports (UCR) present a nationwide view of crime based on the submission of statistics by city, county, and state law-enforcement agencies throughout the country. At present, more than 15,000 agencies are contributing crime data to this reporting program, representing coverage for more than 98 percent of the national population.

The UCR divides its compilations into two categories: "crimes known to the police" and "arrests." Crimes known to the police include all events either reported to, or observed by, the police in those categories of crime that the FBI designates as "Part I offenses"—criminal homicide, forcible rape, aggravated assault, robbery, burglary, larceny-theft, and arson. "Arrests" include compilations of arrests reports for all the Part I offenses, combined with those of 21 additional categories, designated "Part II offenses."

The analysis in this essay is based on arrest reports for all Part I and Part II offenses, with one deviation from the UCR scheme. Historically, arson has been defined as a Part II offense in UCR compilations. In 1979, however, it was redefined as a Part I offense. For the sake of consistency, in this analysis, arson has been included with the Part II offenses for the entire 1964–1982 study period.

FINDINGS

Has crime among the elderly (defined in terms of their rate of arrest) increased? By combining the arrest totals for all Part I and Part II offenses for the nation as a whole and comparing them with those of the elderly population (persons 60 and older) for the years 1964 through 1982, the data in Table 1 suggest that in the aggregate, crime within the senior citizen population has decreased—and decreased quite substantially. In 1964, almost 4.7 million arrests were reported to the FBI, reflecting an arrest rate of 2,448.6 per 100,000 population. During the same year, there were some 196,549 elderly persons arrested, reflecting a rate of 769.0 per 100,000 elderly population. From 1964 to 1982, the general arrest rate increased by 77.5 percent to 4,346.0 per 100,000 population. During this 19-year interval, the arrest rate of the elderly declined by some 33.1 percent to 528.2 per 100,000 elderly population. Moreover, while the number of elderly persons arrested in 1964 represented 4.2 percent of all arrests, by 1982 this pro-

TABLE 1
Total Arrests,[1] Total and Elderly Populations, United States, 1964–1982

Year	Total U.S. Arrests		Total Arrests of Elderly[3]		
	Number	Rate[2]	Number	Percent[4]	Rate[5]
1964	4,685,080	2448.6	196,549	4.2	769.0
1965	5,031,393	2595.9	224,640	4.5	863.2
1966	5,016,407	2561.3	218,526	4.4	824.3
1967	5,518,420	2789.0	225,510	4.1	833.4
1968	5,616,839	2810.4	212,890	3.8	771.3
1969	5,862,246	2903.2	210,259	3.6	747.0
1970	6,570,473	3233.7	224,474	3.4	779.9
1971	6,966,822	3377.8	228,757	3.3	777.2
1972	7,013,194	3368.0	221,187	3.2	735.4
1973	6,499,864	3097.4	192,440	3.0	626.4
1974	6,179,406	2923.2	160,315	2.6	510.8
1975	8,013,645	3760.1	206,371	2.6	643.0
1976	7,912,348	3686.0	191,143	2.4	583.1
1977	9,029,335	4173.8	211,242	2.3	631.0
1978	9,775,087	4482.8	212,875	2.2	622.6
1979	9,506,347	4319.1	198,771	2.1	567.9
1980	9,703,181	4305.9	197,669	2.0	551.4
1981	10,293,575	4492.2	212,964	2.1	581.9
1982	10,062,343	4346.0	197,613	2.0	528.2

[1] Arrest data drawn from Uniform Crime Reports, 1964–1982.
[2] Rate per 100,000 population.
[3] "Elderly" includes all persons 60 and above.
[4] Percent of total arrests.
[5] Rate per 100,000 elderly population.

portion had decreased to 2.0 percent. These arrest trends are illustrated more graphically in Figure 1.

Despite this general finding, an analysis of individual crime categories presents a radically different picture. Tables 2 and 3 examine the arrest trends of the elderly for the Part I offenses of criminal homicide, forcible rape, robbery, aggravated assault, burglary, larceny-theft, and vehicle theft. As such, *the arrest rate for Part I offenses as a whole increased by 200 percent*, from 29.0 to 87.9 per 100,000 elderly population; the rate for violent crime (criminal homicide, forcible rape, robbery, and aggravated assault) increased by 76 percent, from 9.1 to

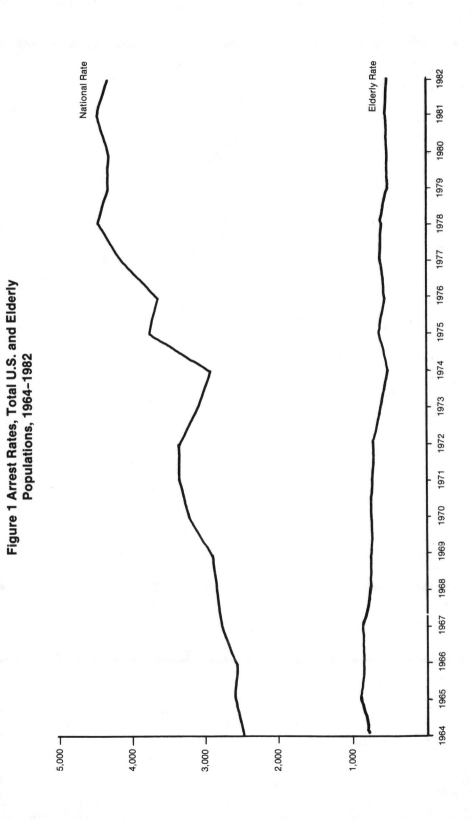

Figure 1 Arrest Rates, Total U.S. and Elderly Populations, 1964–1982

TABLE 2
**Arrest Rates per 100,000 Elderly Population, Part I Offenses,
United States 1964–1972**

	1964	1965	1966	1967	1968	1969	1970	1971	1972
Criminal homicide	1.3	1.5	1.6	2.0	1.8	1.8	1.8	1.9	2.0
Forcible rape	.2	.2	.2	.3	.2	.3	.3	.3	.3
Robbery	.4	.5	.4	.5	.4	.5	.6	.5	.8
Aggravated assault	7.1	7.7	8.6	9.3	8.2	8.8	9.6	9.9	11.1
Burglary	1.6	2.0	1.7	1.9	1.8	1.9	1.9	2.1	2.2
Larceny-theft	18.0	20.7	20.7	23.2	24.5	24.8	30.4	32.9	33.9
Vehicle theft	.3	.4	.4	.4	.4	.4	.6	.9	.7
Total Part I offenses	29.0	33.0	33.8	37.6	37.7	38.5	45.2	48.4	51.0
Total violent crime	9.1	9.9	10.9	12.0	10.6	11.4	12.3	12.5	14.2
Total property crime	19.9	23.1	22.9	25.6	26.7	27.1	32.9	35.9	36.8

Source: Uniform Crime Reports, 1973–1982.
Note: "Violent crime" includes criminal homicide, forcible rape, robbery, and aggravated assault. "Property crime" includes burglary, larceny theft, and vehicle theft. "Index crime" includes all "violent" and "property" crime.

TABLE 3

Arrest Rates per 100,000 Elderly Population, Part I Offenses, United States 1973–1982

	1973	1974	1975	1976	1977	1978	1979	1980	1981	1982
Criminal homicide	1.8	1.5	1.9	1.7	1.6	1.5	1.5	1.3	1.5	1.2
Forcible rape	.4	.3	.4	.5	.6	.7	.7	.6	.8	.6
Robbery	1.1	.8	.8	.6	.8	.9	.8	.9	1.0	.9
Aggravated assault	11.6	10.0	13.1	12.2	13.5	14.4	13.4	13.2	13.9	13.4
Burglary	2.4	1.8	2.5	2.3	2.5	2.9	2.8	3.0	4.0	3.3
Larceny-theft	32.2	31.4	47.3	45.9	50.4	57.4	60.4	62.6	71.1	67.6
Vehicle theft	.7	.6	.7	.7	.7	1.0	.9	.8	1.1	1.1
Total Part I offenses	50.3	46.5	66.7	63.8	70.1	78.9	80.6	82.4	93.4	87.9
Total violent crime	15.0	12.6	16.1	15.0	16.5	17.5	16.5	16.0	17.2	16.0
Total property crime	35.3	33.9	50.5	48.8	53.6	61.4	64.1	66.4	76.2	71.9

Source: Uniform Crime Reports, 1973–1982.
Note: "Violent crime" includes criminal homicide, forcible rape, robbery, and aggravated assault. "Property crime" includes burglary, larceny theft, and vehicle theft. "Index crime" includes all "violent" and "property" crime.

16.0; and the rate for property crime (burglary, larceny-theft, and vehicle theft) increased by 261 percent, from 19.9 to 71.9.

More specifically, with the exception of criminal homicide, where the rate of arrest remained fairly stable over the 19-year period, the rates in all other Part I offense categories increased. For example:

- With *forcible rape*, *aggravated assault*, *robbery*, *burglary*, and *vehicle theft*, the arrest rates either doubled or tripled, although these increases are not particularly significant since the rates were relatively low to begin with;
- With *larceny-theft*, however, the arrest rate almost quadrupled, from 18.0 to 67.6 per 100,000 elderly population.

The bulk of the increase in the Part I offense arrest rate was attributable to the change in the larceny-theft category, an area that includes such property offenses as purse-snatching, shoplifting, pickpocketing, theft of bicycles and motor vehicle accessories, and thefts from coin machines, buildings, and vehicles.

If the arrest rate for larceny-theft offenses significantly *increased* within the elderly population, what accounts for the fact that the overall arrest rate for this age cohort dropped by over 30 percent from 1964 to 1982? The answer lies in the analysis of the Part II offenses (see Tables 4 and 5). In more than half of these crime categories, the arrest rates increased. These increases were only minimal, however, and occurred in areas where the arrest rates were extremely low to begin with. The only Part II offense arrest rate to show any dramatic rise was driving under the influence of alcohol (DUI), which jumped from 38.9 in 1964 to 117.8 in 1982 (with a high of 137.7 in 1978). *The sharp decreases occurred with "victimless crimes," such as gambling, drunkenness, and vagrancy.*

DISCUSSION

In summary, several observations can be made about arrest rates and crime among the elderly.

First, while the arrest rate for the nation as a whole increased dramatically from 1964 through 1982, the rate for the country's elderly population decreased by some 33.3 percent. This is attributable to de-

TABLE 4
Arrest Rates per 100,000 Elderly Population, Part II Offenses,
United States 1964–1972

	1964	1965	1966	1967	1968	1969	1970	1971	1972
Other assaults	12.9	14.7	13.2	14.4	14.9	15.3	17.3	17.7	17.1
Arson	.2	.3	.2	.3	.2	.3	.3	.4	.3
Forgery/counterfeiting	.9	1.0	.8	.9	.8	.7	.8	.8	.9
Fraud	2.9	3.1	3.2	3.1	2.8	2.9	3.5	4.3	4.1
Embezzlement	.5	.4	.4	.3	.3	.4	.3	.3	.2
Stolen property	.6	.7	.6	.6	.8	.9	1.3	1.5	1.5
Weapons violation	3.4	4.1	4.4	5.4	5.9	6.4	8.0	8.5	9.1
Prostitution/vice	1.2	1.6	1.7	1.7	1.4	1.3	1.5	1.4	1.4
Sex offense	6.2	6.6	6.6	6.0	5.3	5.2	4.6	5.1	5.0
Drug law violation	.7	1.1	.8	1.0	1.2	1.5	2.0	1.8	2.1
Gambling	28.9	35.1	29.7	30.2	28.4	29.1	30.3	28.9	25.0
Family offenses	2.0	2.3	1.9	2.1	1.8	1.8	1.9	2.0	1.9
DUI	38.9	44.1	46.8	50.9	54.0	59.9	71.8	83.9	97.3
Drunkenness	474.5	538.8	518.9	515.0	471.0	447.3	463.1	440.7	393.4
Disorderly conduct	63.1	75.2	61.1	56.4	58.4	56.1	51.1	54.3	51.0
Vagrancy	38.4	34.7	29.7	27.3	22.5	19.9	13.8	11.4	6.9
All other	51.0	45.5	56.2	66.1	52.1	46.2	50.2	51.7	53.2

Source: Uniform Crime Reports, 1964–1972.

TABLE 5
Arrest Rates per 100,000 Elderly Population, Part II Offenses,
United States 1973–1982

	1973	1974	1975	1976	1977	1978	1979	1980	1981	1982
Other assaults	14.5	12.7	16.1	16.2	16.5	18.6	17.0	17.1	17.0	16.3
Arson	.3	.3	.4	.4	.5	.5	.5	.5	.6	.5
Forgery/counterfeiting	.8	1.2	.8	.9	.9	1.0	.8	1.1	1.5	1.4
Fraud	3.7	2.9	4.4	5.2	6.6	7.9	7.4	8.2	9.2	8.9
Embezzlement	.2	.2	.2	.2	.1	.2	.2	.2	.2	.2
Stolen property	1.4	1.3	1.9	1.7	1.9	1.9	1.9	2.1	2.3	2.3
Weapon violation	8.5	7.4	8.9	7.8	8.7	8.6	7.7	8.2	9.0	8.7
Prostitution/vice	1.1	1.2	1.1	1.3	1.8	2.2	2.0	2.2	2.6	2.8
Sex offense	5.1	3.7	4.4	4.9	5.2	5.2	5.0	5.1	5.8	5.9
Drug law violation	2.5	1.8	2.7	2.2	3.5	3.6	3.6	5.3	6.6	6.3
Gambling	17.9	13.9	14.8	16.5	14.3	14.0	13.0	11.6	10.0	8.6
Family offenses	1.5	1.0	1.4	1.9	1.4	1.4	1.3	1.2	1.2	1.1
DUI	103.1	90.2	128.5	114.7	134.3	137.7	127.2	125.4	133.9	117.8
Drunkenness	324.3	238.6	276.7	235.5	243.5	207.1	179.8	157.5	152.2	132.1
Disorderly conduct	27.5	36.5	40.8	29.6	34.4	37.2	37.1	37.6	41.2	39.5
Vagrancy	5.8	5.1	8.2	2.7	3.0	2.9	2.2	1.9	2.0	1.7
All other	46.9	36.9	51.5	61.5	69.9	78.4	66.6	68.6	75.8	72.1

Source: Uniform Crime Reports, 1973–1982.

clining rates of arrest for such offenses as gambling, drunkenness, and vagrancy. These declines, furthermore, are not unique to senior citizens, but are reflective of a national trend. During the 19-year study period, the national arrest rates decreased by 56 percent for gambling, 29 percent for drunkenness, and 75 percent for vagrancy. And there are reasons for this. During the last two decades, there has been a gradual shifting away from the rigid enforcement of "victimless crimes." Furthermore, legislative changes have reduced the pool of potential offenders who have traditionally been at risk of arrest for these so-called "nuisance offenses." The proliferation of state-run lotteries and off-track betting parlors have attracted many away from illegal book-making operations and numbers games. In 1974, characteristic of a pattern that has appeared in other jurisdictions, chronic drunkenness was removed from the criminal code of Georgia, placing public drunks under the authority of the public health statutes. And a similar situation has emerged with the crime of vagrancy—loitering, usually because of being broke or having nowhere to go. There has always been some question as to the constitutionality of vagrancy statutes since "being broke" or "having nowhere to go" or "having no visible means of support" are conditions or status rather than behaviors. As a result, vagrancy has been decriminalized in many jurisdictions and, where the laws remain in effect, they are not wholeheartedly enforced.

Second, while the national arrest rate for property crimes increased by 117 percent from 1964 through 1982, the rate for elderly persons increased by 261 percent—more than double the national rate. As to the reasons for this phenomenon, there is one general assumption which seems plausible. Numerous criminal-justice observers interviewed in the cities of Miami, Florida, and Wilmington, Delaware, during 1983 and 1984 maintained that much of the crime among the elderly involves shoplifting and other forms of petty larceny, suggesting that the general economic problems of poverty and inflation may be at the base of the rising tide of elderly crime. Many of the nation's elderly may be committing small thefts—of food, medicine, and other necessities—because they are living on inflation-ridden, fixed incomes. In fact, Albany (New York) police chief Thomas Keegan noted in 1982 that a rash of elderly shoplifters appeared before him at the end of every month, when their Social Security and pension checks had run out.[7] As for other causes, speculation seems to abound. Explanations have been that the elderly feel betrayed, so they must retaliate; that, like juveniles, they are outside the mainstream of American social life and are no longer bound by the rules; and that as revered senior citizens, they will receive no more than a slap on the wrist for committing minor crimes, so "why not?"

Third, from 1964 through 1982, the national arrest rate for violent crime increased by 167 percent—from 336.0 to 730.7 per 100,000 population. This growth was not exceeded, or even matched, by the 60-and-above age cohort. However, the arrest rate for violent crime among the elderly did increase by 76 percent—from 9.1 to 16.0 per 100,000 elderly population, with more than four-fifths of these arrests resulting from aggravated assaults.

The explanation for this upward trend is at best problematic. Without question, the elderly are living longer and in better health than they were just a generation ago. Moreover, with the advancement of the retirement age to 70 years and beyond, more and more of the nation's senior citizens remain in the workplace for longer periods of time. These two factors combine to place elderly persons more often than in years past into situations where interpersonal conflicts can arise. Rather than spending their final years as invalids or in rocking chairs on the porches of retirement or nursing homes, more and more are now in active contact with their neighbors, peers, relatives, colleagues, and other acquaintances. Furthermore, the American social structure has in many ways disenfranchised the elderly, creating the potential for strife between elderly parent and child, worker and management, tenant and landlord, consumer and merchant. In aggravated assaults— the vast bulk of the violent crimes committed by the elderly—victim-offender relationships are typically intimate, close, and frequent, involving family members and close acquaintances. Also, the vast majority of known aggravated assaults result from domestic quarrels, altercations, jealousies, and arguments over money and property.

Fourth, from 1964 through 1982, DUI (driving under the influence) arrests increased dramatically, from a rate of 38.9 to 117.8 over the 19-year period. There are likely many reasons for this. As has been speculated with the increased number of assaults, changes in the retirement age have placed the elderly in social situations and behind the wheels of automobiles for longer periods of time. In addition, due to the advances in medicine, particularly those associated with alcohol-related diseases, problem drinkers are living, and hence remaining on the highways, longer.

Fifth, the surge of crime by elderly citizens presents problems for criminal justice processing. Should aged offenders be arrested, prosecuted, and punished when many of their crimes are thefts undertaken because of need? There are strong differences of opinion on this issue. According to a Miami Beach police official, there is a reluctance among patrol officers to arrest senior citizens "simply because they are hungry." Yet by contrast, a county prosecutor in the same jurisdiction commented: "You can't ignore a crime just because the accused is old. The victim gets outraged; the community becomes outraged. . . . The elderly must take responsibility for their own actions. This office must pursue a case regardless of whether the defendant is 25 or 125."

An even more complex problem is what to do with the elderly, once convicted. Should elderly offenders be sentenced to jail or prison? Not only would they be easy targets for hardened inmate predators, but because of the fragility of old age, a sentence of a few months or even a few weeks could be a sentence of death for many. On the other hand, should state correctional systems construct special facilities for elderly convicts? Certainly the more acute health and mobility problems of the aged might warrant it. Then there is the problem of institutional programs for the elderly. The traditional athletic, recreational, educational, and vocational programs are clearly unsuitable. Can an elderly shoplifter be rehabilitated by teaching him a trade? Can a 75-year-old assaulter's behavior and outlook be altered by group therapy?

Finally, it appears that current trends will continue and that the problem will not automatically correct itself. As advances in medical science and health care continue, the elderly will live even longer. Government figures released in 1984 set the average life expectancy at birth at 74.2—up 0.5 years since 1980.[8] Moreover, futurists maintain that by the year 2033, it will be common for people to live to age 110 and beyond.[9]

NOTES

1. *U.S. News & World Report*, September 23, 1974, pp. 45–48; *Newsweek*, January 6, 1975, p. 35.
2. Freda Adler, *Sisters in Crime: The Rise of the New Female Criminal* (New York: McGraw-Hill, 1975), p. 14.

3. Susan K. Datesman and Frank R. Scarpitti, *Women, Crime, and Justice* (New York: Oxford University Press, 1980), p. 11.
4. *U.S. News & World Report*, March 29, 1982, p. 10.
5. *The National Law Journal*, June 7, 1982, p. 1.
6. See Harry Manuel Shulman, "The Measurement of Crime in the United States," *Journal of Criminal Law, Criminology and Police Science*, 57 (1966), pp. 483–92, James A. Inciardi, "The Uniform Crime Reports: Some Considerations on Their Shortcomings and Utility," *Public Data Use*, 6 (November 1978): 3–16.
7. *The National Law Journal*, June 7, 1982, p. 25.
8. *The New York Times*, July 9, 1984, p. A15.
9. *U.S. News & World Report*, July 16, 1984, p. 104.

APPENDIX A
Population Estimates

Year	Total U.S. Population*	Total Elderly Population**
1964	191,334,000	25,560,000
1965	193,818,000	26,024,000
1966	195,857,000	26,510,000
1967	197,864,000	27,058,000
1968	199,861,000	27,603,000
1969	201,921,000	28,147,000
1970	203,185,000	28,782,000
1971	206,256,000	29,434,000
1972	208,232,000	30,076,000
1973	209,851,000	30,724,000
1974	211,392,000	31,388,000
1975	213,124,000	32,095,000
1976	214,659,000	32,780,000
1977	216,332,000	33,480,000
1978	218,059,000	34,190,000
1979	220,099,000	35,000,000
1980	225,349,000	35,851,000
1981	229,146,000	36,598,000
1982	231,534,000	37,410,000

*Total U.S. population estimates drawn from Uniform Crime Reports.
**Total elderly population estimates (persons 60 and above) drawn from U.S. Bureau of the Census, Current Population Reports.

Alcohol and the Elderly: Abuser and Abused

MICHAEL T. HARTER, Ph.D.

Professor
Health Services Administration
School of Health and Sport Sciences
College of Health and Human Services
Ohio University

CARL D. CHAMBERS, Ph.D.

Professor
Health Services Administration
School of Health and Sport Sciences
College of Health and Human Services
Ohio University

INTRODUCTION

Perhaps alcohol use and abuse among the elderly is not the most important problem they face today. In fact, professional researchers and clinicians continue to disagree about the severity of alcohol-related problems among the elderly, though they agree that any individual who consumes alcohol in amounts that create major life problems—separation or divorce, multiple arrests, deteriorating health, job loss—is an "abuser" or a "deviate," regardless of age (34).

Household surveys conducted since 1968 have consistently shown reduced frequency and volume of alcohol use in older population groups, when compared to younger groups (10). Many researchers have concluded, therefore, that serious drinking problems appear to taper off as people grow older (1, 6). Reasons cited for this change have included health problems, decreased income, underreporting of cases, institutionalization, generational differences, and high early mortality of heavy drinkers (2). Others, particularly clinicians who work with elderly patients, believe that the incidence and severity of alcohol-related problems should not be minimized. While this group agrees that as the population ages, fewer people continue to consume alcohol, they point out that the elderly who continue to drink are at much higher risk than younger cohorts (*1, 2, 10, 29, 32–36, 42, 42–46*). Furthermore, subscribing to the theory that as people age, their alcohol-related problems tend to disappear has resulted in underdiagnosis of the problem (*42*) and diversion of resources to populations other than the elderly (*29*).

The purpose of this chapter, therefore, is fourfold: (1) to place these apparently disparate conclusions regarding the severity of alcohol problems among the elderly into a meaningful framework; (2) to review several of the more recent studies that have focused specifically on the elderly community-based population in order to articulate more clearly the incidence and prevalance of alcohol use among the elderly; (3) to examine several health factors that make the elderly a high-risk population; and (4) to discuss briefly recommendations for addressing several of the problems identified.

THE CONTROVERSY

The concept of a continuum will help establish a context within which to discuss the disparate positions of researchers regarding the severity of alcohol-related problems among the elderly. On one end of the continuum are researchers who have focused primarily on the elderly deviate, the individual who abuses alcohol and who has suffered from a major life problem as a result. However, because survey studies indicate that people both use and abuse alcohol less in older population cohorts, these researchers have concluded that alcohol problems appear to taper off as people age and that the topic of alcohol-related problems among the elderly is a topic relegated to a position of minor importance (*29*). Many of this same group quote an estimate that only 2 percent to 10 percent of the elderly population have severe alcohol problems (*16*).

Based on 1980 national census data, there are 25,549,427 persons aged 65 and older in the United States and 47,252,302 people over the age of 55. Depending on where the analysis begins (whether "elderly" means older than 55 or older than 65), the estimated number of people with severe alcohol-related problems ranges thus:

	Population	2%	10%
55 years or more	47,252,302	945,046	4,725,230
65 years or more	25,549,427	510,989	2,554,943

If numbers of people over 65 with alcohol problems range from 500,000 to 2½ million, sheer numbers indicate that these problems are not of minor importance. Further, Atkinson estimates that with no change from current rates, the *number* of elderly abusers will likely double in the next 50 years, based on the projected increase in the size of the older population (*1*).

At the other end of the continuum is a group of researchers and clinicians who believe that alcohol-related problems among the elderly are legion and that significant programs should be established for prevention, identification, and treatment. Some of these authors contend that not only do the predictable problems exist, but that the elderly are especially vulnerable to alcohol-related morbidities, about which they are usually unaware. The general logic that undergirds this position is this (*6*):

- Physiological changes occur as a result of aging and make the aging human organism more susceptible to the effects of alcohol.
- 40 percent of all persons over the age of 65 have a major health problem.
- The large majority of people above 65 take more than one medication on a regular basis.
- Major changes in life circumstances such as retirement, death of close friends, death of a spouse, create greater possibilities of loneliness and isolation.

Regardless of where the issues are placed on the continuum, the use and abuse of alcohol by the elderly may be more than an issue of deviance.

INCIDENCE AND PREVALENCE

Clark and Midanik summarized six years (1971–1976) of research about alcohol use and alcohol problems in the general adult population of the United States and added data from a 1979 national survey

(*10*). With respect to the two oldest population groups (50 to 64 and 65 and over), findings across the nine-year period were surprisingly consistent.

- Fewer men and women in the 50–64 age group consumed alcohol than their younger cohorts, but more consumed alcohol than older cohorts (65 and over).
- Over the nine-year period, there appeared to be an increase in the number of men and women 65 and over who consumed alcohol.
- The 1979 survey showed fewer heavier drinkers than the average of the other surveys for all age groups *except* the oldest.

To arrive at a gross estimate of the number of persons 65 and older who would be considered "heavier" drinkers by the survey's standards (two or more drinks daily), one can apply the 1979 survey findings to 1980 census figures, a calculation that produces a population of 1.13 million elderly "heavier" drinkers.

Much of the earlier research on incidence and prevalence of alcohol use that specifically focused on the elderly took place in psychiatric facilities (*30*). Depending in large part on the psychiatric treatment setting, estimates of persons with serious drinking problems ranged from 15 to 50 percent (*33*). Other sites included nursing homes, where it was estimated that 20 percent of the patients had serious drinking problems (*36*), and general medical wards, which showed rates of 15 to 20 percent of elderly persons with serious drinking problems (*36*).

Incidence and prevalence of alcohol use data with respect to the elderly living in community settings have been collected primarily in conjunction with broader studies on substance use and abuse in this population. At the present time, no reported study using a national sample has examined patterns of drinking among the elderly population. Therefore, three community-based studies that used somewhat similar collection and analysis techniques will provide a broad perspective on the questions of how many elderly currently drink and, of those, how many drink at least daily (*9, 18, 40*).

A 1978 study by Chien et al. (*9*) included a sample of 242 subjects, all over age 60, predominantly white and recruited from several Washington, D.C., settings: senior citizen centers, housing complexes for the elderly, and a geriatric day care center. The group studied by Stephens et al., consisted of 1,090 randomly selected persons 55 and older in the

Houston area. These subjects were identified through a telephone survey, and data were collected from them in late 1979 and early 1980. To introduce an additional variable—ethnicity—for examination, Harter et al. selected almost equally distributed groups of Whites, Blacks, and Mexican-Americans, all of whom were retired, were 55 and older, and attended one of three senior citizen centers in San Antonio, Texas. This study, directed by Carl Chambers, Ohio University, with assistance from O. Z. White and John Lindquist, Trinity University, focused on the broader issue of substance abuse within this tri-ethnic elderly population. Interviews were conducted during late 1983 at the senior centers.

As indicated in Table 1, in two of the three studies less than 50 percent of two study populations were considered current drinkers and only 53 percent of the third group. However, Harter's and Chien's data both reveal that nearly one-third of the persons who drink consume at least one drink each day, and Stephens' data appear to corroborate that finding. Taken as a function of the total study populations, 17 percent of Chien's study population, 18 percent of Stephens', and over 10 percent of Harter's appeared to be drinking on a daily basis. We recognize that findings from these three isolated studies cannot be used to infer national patterns with any great reliability, but in the absence of any national data, we will do so with caution.

Using 1980 census data, the frequency ranges from these three studies suggest the following:

- From 5 million to 9 million people aged 55 and older drink alcohol daily.
- From 9 million to 25 million people aged 55 and older are current users of alcohol.

Additional relevant findings from these three studies include the following:

- With regard to health status, Chien, et al. found that only 2.5 percent of the study population reported no illness and that 57 percent reported symptoms in 4 to 11 body systems (including 52.9 percent who were receiving medical care for cardiovascular system problems).

TABLE 1
Comparison of Three Studies

Sample	Chien, et al.	Stephens, et al.	Harter, et al.
Size	242	1,090	305
Age	Over 60	55 and over	55 and over (all retired)
Location	Washington, D.C.	Houston	San Antonio
Sex			
Male	32%	38%	38%
Female	68%	62%	62%
Non-Drinkers	47%	60%	55%
Drinkers	53%[a]	40%[b]	45%[c]
Less than 1 drink a day	68%	56%	69%
1 drink or more a day	32%	44%[d]	31%

[a] Current drinkers are not defined.
[b] Current drinkers are defined as having consumed an alcoholic beverage in the past month.
[c] Current drinkers are defined as having consumed an alcoholic beverage in the past year.
[d] Reported data consists only of the number of people who drank the day before the interview, a factor which might account for the difference between this number and the others.

- Stephens et al. reported that 6 percent of their sample used both alcohol and psychoactive substances in the past month, while Harter et al. found that 15 percent of the people who drink at least once each week also take a psychoactive substance each week.
- Both of these studies found that males were more frequent and heavier drinkers than females.
- Harter et al. found that 36 percent of the current drinkers had consumed two or more drinks less than an hour before driving a car and 11 percent were cited by police for operating a motor vehicle while under the influence of alcohol or another drug.
- Additional findings related to ethnicity from the Harter study include the following:
  1. Fewer Blacks were current drinkers than either Whites or Mexican-Americans.
  2. Among the current drinkers, the Black group drank far more frequently than either of the other two groups (52 percent drank at least once a day, while 72 percent drank at least once each week).

3. Fully 55 percent of the Black drinkers admitted to having consumed two or more drinks less than an hour before driving a car, a rate twice that of either of the other two ethnic groups.
4. Black current drinkers were cited at triple the rate of the other two ethnic groups for driving while intoxicated.

- Harter et al. also found that persons 70 and over drink less frequently than their younger cohorts.

In summary, research evidence suggests that significant numbers of persons continue to drink alcohol in old age, and a high percentage of the drinkers consume alcohol at least once a day.

BIOLOGICAL ASPECTS OF AGING

The elderly differ from younger populations in their ability to absorb and distribute alcohol in the body (3). Not all the biological reasons for this phenomenon are known at this time, primarily because most of our understanding of therapeutics, clinical pharmacology, and pharmokinetics is based on studies in young people (17). In general, lean body mass declines and adipose-tissue mass increases in relation to total body weight as a person ages (27). It is generally recognized that this change, combined with a smaller volume of body water in the elderly, explains why the elderly often experience higher peak alcohol levels in blood water and increased pharmacologic effects when compared to younger subjects (41). In short, given the biological changes related to aging, it is likely that the use of alcohol in amounts that are relatively safe for younger populations could produce adverse effects in the elderly (3). As Schuckit contends, alcohol consumed in even moderate amounts is more likely to contribute to accidents and general disorientation for the elderly than for younger counterparts (33).

Perhaps of even greater significance is the potential for compounding the effects of alcohol by combining it with certain medications. As noted earlier in this chapter, upwards of 50 percent of persons over 65 drink alcohol; given that persons 65 and older (11 percent of the total population) account for over 25 percent of all prescriptions and over-the-counter drug purchases in the United States, the probability of potential alcohol and other drug interaction appears high (15). Of particular concern is the combined impact of central nervous system

(CNS) depressants and alcohol. Gerbino reviewed the research literature on alcohol and the major CNS-depressant medications and reported the following (*15*):

- *Benzodiazepines.* Studies of the elderly indicate that alcohol alters
  the metabolism and plasma levels of diazepam, the most commonly
  prescribed drug in the United States. Alcohol mixed with diazepam
  can cause substantial psychomotor impairment, especially in driving
  proficiency and other motor tasks.
- *Barbiturates and meprobamate.* The actions of barbiturates and
  meprobamate combined with alcohol are very complex. However,
  the worst possible circumstance in the elderly patient is addictive
  therapeutic effects with synergistic CNS depression.
- *Chloral hydrate.* Chloral hydrate and alcohol can be a dangerous
  combination in the elderly. High levels of both alcohol and trichlor-
  ethanol (a reduced form of chloralhydrate) can be potentially lethal
  in elderly patients because of their combined CNS hypnotic and depressive effects.
- *Psychotropic drugs.* The effects of alcohol combined with psychotropic drugs are less predictable than the effects of other CNS depressants and alcohol. Patients who use chlorpromazine and alcohol
  have driving skills and other psychomotor functions impaired.
- *Narcotic analgesics.* Morphine, codeine, or meperidine combined
  with alcohol can have an addictive effect on CNS and respiratory
  depression. It is a potentially hazardous combination.

In addition, when taken with alcohol, medications prescribed for cardiovascular problems and antidiabetic drugs can also have serious side
effects.

It is obvious that among clinicians, increased awareness must be
created with regard to the dangers of combining alcohol and any
number of medications.

MORE HEALTH IMPLICATIONS

Even though significant numbers of elderly people have always consumed alcohol, little research prior to 1975 focused on the health implications of alcohol on the aging human organism (*2, 16*). Recent

medical evidence convincingly shows that excessive use of alcohol not only affects the liver negatively (the liver being the organ most often associated with alcohol), but can have negative effects on many other organs. Within the cardiovascular system, for example, as the liver metabolizes alcohol, it produces acetaldehyde, which inhibits heart protein synthesis. Continuous exposure of the heart to acetaldehyde interferes with normal replenishment of heart protein, which can lead to protein deficiency and heart damage (25).

Over the years, the results of studies which attempted to analyze the impact of alcohol on blood pressures were inconsistent. Current researchers have attributed some of the inconsistencies to uncontrolled confounding variables. Fortmann et al. found that when the age variable is controlled, alcohol is independently associated with blood pressure; in a large study population of persons aged 50 to 74, as alcohol intake increased from one to three drinks per day, blood pressure increased proportionately (13).

In a study of health maintenance organization subjects, Klatsky et al. found that men and women of three races who took three or more drinks per day had higher blood pressures than either nondrinkers or drinkers who took two or fewer drinks (22). Kannel and Schatzkin reported that cardiovascular mortality is tripled in the hypertensive elderly, compared to those of the same age with normal blood pressure (20). In general, elderly people with decreased cardiac functioning have a greater chance of developing more serious cardiac problems if they continue to consume alcohol (3).

For the elderly drinker, the health consequences of heavy drinking on the cardiovascular system are quite clear. For the elderly drinker who consumes alcohol more moderately (and the definition of moderate shifts across studies), one series of studies concluded by extolling the potential virtues of using alcohol.

Kastenbaum (with others) conducted several studies with regard to the value of using wine or beer with elderly patients in geriatric hospital settings (24). Major findings included heightened group interaction and sustained group relationships. Other projects reported that long-term patients "griped" less about life, slept better, and ate better (24). In all reported studies, data collection took weeks or months, with very little data about long-term impact. Given the current evidence that nursing home patients take on the average four to six medications daily (9), one wonders about the potential for alcohol-drug interactions, especially if the results of these studies motivate personnel in long-term geriatric settings to supply alcohol to patients on a regular basis.

For some time, chronic alcohol abuse has also been associated with brain damage (47). Chronic brain syndrome normally associated with alcoholism includes major subtypes of dementia (general loss of cognitive abilities) and the amnestic syndrome (loss of specific recent memory, and to a lesser extent remote memory) (28). Using neuropsychological functioning instruments to compare alcoholics with control groups, researchers have consistently found that alcoholics were significantly lower in nonverbal abstracting performance, tactual-spatial problem-solving speed, and perceptual motor speed (28). Within the past decade, employing computer-assisted tomography (CT scan), scientists have been able to document degenerative cortical changes which are significantly correlated with excessive consumption of alcohol and with age (5). Using an event-related (ERP) technique, Beck et al. found that young alcoholics and elderly normal people had similar brainwave responses, thus supporting the notion of premature aging among alcoholics (28).

Recently, investigators have moved beyond clinical-based studies involving alcoholic patients to analysis of drinking patterns of people in community settings (27). Studying a randomly selected group of men living in a suburban California community, Parker and Noble concluded that both social drinking practices and age are significantly and inversely related to performance on tests of nonverbal abstracting, adaptive abilities, and concept formation (26). In a related study involving men who were sober when tested, Parker et al. concluded that the combination of being older *and* being a heavy social drinker is associated with lower performance on tests of abstraction than is true when either factor is present alone (27). Jones and Jones studied the relationship of age and drinking habits on memory in women (19) and concluded that drinking habits and age have an additive effect on women social drinkers with respect to impairment of short-term memory.

In summary, the combination of the normal aging process with the consumption of alcohol, especially substantial amounts, can have synergistic effects on the elderly, contributing at one end of the scale to decreased cognitive and psychomotor functioning, in the middle of the scale to confusion and quasi-incompetence, and—at the most extreme end—to chronic brain syndrome.

Nutrition-related health problems associated with excessive use of alcohol have also been identified (3). For example, alcohol inhibits absorption of thiamine from the intestine, an effect that may be responsible for the thiamine deficiency often exhibited by alcoholics. Excessive alcohol use damages the liver and often results in depletion of the vitamin A stored there. In addition to effects on absorption of nutrients, alcohol promotes the loss from the body of essential minerals such as magnesium, calcium, and zinc. Evidence further suggests that a combination of factors—reduced appetite, altered eating habits, low income, and low expenditures for food—might even compound the nutritional effects of alcohol in the elderly (3).

Many other health-related consequences of excessive alcohol use have not been fully documented, but recent research in, for example, cancer of the larynx shows a somewhat higher probability of laryngeal cancer among excessive drinkers (11). More important, however, is the apparent potentiation and synergism observed when smoking and drinking are combined. Risk potential of drinking and smoking combined is at least 50 percent greater than the effect of either alone (11).

A last note on alcohol, the elderly, and health implications: elderly people are three times more vulnerable to automobile accidents at low blood-alcohol concentrations than at zero blood-alcohol levels (3). Therefore, drinking and driving, even within the legal limits of blood alcohol levels, appears risky for the elderly.

To this point, our discussion has focused on establishing a broad understanding of the incidence and prevalence of alcohol use and abuse among the elderly and the health problems associated with both abuse and "moderate" use. The remainder of the discussion will focus on what is known about the causes of alcohol abuse, the prognosis for successful treatment of elderly abusers, and techniques for solving problems that might accompany even moderate alcohol use by the elderly.

CAUSATION AND TREATMENT

Examination of the research literature supports the conclusion that the causes of alcoholism among the elderly are not known (35). There is some reason to believe, however, that there are at least two types of elderly abusers: (1) those who have become alcoholics later in life and

(2) those who have long histories of alcohol abuse and who carry this behavior into old age (45).

Results of some studies have been interpreted in general to mean that the late onset of alcoholism is often related to stresses associated with aging: bereavement, loneliness, retirement, marital stress, health problems, and depression; the early onset of alcoholism appears likely to be related to more deep-rooted psychological problems, which might be exacerbated by stresses associated with aging (16). Recognizing the distinction between these two types of alcoholism has apparently been important for establishing viable treatment plans (46).

A significant first step in treatment is to have the problem diagnosed. However, diagnosis is complicated. Often, an alcohol problem is denied and hidden by the elderly and often even by their families (16). Physicians, too, may be unable or unwilling to identify alcoholism in their patients (46). Therefore, an essential first step is public education, to help the general population recognize the symptoms of alcohol abuse in their own family members and understand that continued abuse will not result in an improved quality of life. Further, medical education programs both at the undergraduate and continuing-education levels need to be strengthened in order to provide practitioners with adequate information and skills to identify alcohol-related problems where they exist.

Although magic cures for alcoholism do not exist at any age (33), there are numerous treatment techniques reputed to be successful. Zimberg, for example, reported that a combination of a therapeutic regimen, including antidepressant medication and socialization programs, could be successful in treatment of both late-onset and early-onset alcoholics (45).

From the literature cited, there also appears to be a substantial population of elderly who consume alcohol at what many would consider "moderate" levels, but who also risk numerous health complications as a result of using alcohol in combination with other factors. Because the process of examining the pharmacological effects of most drugs has involved populations other than the elderly, little is known about the effects of age. Therefore, we recommend that during clinical trials, special attention be paid to the effects of drugs consumed by the elderly and to the potentiating effects of alcohol. Pharmaceutical companies also should be required to communicate significant findings to physicians and others who will be prescribing the drugs. Much better education of health practitioners to the potential existence of these problems must occur if elderly patients are to have adequate opportunities to understand the dangers of alcohol use. Certainly, a combination of better-informed health professionals and members of the general public (including the elderly and family members) would decrease the probability of unnecessary illnesses, alcohol-related visits to the emergency room, alcohol-related confinement in mental health and other long-term care facilities, and—most important—early death.

REFERENCES

1. Atkinson, R. M., and L. L. Kofoed. 1982. Alcohol and drug abuse in old age: A clinical perspective. *Substance and Alcohol Actions/Misuse* 3:353–68.
2. Atkinson, R. A. 1984. Substance use and abuse in late life. In R. Atkinson, ed., *Alcohol and Drug Abuse in Old Age*. Washington, D.C.: American Psychiatric Press.
3. Barnes G. M., E. L. Abel, and C. A. Ernst. 1980. *Alcohol and the elderly: A comprehensive bibliography*. Westport: Greenwood Press.
4. Barrett-Conner, E., and L. Suarez, L. A community study of alcohol and other factors associated with the distribution of high density lipoprotein cholesterol in older vs. younger men. *American Journal of Epidemiology* 115:888–93.
5. Bergman, H., S. Borg, T. Hindmarsh, C. M. Idestrom, and S. Mutzell. 1980. Computed tomography of the brain, clinical examination and neuropsychological assessment of a random sample of men from the general population. *Acta Psychiatrica Scandinavica* 286:47–55.
6. Brody, J. A. Aging and alcohol abuse. 1982. *Journal of the American Geriatric Society* 30:123–26.
7. Calahan, D., I. H. Cisin, and H. M. Crossley. 1969. *American drinking practices: A national study of drinking behavior and attitudes*. New Haven: College and University Press.
8. Carlen, P. L., and D. A. Wilkenson. 1978. Alcoholic brain damage and reversible deficits. *Acta Psychiatrica Scandinavica* 286:103–17.
9. Chien, C. P., E. J. Townsend, and A. Ross-Townsend. 1978. Substance use and abuse among the community elderly: The medical aspect. *Addictive Diseases: An International Journal* 3:357–72.
10. Clark, W. B., and L. Midanik. 1980. Alcohol use and alcohol problems among U.S. adults: Results of the 1979 National Survey. In *Alcohol and health monograph I, alcohol consumption and related problems*. Rockville, Md.: National Institute on Alcohol Abuse and Alcoholism.
11. Cowles, S. R. Cancer of the larynx: Occupational and environmental association. *Southern Medical Journal* 76:894–98.
12. Dunham, R. G. 1981. Aging and changing patterns of alcohol use. *Journal of Psychoactive Drugs* 13(2):143–51.

13. Fortman, S. P., W. L. Haskell, K. Vranizan, B. W. Brown, and J. W. Farquhar. 1983. The association of blood pressure and dietary alcohol: Differences by age, sex, and estrogen use. *American Journal of Epidemiology*, 118:497–507.

14. Freund, G. 1982. The interaction of chronic alcohol consumption and aging on brain structure and function. *Alcoholism: Clinical and Experimental Research* 6(1):13–21.

15. Gerbino, P. 1982. Complications of alcohol use combined with drug therapy in the elderly. *Journal of the American Geriatric Society* 30(11) Supplement: 588–93.

16. Glanz, M. 1981. Predictions of elderly drug abuse. *Journal of Psychoactive Drugs* 13(2):117–26.

17. Greenblatt, D. J., E. M. Sellers, and R. I. Shader. 1982. Drug disposition in old age. *New England Journal of Medicine* 306(18):1081–88.

18. Harter, M., C. Chambers, J. Lindquist, and O. White, 1984. Drinking patterns and the elderly. Presented at the 79th Annual Meeting of the American Sociological Association, San Antonio, Texas, August.

19. Jones, M. K., and B. M. Jones. 1980. The relationship of age and drinking habits to the effects of alcohol on memory of women. *Journal of Studies on Alcohol* 41(1):179–86.

20. Kannel, W. B., and A. Schatzkin. 1983. Risk factor analysis. *Progress in Cardiovascular Diseases* 26(4):309–32.

21. Klatsky, A. L., G. D. Friedman, and A. B. Siegelaub. 1981. Alcohol use and cardiovascular disease: The Kaiser-Permanente experience. *Circulation* 64 Supplement III: III-32-III, 41.

22. Klatsky, A. L. 1982. The relationship of alcohol and the cardiovascular system. In *Alcohol and health monograph II Biomedical processes and consequences of alcohol use*. Rockville, Md.: National Institute on Alcohol Abuse and Alcoholism.

23. Medd, B. H. 1983. The benzodiazepines: Public health, social and regulatory issues. An industry perspective. *Journal of Psychoactive Drugs* 15(1–2):127–35.

24. Mishara, B. L., and R. Kastenbaum. 1980. *Alcohol and old age*. New York: Grune and Stratton.

25. Oratz, M. 1982. *Alcohol and protein synthesis*. Rockville, Md.: National Institute on Alcohol Abuse and Alcoholism.

26. Parker, E. S., and E. P. Noble. 1980. Alcohol and the aging process in social drinkers. *Journal of Studies on Alcohol* 41(1):170–78.

27. Parker, E. S., D. A. Parker, J. A. Brody, and R. Schoenberg. 1982. Cognitive patterns resembling premature aging in male social drinkers. *Alcoholism: Clinical and Expermental Research* 6(1):46–52.

28. Parsons, O. A., and W. R. Lebar. 1982. *Alcohol, cognitive dysfunction, and brain damage*. Rockville, Md.: National Institute on Alcohol Abuse and Alcoholism.

29. Peppers, L. G., and R. G. Stover. 1979. The elderly abuser: A challenge for the future. *Journal of Drug Issues* 9(1):73–83.

30. Peterson, D. M., and F. J. Whittington. 1977. Drug use among the elderly: A review. *Journal of Psychedelic Drugs* 9(1):25–37.

31. Rosin, A. J., and M. M. Glatt. 1971. Alcohol excess in the elderly. *Quarterly Journal of Studies on Alcohol* 32:53–59.

32. Schuckit, M. A. 1977. Geriatric alcoholism and drug abuse. *Gerontologist* 17(2):168−74.
33. _____. 1982. A clinical review of alcohol, alcoholism, and the elderly patient. *Journal of Clinical Psychiatry* 43(10):396−99.
34. _____. J. A. Atkinson, P. L. Miller, and J. Berman. 1980. A three year follow-up of elderly alcoholics. *Journal of Clinical Psychiatry* 41(12):412−16.
35. Schuckit, M. A., E. R. Morrissey, and M. R. O'Leary. 1978. Alcohol problems in elderly men and women. *Addictive Diseases: An International Journal* 3(3): 405−16.
36. Schuckit, M. A., and P. A. Pastor. 1978. The elderly as a unique population: Alcoholism. *Alcoholism: Clinical and Experimental Research* 2(1):31−38.
37. Seller, E. M., R. C. Frecker, M. K. Romach. 1983. Drug metabolism in the elderly: Confounding of age, smoking, and ethanol effects. *Drug Metabolism Reviews* 14:225−49.
38. Siassi, I., G. Crocetti, and H. R. Spiro. 1973. Drinking patterns and alcoholism in a blue collar population. *Quarterly Journal of Studies on Alcohol* 34:917−26.
39. Simon, A., and L. J. Epstein. 1968. Alcoholism in the geriatric mentally ill. *Geriatrics* 125−31.
40. Stephens, R. C., C. A. Haney, and S. Underwood. 1982. *Drug taking among the elderly*. Rockville: Department of Health and Human Services Pub. No. (ADM 83-1229).
41. Vestal, R. E., E. A. McGuire, J. D. Tobin, R. Andres, A. H. Norris, and R. Mezey. 1977. Aging and ethanol metabolism in man. *Clinical Pharmacology and Therapeutics* 21:343−354.
42. Wattis, J. P. 1983. Alcohol and old people. *British Journal of Psychiatry* 143:306−7.
43. Wells-Parker, E., S. Miles, and B. Spencer. 1983. Stress experiences and drinking histories of elderly drunken driving offenders. *Journal of Studies on Alcohol* 44(3):429−37.
44. Zimberg, S. 1974. The elderly alcoholic. *Gerontologist* June, 221−224.
45. _____. 1974. Two types of problem drinkers: Both can be managed. *Geriatrics* (August): 135−38.
46. _____. 1978. Diagnosis and treatment of the elderly alcoholic. *Alcoholism: Clinical and Experimental Research* 2(1):27−29.
47. Zornetzer, S. F., D. W. Walker, B. E. Hunter, W. C. Abraham. 1982. Neurophysiological changes produced by alcohol. Rockville, Md.: National Institute on Alcohol Abuse and Alcoholism.
48. Zung, B. J. 1979. Sociodemographic correlates of problem drinking among DWI offenders. *Journal of Studies of Alcohol* 40:1064−72.

The Older Drunk Driving Offender

HARVEY A. SIEGAL, Ph.D.

Professor
School of Medicine and
Department of Sociology and Anthropology
Wright State University
Dayton, Ohio

INTRODUCTION

The offense of driving while intoxicated (DWI) or driving under the influence (DUI) of liquor, alcohol, or drugs has gained much public notoriety, thanks to several very vocal, single-issue, grass-roots organizations that came into existence approximately a half decade ago. While formerly our views of the offense and offender cast them in either comic or sympathetic terms, we have recently grown intolerant of the risks they pose. We need only look to the recent legislation enacted by many states mandating harsher sanctions for convicted offenders; the stepup in enforcement activities, including the use of such measures as roadblocks; and the ongoing support from Congress to confirm this observation.

The goals of each group are essentially the same: reduce automobile fatalities and injuries. Prevention strategies on both the *general* and *specific* level have subscribed to classic theories of social control. *General deterrence*—keeping people from driving after drinking—has focused on the enactment and publicizing of laws calling for harsher penalties and awareness campaigns about the risks associated with drunk driving. *Specific deterrence* has involved devising ways of keeping convicted offenders from repeating their crimes. Often, the effort has relied on harsh sanctions—usually involving incarceration—to motivate behavioral change.

The belief in punishment as a deterrent has provided the grass-roots organizations with a common objective. Members have seen imprisonment as worthy because it represents a recognition of the seriousness of the offense. Jail has a strong symbolic value. Moreover, on a common-sense level, at least, it does seem to work. Proponents of "deterrence through certain detection" and "sure and swift punishment" would confidently point to the reduction in the incidence of skyjacking after the introduction of airport security measures. Or, more specifically, they would call attention to the experiences of the Scandinavian countries, whose harsh laws and aggressive police action successfully reduced the incidence of drunk driving.

While certainly appealing, these comparisons invite challenge. Criminologists would dispute the comparison of skyjacking—which is a form of robbery—to DWI, which is a victimless crime unless there is an accident (Inciardi, 1984). Others might caution against making monolithic, cross-cultural comparisons and simplistically assuming that what works in one part of the world will be successful in another.

A discussion of these larger, theoretical issues falls well beyond the scope of this chapter. The efficacy of punishment, especially incarceration, has not been universally accepted. To date, no data exist to suggest that imprisonment has a decisive impact on either general or specific deterrence. While many legislators initially acquiesced to political pressures from the grass-root organizations, they have come to appreciate the complexity of the entire issue. Problems have ranged from a shortage of jail facilities for those convicted, to additional and even greater burdened courts. Dissatisfaction with legislation calling for the mandatory incarceration has been widespread. Judges argue that when the option of sentencing discretion is removed, the role of the courts is severely limited. When they no longer have the ability to individualize sentences, rehabilitation is less likely and the needs of society are not as well served. Moreover, overcrowded facilities in many communities have made judges reluctant to sentence first-time DWI offenders to jail terms.

To address these problems, communities have developed alternatives to incarceration. These provide some form of confinement to DWI offenders outside of prison or jail, allowing them to "serve time" and perhaps even benefit from the experience so that the risk of repeat offenses is reduced.

THE SETTING AND THE STUDY

One such program is the Weekend Intervention Program (WIP), orig-
inated and operated by the School of Medicine at Wright State University, Dayton, Ohio. The program emerged in 1978 and has been used as
an alternative to incarceration by judges in the greater Miami Valley
area of Ohio. Similar programs have been implemented in several
states and in other institutions in Ohio.

The WIP approach differs from previous attempts at affecting specific deterrence because it is not an *educational* program aimed at convincing convicted offenders that they should not drive under the influence. Nor is it a *short-term rehabilitation* program, aimed at equipping
offenders with specific social and psychological skills or offering ther-
apies that would modify their behaviors. Instead, its thrust is directed
toward *identifying* the problem drinker or alcoholic within the larger
population of DWI offenders. It operates on the premise that recidivism and subsequent alcohol-related crashes could be avoided if problem drinkers were identified and received medical, psychological, or
other treatment.

The three goals of WIP are:

1. Diagnosis or assessment—identifying problem drinkers and documenting the extent and severity of their problems.
2. Breaking through denial—helping problem drinkers see that the
   "cause" of their difficulties is actually their drinking.
3. Preparation for treatment—directing them to the specific programs
   or agencies that can meet their needs and equipping them to obtain
   these services.

The program obtains extensive data on each participant. These
data—including usage patterns, alcohol-induced difficulties, and risk
factors—are carefully considered by the professional staff as they pre-
pare their assessments of each participant. An individualized post-
WIP treatment referral plan is constructed for each participant who
needs additional service.

The WIP has been in operation for seven years and has had over
10,000 offenders remanded to it. In the fall of 1983, the National
Highway Traffic Safety Administration (NHTSA) provided the resources to evaluate the program. In addition to examining the WIP

population, the study identified the larger population convicted of DWI throughout southwestern Ohio. Ultimately, the study will examine the relationship of sentencing alternatives to recidivism, and these data will be in the NHTSA final report, which will be produced in December 1986. The data we will present come from this study and reflect a one-year period from spring 1983 to spring 1984.

The setting for this research is the greater Miami Valley region of Ohio. This region encompasses several counties in the southwestern quadrant of the state, excluding the metropolitan Cincinnati area (see Figure A). To maximize subject comparability, only courts that regularly referred offenders to the WIP were included. The areas encompassed represent urban, suburban, and rural settings.

When convicting, the courts could exercise one of several sentencing options:

1. Remanding the offender to the Weekend Intervention Program.
2. Incarcerating the offender for 72 hours.
3. Giving a suspended sentence or fine.
4. Requiring driver education, a DWI school, direct entrance to treatment, etc.

Table 1 displays the frequencies and relative distribution of these alternatives.

TABLE 1
DWI Dispositions by Sentencing Alternative

WIP	Jail	Suspended Sentence/Fine	Other
1405 (29.4%)	1571 (32.9%)	814 (17.0%)	988 (20.7%)

THE DWI OFFENDER: AGE AND SEX

The DWI population is young and predominantly male (see Table 2). Some 84.8 percent (4,387 cases) are male, while 14.8 percent (768 cases) are female. Data are missing on only 16 subjects.

LEGEND

⊙ Places of 100,000 or more inhabitants
● Places of 50,000 to 100,000 inhabitants
□ Central cities of SMSA's with fewer than 50,000 inhabitants
○ Places of 25,000 to 50,000 inhabitants outside SMSA's

Standard Metropolitan
Statistical Areas (SMSA's)

SCALE

Bureau of the Census: 1970

Table 3 represents the age distribution of the study population. More than half (51 percent) are under 30 years of age; just about one-third (32 percent) are younger than 25. The age-frequency distribution consistently declines in older cohorts.

TABLE 2
Study Population
Age Distribution by Sentencing Alternative in Percentages

	WIP	Jail	Suspended Sentence/Fine	Other	
16–20	12.2	13.2	14.3	14.6	
21–25	26.2	24.9	26.7	25.5	
26–30	17.8	17.5	19.0	17.2	
31–35	12.3	12.4	11.7	13.1	
36–40	9.0	9.9	8.8	9.9	
41–45	6.2	7.0	6.8	5.6	
46–50	5.3	5.1	4.8	4.9	
51–55	4.5	4.4	4.3	3.8	
56–60	3.0	2.9	1.6	2.1	
61–65	1.9	1.9	1.0	2.1	
65+	1.7	.8	1.1	1.2	
N=	1346	1539	798	971	N=4654
Missing	4.2	2.0	2.0	1.7	
N=	1405	1571	814	988	N=4778
Missing data total = 2.6%					

TABLE 3
Study Population
Sex Distribution by Sentencing Alternative in Percentages

	WIP	Jail	Suspended Sentence/Fine	Other	
Male	82.1	89.6	84.1	82.0	
Female	17.9	10.4	15.9	17.9	
N=	1386	1563	813	987	N=4749
Missing data	1.4	.5	.1	.1	
N=	1405	1571	814	988	N=4778
Missing data total = .06%					

These findings are consonant with other studies that document the preponderance of younger people in the offender population. One interesting finding, however, concerns the sentencing of older offenders. While one might expect that judges are reluctant to sentence older offenders to jail, the data do not support this hypothesis.

WIP POPULATION DATA

Considerable additional data about the WIP population are available because they could be interviewed and observed. In addition to the specific data obtained as part of the alcohol assessment process at the WIP, other social-category data and demographics are available.

Race

The population of the area served by the WIP is predominantly white, with sizable concentrations of minorities found only in the central cities. (Race data on the general study population is unavailable because it is not recorded on the operator's license or court docket.)

Although the actual numbers are *not* great, the representation of black people is significantly greater in the older population. Consider the data in Table 4.

TABLE 4
WIP: Distribution by Race

Race	Percentage Representation	
	Under Age 50	Over Age 50
White	92.8	84.1
Black	6.3	15.9
Other	.9	0.0
Missing data	2.2%	N=1405

The actual assignment to any of the sentencing alternatives occurs solely at the level of the court. This suggests either that judges are more likely to remand older minority offenders to the WIP, or older offenders *choose* this alternative.

Marital Status

DWI offenders are essentially young. The data on marital status in Table 5 reflect this observation.

TABLE 5
WIP: Distribution by Marital Status

	Age	
Status	Under 50	Over 50
Married	31.4%	84.1%
Widowed	1.1%	15.6%
Divorced	20.5%	25.9%
Separated	3.1%	2.0%
Never married	43.9%	5.4%
Missing	3.4%	N=1405

The categories reflect the *current* status of respondents. The "married" category reflects involvement in a stable relationship (legal or informal) in which the respondent shares a household with another. In either age cohort, a very large proportion of the respondents (69 percent of those under 50; 49 percent of those over 50) do not enjoy the benefit of such support. These data have specific relevance in any program plans formulated for the individual.

They also suggest that elements of the individual's lifestyle place him at risk for the offense that was responsible for his attendance in the program. Until these elements change, the risk of repeating the offense will probably remain at a similar level. As data on recidivism are collected by the study, it will be possible to explore the hypothesis that younger cohorts are at risk because of lifestyle, while older cohorts are at risk because more of them experience drinking problems or alcoholism.

Alcohol Problems

Some data already available however, suggest that drinking problems are *more* prevalent among the young WIP population.

TABLE 6
WIP: Representation of Alcohol Problems by Age Cohort

Problem Level*	Under Age 50	Over Age 50
No problem	23.9%	25.0%
Mild problem	29.7%	17.6%
Moderate problem (no dependence)	18.9%	20.9%
Moderate problem	18.1%	23.6%
Severe problem	8.6%	12.8%
Missing	4.2%	N=1405

*"No problem" denotes an individual who appears to be entirely in control of his drinking. The offense which brought him to the program is isolated and situational. There is only a minimal probability of subsequent difficulties. "Mild problem" suggests only slight harm to one or two areas of an individual's life. It suggests as well that the individual can still control his drinking, if he elects to do so. A *"moderate problem"* suggests more extensive, larger impairment. In some cases, it reflects evidence of alcohol dependence—either physiological or psychological. In these cases, the drinking has substantially exceeded the realm of the individual's control. The *"severe problem"* category designates extensive harm in each area of the individual's life and alcohol dependence.

The determination of an alcohol problem is made by the professional WIP staff after having extensive contact with participants in both group and individual counseling sessions, analyzing results of standard diagnostic tests, and obtaining extensive personal histories. All these data focus on the specific impact that alcohol has had on the individual's life. The findings do suggest a more *negative* general impact on the older cohort. For example:

- Thirteen percent of the older cohorts indicated that their drinking was responsible for a divorce, separation, or similar marital problem, while only 11 percent of the younger cohorts offered this report.
- Ten percent of the older cohorts reported severe (current) alcohol-related job problems, while only 8 percent of the younger cohorts reported current difficulties.

It is in the areas of alcohol's impact on the individual's health and his dependence on alcohol that some of the most striking differences between cohorts arise (see Tables 7 and 8).

TABLE 7
WIP Population: Representation of Dependence on Alcohol

Dependence	Under Age 50	Over Age 50
No dependence	65.4%	58.9%
Psychological dependence	22.3%	20.5%
Physiological dependence	4.4%	6.8%
Both	7.9%	13.7%
Missing	4.4%	N=1405

TABLE 8
WIP Population: Representation of
Alcohol-Related/Exacerbated Health Problems

Health Status	Under Age 50	Over Age 50
Satisfactory/no reported problems	69.1%	46.3%
Some problems, [health] professional suggested change in consumption pattern	22.6%	32.9%
Major problems, [health] professional ordered need for abstinence	8.3%	20.8%
Missing	3.4%	N=1405

These data, especially the observations on alcohol-related health conditions, are striking.

- Fifty-seven percent of the over-50 group have a moderate to severe drinking problem, while only 46 percent of the younger group does.
- The representation of alcohol dependence on both the psychological and physiological level is *almost double* for the older cohort.
- Alcohol-related health impairment affects more than half (54 percent) of the older group, but less than one-third (30 percent) of the younger.

These data should sensitize us to the fact that if an older person's drinking has caused involvement with the criminal justice system, there is a greater chance that the incident indicates a more extensive problem with alcohol. This implies that for this population, at least, a comprehensive assessment is most appropriate.

The *most* striking observation involves the very heavy use of Alcoholics Anonymous (AA) referral option for the older population. This, I suspect, reflects the couselor's bias toward its use as a way of helping to provide both sociability and assistance in the management of time. However, it can be a somewhat myopic referral, in that the only possible problem area to be addressed will be the individual's drinking. It is likely that other problems, such as health needs, will not receive any attention. Given the very high representation of health problems within the elderly population, this may constitute a serious shortcoming.

TABLE 9
WIP Population: Post-Program Service Recommendation in Percentages

Service Recommendation*	Under 50 Age Group	Over 50 Age Group
No problem/No recommendation	45.0%	44.3%
Short-term alcohol education	15.6%	4.7%
"Standard" outpatient treatment	22.3%	18.1%
"Daycare" treatment	1.1%	2.7%
Detoxification/inpatient treatment	4.8%	3.4%
Alcoholics anonymous	5.4%	20.8%
Other	5.8%	6.1%
	N=1202	149

N=1405 (Missing observations = 3.8%)

*Short-term education involves 6 to 8 additional hours supporting or reinforcing the information offered by the WIP. A "Standard Outpatient" program involves 12 to 22 weeks of twice-weekly counseling sessions supported by Alcoholics Anonymous involvement. A "Daycare Treatment" programs offers 6 to 8 weeks of daily service (Monday through Friday) for 4 to 6 hours per day; it offers counseling and education. "Detoxification/Inpatient" provides live-in treatment for 28 days typically followed by a formal aftercare program. "Self Help/Alcoholics Anonymous" involves weekly or more frequent attendance at A.A. (or similar) meetings for 12 to 26 weeks. Other counseling/therapy involves referral to community mental health center (or private therapists). The terms and specifications of this service are negotiated between the patient and the agency/therapist.

DISCUSSION

To begin, it must be emphasized that this is just the first rough cut at a sizable body of data. Analyses will be undertaken to explore the characteristics of each cohort and the various groups within each. Moreover, because assignment to the WIP (or any other alternative) represents the operation of a complex system, whose component parts operate differently, there is really no way to confidently offer generalizations. Futhermore, the relatively small representation of older individuals within the WIP population makes conclusions problematic. Nevertheless, older people do appear in the offender population and data on them are collected. Given the usual qualifications and cautions, some observations are appropriate.

Abusive drinking, drinking and driving, and perhaps even drinking itself seem to present special risks for the older population. The older person is more likely to be taking medications, many of which can have interactive effects with ethanol. In addition to the general health risk involved, the possibility of impaired performance on such tasks as driving is increased. On the average, older persons with equivalent patterns of alcohol consumption perform less well on standard psychological tests than younger ones (Carlen, et al., 1981). Changes in the body's ability to metabolize alcohol and changes in central nervous system function may make the older person more vulnerable to the deleterious effects of alcohol (Wood and Armbrecht, 1982). Hence, some involvement with the criminal justice system through offenses such as DWI would be expected if older persons continue to drink and drive.

These observations should be of particular importance to those interested in highway safety, especially prevention. Older drivers need to be educated that if they drink at all, they are at special risk for driving problems.

The findings about the extent of alcohol problems in the older group come as something of a surprise. One finding, although not entirely unexpected, is noteworthy: this is the incidence of self-reported health problems (e.g., coronary and circulatory disease) that are likely to be exacerbated by any drinking and especially abusive drinking. This evidence demands that when the older individual is present for either assessment or service, a more comprehensive examination be recommended. A complete risk-management plan, pulling together all available data, needs to be developed and incorporated into the professional's strategy.

Our experience suggests that alcoholism counselors often overlook this aspect. Hence, they focus almost exclusively on the social and psychological dimensions, and the plans they formulate tend to reflect this. There is a great tendency to encourage the older client to affiliate with and participate in AA. Counselors tend to see this as a desirable avenue for time management, sociability, and support, especially among retired persons.

While at this time there is no justification for recommending special or exclusive alcohol-treatment services or modalities for older people— indeed, the integration of varying age cohorts in treatment activities appears more desirable—assistance in accessing activities that will provide a health-risk management appraisal for the older client should be strongly encouraged by any alcoholism or social service professional that he comes into contact with.

Again, how typical the WIP population is of the general DWI population is not known at this time. It appears however, that age (unlike sex) is *not* a good predictor of sentence alternative; therefore, some similarities might be apparent. If this is the case, special screening programs could be justified.

RECOMMENDATIONS

Right now, several recommendations could be confidently offered. These associate with both the general and specific levels of prevention.

1. Specially focused prevention activities aimed at appraising the older driver of the risks involved with *any* alcohol use and driving need to be formulated and offered to this population.
2. Work on the incidence and prevalence of alcohol use and abuse, and medication use and misuse when driving must be continued or undertaken.
3. Professionals at each level and specialty of the health care delivery system must broaden their perspective when it comes to the assessment and management of older patients or clients. *Physicians* need to become more sensitive to the possibilities of alcohol problems among this population. In their initial evaluations, *alcoholism pro-*

fessionals need to broaden their perspectives to include resources that assess their clients' health needs and situations and then assure that their findings become part of the case-management plan.

REFERENCES

Brody, J. A. 1982. Alcohol and aging: Extent of the problem viewed from limited data. 6th Annual Conference on Addiction Research and Treatment, Drugs, Alcohol and Aging, Cartersville, Pa.

Carlen, P. L., et al. 1981. Cerebral atrophy and functional deficits in alcoholics without clinically apparent liver disease. *Neurology* 31:377–85.

Inciardi, J. A. 1984. *Criminal justice.* Academic Press: Orlando, Fla.

Wood, W. G., and H. J. Armbrecht. 1982. Behavioral effects of ethanol in animals: Age difference and age change. *Alcoholism: Clinical and Experimental Research* 6:3–12.